FACING
SCLERODERMA
A Guide for Patients and Their Families

EDITORS
Marcy B. Bolster, MD
Theodore A. Stern, MD

FACING
SCLERODERMA

A Guide for Patients and Their Families

Facing Scleroderma – A Guide for Patients and Their Families

Copyright ©2020 by The Massachusetts General Hospital Psychiatry Academy. All rights reserved. Printed in the United States of America. Except as permitted under the United States Copyright Act of 1976, no part of this publication may be reproduced or distributed in any form or by any means, or stored in a data base or retrieval system, without the prior written permission of the publisher.

ISBN-13: 978-1-951166-05-2 (Print)
ISBN-13: 978-1-951166-04-5 (Ebook)

Cover Design: Falcone Creative Design, LLC
Book Design: Dianne Russell, Octal Productions, LLC
Book Production: Octal Productions, LLC
Copyeditor: Bob Russell, Octal Publishing, LLC
Managing Director: Jane Pimental, MGH Psychiatry Academy
Program Managers: Heather Giza and Grace Shanks, MGH Psychiatry Academy
Clinical Research Assistant: Julia Chippari, MGH Psychiatry Academy
Printing and Binding: RP Graphics
This book is printed on acid-free paper.

ABOUT THE EDITORS

Marcy B. Bolster, MD is a rheumatologist and the Director of the Rheumatology Fellowship Training Program at the Massachusetts General Hospital, Boston, Massachusetts. She is an Associate Professor of Medicine at Harvard Medical School. Dr. Bolster has both expertise and a special interest in taking care of patients with scleroderma. She has a strong interest in medical education and has helped to train more than 50 physicians to become rheumatologists. She is the author of articles and textbook chapters on scleroderma as well as a variety of other rheumatic diseases. She is the co-editor of *Facing Osteoporosis, Facing Lupus,* and *Facing Rheumatoid Arthritis.*

Theodore A. Stern, MD is the Ned H. Cassem Professor of Psychiatry in the field of Psychosomatic Medicine/Consultation, Harvard Medical School and Chief Emeritus of the Avery D. Weisman Psychiatry Consultation Service, Director of the Thomas P. Hackett Center for Scholarship in Psychosomatic Medicine, and Director of the Office for Clinical Careers, at the Massachusetts General Hospital in Boston, Massachusetts. Dr. Stern has written more than 450 scientific articles and book chapters and edited more than 25 books, including the *Massachusetts General Hospital Handbook of General Hospital Psychiatry* (4/e–7/e), *Massachusetts General Hospital Comprehensive Clinical Psychiatry* (1/e, 2/e), *Massachusetts General Hospital Guide to Primary Care Psychiatry* (1/e, 2/e), *Massachusetts General Hospital Psychiatry Update and Board Preparation,* (1/e–4/e), and *Facing Cancer, Facing Heart Disease, Facing Diabetes, Facing Immunotherapy, Facing Lupus, Facing Rheumatoid Arthritis, Facing Osteoporosis, Facing Psoriasis, Facing Cystic Fibrosis,* and *Facing Overweight and Obesity.* He is also the Editor-in-Chief of *Psychosomatics.*

DEDICATION

*To our patients with scleroderma, their families,
our students, our colleagues, our mentors,
and our families . . .*

MBB & TAS

ACKNOWLEDGMENTS

OUR THANKS

This book would not have come into being if not for our patients. They expressed to us their need for a guide to the experience of having scleroderma and were so generous in including us in their day-to-day triumphs and struggles. We hope that through this book we were able to fulfill that goal and repay their faith and trust in us.

Without the contributions of so many physicians and related health care professionals, this book would never have been completed. We thank our contributors for their thoughtfulness and gifted writing as well as their tolerance of our deadlines and edits. We also thank our teachers and mentors for imbuing in us a sense of responsibility to educate, to write with rigor, and, most importantly, to provide exceptional care to our patients.

At the Massachusetts General Hospital Psychiatry Academy, we thank Jane Pimental our managing director, Heather Giza and Grace Shanks our program managers, and clinical research assistant Julia Chippari for their assistance and support. At Octal Publishing, LLC, our thanks go to Bob Russell for his yeoman's efforts related to copyediting, and to Dianne Russell at Octal Productions, LLC for overseeing the production of this book, with grace and style.

MBB
TAS

TABLE OF CONTENTS

Contributors xiv
Foreword xvii
Preface xix

CHAPTER 1
What Is Scleroderma? 1
Sara Schoenfeld, MD and Chio Yokose, MD

Introduction 2
What Are the Different Types of Scleroderma? 2
What Causes Scleroderma and Who Gets Scleroderma? 2
What Are the Signs and Symptoms of Scleroderma? 3
Will My Appearance Change with Scleroderma? 8
How Will I Know Whether I Am Starting to Have a Problem? 8
Summary 9

CHAPTER 2
Can Scleroderma Be Identified Early During the Disease? 11
Naomi Serling-Boyd, MD and Flavia V. Castelino, MD

What Does the Assessment of Scleroderma Involve? 12
What Elements of My History Will Be Obtained? 12
Why Is the Physical Examination Important? 14
How Will My Doctor Know Whether I Have Scleroderma? 18
What Are the Different Types of Scleroderma? 19
What Factors Increase My Risk of Developing Organ Involvement in Scleroderma? 19
Can I Pass Scleroderma Along to My Children or Grandchildren? 21

CHAPTER 3
How Are Complications of Scleroderma Recognized and Treated?................... 23
Nancy Elorreaga, LCSW and Tracy M. Frech, MD, MS

What Can My Doctor Learn from Talking to Me About My Symptoms?...............................24
What Tests Are Used to Diagnose Scleroderma? 24
What Screening Tests Should I Expect My Doctor to Perform? 25
Which Screening Tests Will Need to Be Repeated?...26
What Is the Role of Preventative Measures for Avoiding Complications? 28

CHAPTER 4
How Can Scleroderma and Its Complications Be Treated? 31
Chase Correia, MD and Monique Hinchcliff, MD, MS

Overview..32
How Can Skin Thickening Be Treated? 32
How Can Raynaud Phenomenon Be Treated? 35
How Can the Gastrointestinal Manifestations of Scleroderma Be Treated? 38
How Can Pulmonary Complications of Scleroderma Be Treated? 40
How Can Renal Complications of Scleroderma Be Treated?..45
How Can Muscle and Joint Symptoms of Scleroderma Be Treated? 46
Summary..47

CHAPTER 5
What Should I Consider If I Want to Become Pregnant? 49
Jessica L. Sheingold, MD and Virginia Steen, MD

Will I Be Able to Have Children? 50
What Are the Risks to My Health If I Become Pregnant?..51
What Are the Risks to My Baby If I Have Scleroderma?..54
Which Medications Are Safe, and Which Should Be Avoided If I Want to 57
  Become Pregnant?
Will I Be Able to Breastfeed? 61
Is My Child at Risk of Developing Scleroderma?..62

CHAPTER 6
How Am I Likely to Feel When I Learn That I Have Scleroderma?................. 65
Daniel J. Daunis, Jr., MD; Christopher M. Celano, MD; and Marcy B. Bolster, MD

Should I Blame Myself for Developing Scleroderma? 66
What Can I Do If I Feel Depressed, Angry, or Scared? 66
Are My Feelings of Depression Normal?...67

How Long Will It Take Me to Regain My Emotional Equilibrium?..68
Should I Tell Others About the Diagnosis and the Prognosis? 68
What Should I Tell Others About My Condition?..69
How Can I Manage My Fear of Having a Complication from Scleroderma? 70
How Can I Learn to Be Less Stressed and More Hopeful and Optimistic? 70

CHAPTER 7
How Can I Learn More About Scleroderma?... 73
Maria C. Prom, MD and Chris Derk, MD

Where Can I Turn for More Information About Scleroderma? 74
Should I Seek a Second Opinion? 74
Should I Obtain Professional Counseling or Psychiatric Care? 75
Should I Seek Care at a Specialized Center for My Scleroderma? 76
How Can My Local Library or the Internet Be of Assistance to Me? 77
What Are the Most Reliable Internet Resources for Me to Use for Information? 78
What Local, Regional, or National Organizations Provide Useful Information 80
    About Scleroderma and Its Complications?
What Articles or Videos Offer Sound Advice or Information? 81
Would It Be Helpful for Me to Speak with Someone Who Has a Similar Condition? 81
What Is the Role of Social Media in Learning About Scleroderma? 82
Summary..83

CHAPTER 8
How Can Members of My Health Care Team Help Me Manage 85
My Scleroderma?
Mark A. Matza, MD, MBA and Vivien Hsu, MD

What Role Will My Primary Care Provider Play in Helping to Take Care of 86
    Me and My Scleroderma?
What Role Will My Rheumatologist Play in Taking Care of Me?..87
What Role Might Other Subspecialists Play in Taking Care of Me? 88
How Can Occupational Therapy and Physical Therapy Help Me with 92
    My Scleroderma?
How Can Other Members of My Health Team Improve My Function and 92
    Help Me Cope?
Summary..93

CHAPTER 9
How Can I Reduce My Risk of Scleroderma and Its Complications? 95
Karen L. Smarr, PhD and Zsuzsanna H. McMahan, MD, MHS

Can Exercise, Dieting, Quitting Smoking, or Reducing Stress Prevent 96
  Scleroderma or Improve Its Treatment?
What Role Does My Diet Play in How I Am Feeling? Can Dietary Modifications 103
  Improve My Health?
What Can I Do to Change My Exercise Habits?...104
Can I Make Lasting Changes on My Own or Will I Need the Help of Others?........................106
Should I Build a Support System?..107

CHAPTER 10
How Do Family Members Respond to a Family Member with........................ 109
  Scleroderma?
Maria C. Prom, MD and Kevin M. McKown, MD

Should I Talk to Family and Friends About the Changes My Body Is Experiencing? 110
Who in My Family and Circle of Friends Is at Risk for Becoming Stressed? 110
What Are Some Indicators That a Family Member Is Not Coping Well? 111
What Are Some Ways to Improve Coping in Family Members? 113
Are Support Groups Available to Family Members?...114
Summary..115

GLOSSARY 116

REFERENCES 148

INDEX 164

CONTRIBUTORS

Marcy B. Bolster, MD
Associate Professor of Medicine,
Harvard Medical School;
Director, Rheumatology Fellowship Training
Program, Massachusetts General Hospital;
Boston, MA

Flavia V. Castelino, MD
Assistant Professor of Medicine,
Harvard Medical School;
Director, Scleroderma Program,
Massachusetts General Hospital;
Boston, MA

Christopher M. Celano, MD
Assistant Professor of Psychiatry,
Harvard Medical School;
Associate Director, Cardiac Psychiatry
Research Program,
Massachusetts General Hospital;
Boston, MA

Chase Correia, MD
Instructor of Medicine, Northwestern
University Feinberg School of Medicine,
Division of Rheumatology;
Chicago, IL

Daniel J. Daunis Jr., MD
Clinical Fellow in Psychiatry,
Harvard Medical School;
Fellow in Psychosomatic Medicine/
Consultation-Liaison Psychiatry,
Massachusetts General Hospital;
Boston, MA

Chris Derk, MD
Associate Professor of Medicine,
University of Pennsylvania;
Director, Fellowship Program,
Division of Rheumatology,
University of Pennsylvania;
Philadelphia, PA

Nancy Elorreaga, LCSW
University of Utah Hospital and Clinics;
Salt Lake City, UT

Tracy M. Frech, MD, MS
Associate Professor of Medicine, Department of
Internal Medicine, Division of Rheumatology,
University of Utah Hospital and Clinics;
Salt Lake City, UT

Monique Hinchcliff, MD, MS
Associate Professor of Medicine,
Yale School of Medicine;
Director, Yale Scleroderma Program, Section of
Rheumatology, Allergy, & Clinical Immunology;
New Haven, CT

Vivien Hsu, MD
Professor of Medicine,
Robert Wood Johnson Hospital;
Director, Rutgers-Robert Wood Johnson
Scleroderma Program,
Director, Rutgers-Robert Wood Johnson
Rheumatology Fellowship Program;
New Brunswick, NJ

Mark A. Matza, MD, MBA
Fellow, Division of Rheumatology,
Allergy, and Immunology,
Massachusetts General Hospital;
Boston, MA

Kevin McKown, MD
Professor of Medicine and
Head, Division of Rheumatology
Department of Medicine,
University of Wisconsin School of
Medicine & Public Health;
Madison, WI

Zsuzsanna H. McMahan, MD, MHS
Assistant Professor of Medicine,
Johns Hopkins Hospital;
Division of Rheumatology,
Johns Hopkins Scleroderma Center;
Baltimore, MD

Maria C. Prom, MD
Clinical Fellow in Psychiatry,
Harvard Medical School;
Fellow in Psychosomatic Medicine/
Consultation-Liaison Psychiatry,
Massachusetts General Hospital;
Boston, MA

Sara R. Schoenfeld, MD
Instructor in Medicine,
Harvard Medical School;
Division of Rheumatology,
Allergy, and Immunology,
Massachusetts General Hospital;
Boston, MA

Naomi Serling-Boyd, MD
Fellow, Division of Rheumatology,
Allergy, and Immunology,
Massachusetts General Hospital;
Boston, MA

Jessica L. Sheingold, MD
Assistant Professor of Medicine,
Medstar Georgetown University Hospital;
Washington DC

Karen L. Smarr, PhD
Clinical Assistant Professor of Medicine,
University of Missouri-Columbia
School of Medicine;
Division of Immunology and
Rheumatology, Psychologist,
Harry S. Truman Memorial Veterans' Hospital;
Columbia, MO

Virginia Steen, MD
Professor of Medicine,
Georgetown University School of Medicine;
Washington DC

Theodore A. Stern, MD
Ned H. Cassem Professor of Psychiatry in the
Field of Psychosomatic Medicine/Consultation,
Harvard Medical School;
Chief Emeritus, Avery D. Weisman, M.D.
Psychiatric Consultation Service,
Massachusetts General Hospital;
Director, Thomas P. Hackett Center for
Scholarship in Psychosomatic Medicine,
Massachusetts General Hospital;
Director, Office for Clinical Careers,
Massachusetts General Hospital;
Editor-in-Chief, *Psychosomatics;*
Boston, MA

Chio Yokose, MD
Fellow, Division of Rheumatology,
Allergy, and Immunology,
Massachusetts General Hospital;
Boston, MA

FOREWORD

THE BEST INFORMATION SOURCE IN CONFRONTING SCLERODERMA

Facing Scleroderma is for anyone whose life is affected by this diagnosis. Written by leading health care providers in their fields, *Facing Scleroderma* combines top-tier medical information and compassionate counsel on the management of scleroderma, with a caring and sensible approach to the emotional aspects of living with scleroderma and its complications. This book provides easily readable and trustworthy information; it is divided into ten chapters that asks and answers pertinent questions about scleroderma and its medical and psychiatric/psychological care. A glossary of terms provides important background information to readers (e.g., about nutrition, diet, exercise, risk-reduction); online resources and references are also offered; words italicized in the text are defined in the glossary.

Each of the chapters is accompanied by selected references, internet resources, illustrations, and photographs.

PREFACE

Facing Scleroderma employs a user-friendly question and answer format to provide practical information on the dermatological, vascular, lung, gastrointestinal, kidney, musculoskeletal, and psychiatric aspects of scleroderma. Written in an approachable style, this guide is intended for people with scleroderma, their family members, and caregivers.

MBB
TAS

WHAT IS SCLERODERMA?

Sara Schoenfeld, MD and Chio Yokose, MD

CHAPTER

In This Chapter

- Introduction
- What Are the Different Types of Scleroderma?
- What Causes Scleroderma and Who Gets Scleroderma?
- What Are the Signs and Symptoms of Scleroderma?
- Will My Appearance Change with Scleroderma?
- How Will I Know Whether I Am Starting to Have a Problem?
- Summary

Introduction

Scleroderma is a complex disease that can affect the skin and vital *internal organs*. Scleroderma literally means "hardening of the skin" in Greek, which describes the hallmark of the condition. The same process that results in hardening of the skin affects your internal organs, leading to complications of scleroderma (also called *systemic sclerosis*). There is a wide spectrum of how the condition reveals itself *(clinical manifestations)*. Some people have mild and slowly progressive disease, whereas others have a much more aggressive condition. Scleroderma is considered an *autoimmune condition*, although the exact causes of the disease are still poorly understood (Gabrielli et al, 2003).

What Are the Different Types of Scleroderma?

There are two main sub-types of scleroderma (or systemic sclerosis): *limited* and *diffuse*. These are distinguished from each other primarily by the degree of skin involvement. The limited form of the disease, called *limited scleroderma*, is characterized by skin thickening that might involve the skin on your face and is otherwise restricted to the lower aspects of your arms (below your elbow) and/or your legs (below your knee). The diffuse form of the disease, called *diffuse scleroderma*, is characterized by more extensive skin thickening that usually starts in your hands and feet, but it can progress to involve areas above your elbows and knees as well as your chest and abdomen. Facial skin involvement can occur in those with limited or diffuse scleroderma. In general, those with limited scleroderma have milder or more slowly progressive internal organ involvement compared to individuals with diffuse scleroderma. There is a third sub-type of scleroderma in which internal organ *fibrosis* is present without any skin involvement; however, this form of the disease, called *systemic sclerosis sine scleroderma*, is quite rare (Kucharz and Kopec-Medrek, 2017). People with systemic sclerosis sine scleroderma tend to follow a disease course similar to those with limited scleroderma. Aside from the three sub-types of systemic sclerosis, there is *morphea*, another condition characterized by skin hardening. This condition is not likely to be confused with limited or diffuse scleroderma, though a skin biopsy of morphea has the same appearance as a skin biopsy from an individual with limited or diffuse scleroderma. Morphea, however, is localized to the skin and the *tissue* just below the skin; it does not affect internal organs. Morphea is sometimes called *localized scleroderma*. Localized scleroderma is a category of conditions that includes morphea, *generalized morphea*, *linear scleroderma*, and *en coup de sabre*.

What Causes Scleroderma and Who Gets Scleroderma?

The exact causes and *risk factors* for developing scleroderma are unknown. Women are four times more likely to develop scleroderma than are men (Black, 1993). A family history of scleroderma also increases your risk of developing scleroderma, but this is only one factor that can increase your risk. Individuals of African ancestry are more likely to be diagnosed with scleroderma at a younger age and to develop diffuse and more severe disease (Laing et al, 1997). Environmental exposures might also play a role in the development of scleroderma. Numerous environmental exposures (e.g., silica, vinyl chloride, organic solvents, silicone breast implants) have been linked with the development of scleroderma, but none of them is believed to definitively cause scleroderma (Chifflot et al, 2008). However, in most people who develop scleroderma, no clear trigger is ever identified.

What Are the Signs and Symptoms of Scleroderma?
Constitutional

Fatigue is a common and early symptom of scleroderma. Although the degree of fatigue varies, it can be severe and even debilitating. Fatigue can adversely affect your sense of well-being and quality of life and can contribute to mood disturbances such as depression.

By Organ System
Dermatologic

As the name of the condition implies, skin hardening is a hallmark of scleroderma. However, it can be preceded by other, more subtle, skin changes, such as *puffy fingers*. You might also notice *telangiectasias*, which are abnormal networks of blood vessels that might appear on your face, trunk, or hands. Itchy skin can also be a prominent feature with early skin disease and can interfere with your quality of life and sleep. The itching is related to the *inflammatory process* in the skin that eventually leads to skin fibrosis. After skin thickening begins to develop, although it might not be life threatening, it can reduce your quality of life. Skin thickening that involves your face can limit the ability of your mouth to open and to vary your facial expressions, and this can be upsetting. Skin thickening that involves your fingers and toes can lead to *sclerodactyly*, which can be disfiguring and lead to reduced function of your hands. Changes in the skin pigment of your hardened skin will depend on your underlying skin tone, making your skin look lighter or darker, or giving it a "salt-and-pepper" appearance, which is the result of pigment loss that occurs in small patches of skin, thus giving it a speckled appearance compared to the darker skin that surrounds it. Some people also develop areas of *calcinosis* (Figure 1-1), which occur when calcium deposits form in the skin and soft tissues. This can be associated with pain and chronic wounds that can place you at risk for infection.

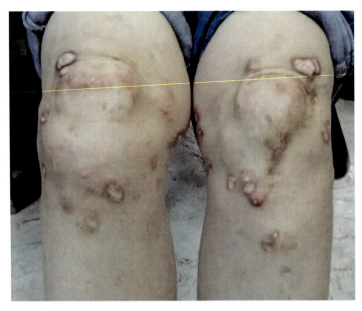

Figure 1-1: Calcinosis. (Source: Düzgün N: Cutaneous calcinosis in a patient with limited scleroderma: CREST Syndrome. *European Journal of Rheumatology*. 2017; 4: 305–306.)

Vascular

Nearly everyone with scleroderma has *Raynaud phenomenon* (Figure 1-2). Raynaud phenomenon is caused by abnormalities of the small blood vessels that supply your fingers. The toes are less commonly involved than are the fingers. With exposure to cold and/or stress, these blood vessels often spasm and temporarily restrict the blood flow to the affected areas, leading to color changes in your fingertips (usually progressing from white to blue to red), and you might experience tingling and discomfort in addition to the color changes. Raynaud's can start before the other symptoms of scleroderma by many years, or it can develop suddenly, around the time that your skin thickening begins, especially if you have a rapidly progressive form of diffuse scleroderma. Sometimes, blood vessel abnormalities can become so severe that they can lead to ulcerations (Figure 1-2) and *pitting scars* of your fingertips. These *lesions* can be associated with severe pain as well as with other less common complications (e.g., infection, gangrene, and, in severe situations, *amputation*). However, Raynaud phenomenon is relatively common in healthy individuals, especially in young women, termed *primary Raynaud phenomenon*. A careful history and physical exam (including examination of your *nailfold capillaries*) and select blood tests for *autoimmune disease* can help your doctor distinguish Raynaud phenomenon that might progress to scleroderma *(secondary Raynaud phenomenon)* from the harmless primary Raynaud phenomenon variant (Desbois and Cacoub, 2016).

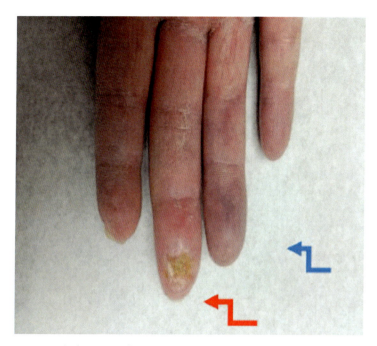

Figure 1-2: Digital ulceration (bottom arrow); Raynaud's phenomenon (top arrow). (Source: Young, et al: Hand impairment in systemic sclerosis: Various manifestations and currently available treatment. *Current Treatment Options in Rheumatology.* 2016; 2(3): 252–269.)

Pulmonary

About 30% to 40% of people with scleroderma develop significant lung involvement at some point during their illness (Denton and Black, 2004; McNearney et al, 2007). Scleroderma can affect your lung tissue (leading to *interstitial lung disease* [ILD] or *pulmonary fibrosis*), the blood vessels that supply your lungs (leading to *pulmonary hypertension*), or both. Lung involvement is an important and serious internal organ manifestation of scleroderma that can reduce your quality of life and lead to early mortality.

The most common *symptoms* of ILD are shortness of breath and cough. At the beginning, you might feel short of breath only with exertion. However, in some cases, it can progress and cause symptoms at rest. Those with ILD often develop a chronic cough, which can be *productive.* The most common symptom of pulmonary hypertension is shortness of breath. However, cough is generally not noted unless you also have ILD. Treatments are available for both types of lung involvement (ILD and pulmonary hypertension) that can help slow the progression of these conditions (see Chapter 4).

Gastrointestinal

Involvement of the *gastrointestinal* (GI) tract is very common in those with scleroderma, but it can range in its severity and symptoms. Any area of the GI tract can be involved; symptoms vary widely depending on the site of involvement. Many GI symptoms relate to *dysmotility*, which occurs due to fibrosis of the GI tract that inhibits the coordinated movement of contents from the *esophagus* all the way down to the *colon*. However, the specific manifestations differ depending on which portion of the GI tract is most affected by this process.

With upper GI tract involvement (i.e., the esophagus and *stomach*), *acid reflux* or *heartburn* is very common; difficulty with, or pain from, swallowing can also occur. Food can feel as if it becomes "hung up" in the esophagus. At first, you might notice difficulty swallowing solid foods, which can progress to having difficulty with liquids. Some people develop additional esophageal complications, such as *strictures* (mechanical narrowing of the esophagus) or *Barrett's esophagus* (a *precancerous* condition of the esophagus related to high levels of acid). Often, nausea and vomiting (frequently of undigested foods) are prominent and very troubling symptoms. People with severe upper-GI involvement might be at increased risk of *aspiration*, which occurs when the stomach contents go down the wrong tube (i.e., the windpipe) into the lungs. This occurs when food is regurgitated (due to dysmotility) as opposed to traveling down the intestine as it normally should. Sometimes, aspiration results in a *pneumonia* or a worsening of lung function.

With lower GI tract involvement (i.e., small intestines, colon), there can be changes in bowel habits (e.g., constipation, diarrhea, or, in severe cases, *incontinence*). With advanced disease, bacterial overgrowth can develop in the GI tract, and there can be trouble with absorption of nutrients, which can lead to malnutrition and severe weight loss (Denton and Khanna, 2017). If there is bacterial overgrowth in the GI tract, *antibiotics* can be administered. It is important to talk to your doctor about any GI symptoms (including diarrhea, constipation, bloating, or incontinence) because these could be due to scleroderma and might be alleviated with proper treatments. Liver involvement is uncommon in those with scleroderma.

Cardiac

It is important to recognize *cardiac* (heart) involvement in scleroderma; however, it can be difficult to detect. One possible reason for this is that symptoms of cardiac involvement are similar to those of scleroderma lung disease. The most frequent cardiac complication of scleroderma relates to abnormalities in your heart's rate and rhythm, called *arrhythmias* (Fernandz-Codina et al, 2017). People can experience a racing heartbeat, *palpitations*, lightheadedness, and/or fainting (also called *syncope*). Scleroderma can also weaken and/or stiffen the heart muscle and decrease the heart's ability to pump effectively; this can lead to *congestive heart failure*. Symptoms of heart failure include weight gain, swelling in the legs and/or abdomen, and shortness of breath. Scleroderma can sometimes affect the tissue that surrounds the heart, called the *pericardium*. In addition, chest pain can develop if there is inflammation of the pericardium, called *pericarditis*. Sometimes, inflammation can lead to fluid accumulation beneath this lining, called a *pericardial effusion*. Your symptoms will depend on the amount of fluid that has accumulated and the speed at which it has accumulated. Some individuals might not have any symptoms from this fluid around the heart, and it might be discovered as an incidental finding on *imaging tests*. If there is a lot of fluid, or if it accumulates quickly, you might develop dizziness, chest discomfort, or breathlessness.

Renal

Kidney involvement in scleroderma was formerly the leading cause of scleroderma-associated death (Denton and Black, 2004). However, significant improvements have been made in the detection and treatment of kidney disease in scleroderma; this has led to improved outcomes. In particular, the use of a certain class of blood pressure medications called *ACE-inhibitors* has improved the survival of those with kidney involvement. Often, the earliest sign of kidney trouble in scleroderma is elevated blood pressure; if you have had a normal blood pressure at baseline, blood pressures above 130/80 *mm Hg* could be concerning (however, the exact threshold should be determined on a case-by-case basis with your doctor). Kidney disease is much more common in those with diffuse scleroderma. Thus, if you have diffuse scleroderma, you should check your blood pressure at home daily or weekly and promptly report any changes to your doctor. The most feared form of kidney involvement in scleroderma is called *scleroderma renal crisis* (SRC), which most commonly affects those who have diffuse scleroderma within the first few years of disease onset. In SRC, people often present with a marked elevation of their blood pressure, which can lead to symptoms (e.g., headache, vision changes, chest discomfort). Some individuals who have SRC can develop kidney failure; fortunately, this is becoming less common with better screening and early treatment.

Musculoskeletal

Joint pain and stiffness are the most common symptoms of *musculoskeletal* involvement in those with scleroderma; typically, pain is experienced in multiple joints, but sometimes only one joint is affected. Swelling, redness, or warmth can appear in one or more joints. Over time, about 30% of affected individuals develop *joint contractures*, in which the joints can no longer straighten fully (Morrisroe et al, 2015). Joint contractures can lead to loss of function and can significantly affect quality of life. In addition to joints, *tendons* can also be involved in scleroderma. Your doctors might test the range of motion of your joints and assess for *tendon friction rubs*, which are leathery, rubbing sensations felt over the tendon as the tendon moves with the joint going through its motion. Your muscles can also be affected in scleroderma, typically manifesting by muscle aches and weakness. When muscle weakness occurs, it is usually in the muscles of the upper arms and upper legs, such as the muscles that help the shoulders and hips to move. Weakness might be noted when trying to reach overhead to put things into a cabinet or when standing up from a low-seated chair.

Psychiatric

Depression and anxiety are common, found in roughly half of those with scleroderma. These conditions are often related to functional disability from scleroderma and from reduced, health-related quality of life (Nguyen et al, 2014). In particular, GI involvement appears to be closely tied to anxiety and depression. Some people find it difficult to leave the house due to frequent episodes of diarrhea. Others find it difficult to go out for meals or to eat in front of others due to difficulty swallowing, nausea, and vomiting. These symptoms can significantly interfere with social activities; activities once enjoyed might now contribute to depressed mood.

Furthermore, sexual dysfunction is common in those with scleroderma; moreover, sexual dysfunction might not be routinely discussed with your doctors. Sexual dysfunction can also worsen depression and anxiety. *Erectile dysfunction* (ED) has been reported in up to 80% of sexually active male patients with scleroderma. Female sexual dysfunction is also more common among women with scleroderma than it is in the general population. Symptoms of female sexual dysfunction can include vaginal dryness and tightness, *dyspareunia* (painful sexual intercourse), reduction in orgasm intensity, decreased desire, and decreased sexual arousal and satisfaction (Bruni et al, 2015).

Will My Appearance Change with Scleroderma?

For some people with scleroderma, appearance can change a lot, whereas for others, appearance changes very little or not at all. With diffuse scleroderma, the skin on your face, trunk, hands, arms, and legs can become hardened and can change color, looking darker in some areas and lighter in other areas. *Flexion contractures* (inability to straighten joints) can also change your appearance. Additionally, some people develop ulcers at their fingertips. For those with a milder form of scleroderma (i.e., limited scleroderma) the changes to appearance might not be dramatic, and there might be only mild thickening of the skin in the fingers (i.e., sclerodactyly). In fact, some people who have sclerodactyly never realize that their skin has undergone changes because the skin change occurs slowly and might be mild. Others with scleroderma can develop what are called *telangiectasias*, which are small red spots made up of tiny blood vessels. Often these appear on the palms of the hands, but they can appear on the chest, face, or lips, as well. Telangiectasias can be infrequent or there could be many. Certainly, the physical changes in your body, including changes in appearance, can challenge your ability to cope. Discussing these feelings and concerns with your friends, family members, and doctor can help.

How Will I Know Whether I Am Starting to Have a Problem?

Depending on the type of scleroderma you have (i.e., diffuse versus limited) and also some of the blood tests associated with scleroderma, certain complications of scleroderma might be more or less likely. Those who have limited scleroderma are more likely to develop pulmonary hypertension, whereas others who have diffuse scleroderma are more likely to develop ILD. Your doctor will monitor you for any complications of scleroderma based on your symptoms, physical exam findings, and test results. Many of the complications of scleroderma develop within the first 3 to 5 years after scleroderma is diagnosed, so this will be an especially important time for your doctors to monitor you for any new symptoms. However, certain complications, such as pulmonary hypertension, can occur later in the disease course, so it is important to continue to follow up with a *rheumatologist* regularly

(Avouac et al, 2010). Most complications of scleroderma are either related to fibrosis or *vascular* changes that can occur in scleroderma. For example, pulmonary hypertension, Raynaud phenomenon, finger ulcerations, and kidney problems are more closely associated with vascular problems, whereas lung disease, skin thickening, and GI involvement tend to be complications linked with fibrosis. Often a person will begin to have new symptoms when a complication is developing. For example, pulmonary hypertension and pulmonary fibrosis can cause shortness of breath. GI involvement can cause symptoms such as acid reflux (heartburn), constipation, bloating, or diarrhea. Some complications, however, are less likely to cause obvious *signs* and symptoms, and that is why a rheumatologist will also screen for these complications by checking blood work and other tests (e.g., an *echocardiogram* of the heart or *pulmonary function tests*). Routine blood pressure monitoring is an important component of screening for kidney involvement, which can be evaluated further with blood and urine tests. Symptoms and signs associated with kidney involvement include confusion, decreased amount of urination, swelling of the legs, persistent headaches, and blurry vision (these last symptoms are often due to the high blood pressure that can go along with kidney involvement).

Summary

Scleroderma is a serious autoimmune condition that is characterized by fibrosis of tissues and by vascular abnormalities. Although skin fibrosis is often the most striking feature of this condition, the same process can occur in internal organs and lead to troubling signs and symptoms. There is a wide spectrum of manifestations of scleroderma; some individuals have mild and slowly progressive disease, whereas others have severe and rapidly progressive forms. Your doctor can help diagnose scleroderma with a thorough history and examination and also prescribe medications to help slow the progression of disease and improve your symptoms.

CAN SCLERODERMA BE IDENTIFIED EARLY DURING THE DISEASE?

Naomi Serling-Boyd, MD and Flavia V. Castelino, MD

CHAPTER

In This Chapter

- What Does the Assessment of Scleroderma Involve?
- What Elements of My History Will Be Obtained?
- Why Is the Physical Examination Important?
- How Will My Doctor Know Whether I Have Scleroderma?
- What Are the Different Types of Scleroderma?
- What Factors Increase My Risk of Developing Organ Involvement in Scleroderma?
- Can I Pass Scleroderma Along to My Children or Grandchildren?

What Does the Assessment of Scleroderma Involve?

Assessment of scleroderma includes a complete history and a physical examination by a *rheumatologist* as well as supplementary laboratory and diagnostic testing, which will be outlined in this chapter and in Chapter 3. At the initial visit, the rheumatologist will ask you about *symptoms* that relate to different *organ systems*. Some questions the rheumatologist might ask initially include whether you have noticed *puffy fingers*, skin changes or skin thickening, trouble swallowing, *heartburn* or *acid reflux*, color changes of your fingers or toes (caused by exposure to cold temperatures or stress, called *Raynaud phenomenon*), respiratory symptoms (e.g., cough, shortness of breath), or other changes in your general condition.

The physical exam will focus on multiple body systems, including the skin. The most common finding on physical examination in those with scleroderma is thickening of the skin. Your rheumatologist will measure the amount of skin thickening or tightening of different regions of the body, look for dilated blood vessels (called *telangiectasias*), and assess for any calcium deposits that can be present along the fingertips, elbows, knees, and other body areas, particularly occurring at areas of pressure points. There might also be an examination of the blood vessels along the base of the fingernails, called *nailfold capillaroscopy*. Your doctor will also perform a complete physical examination of your internal organs (including your heart, lungs, and abdomen) that can be affected by scleroderma.

As part of your initial visit, blood will also be drawn to evaluate for *autoantibodies* (antibodies directed against the body's own tissues) that might support the diagnosis of scleroderma. Additional tests such as an *ultrasound* of the heart *(echocardiogram)*, *computed tomography* (CT) scan of the chest, or tests to measure the lung function *(pulmonary function tests)* might be performed to assess for organ involvement from scleroderma.

What Elements of My History Will Be Obtained?

Scleroderma can present with symptoms related to involvement of different internal organs. Some people might have visible changes, such as skin tightening or Raynaud phenomenon, which might prompt them to see a doctor. Others have more subtle *signs* and symptoms, such as puffy hands, or trouble with swallowing or breathing that might prompt an evaluation for scleroderma.

Raynaud phenomenon is one of the most classic manifestations of scleroderma, though it can also be seen in other rheumatic conditions such as lupus, and it can also occur in people who do not have a rheumatic disease (Figure 2-1). Your doctor will ask whether your fingers change color when exposed to the cold or when you are under stress. Raynaud phenomenon involves the spasm of arteries that affects the circulation of blood to the tips of your fingers or toes (or sometimes to your ears, tongue, or nose). Cold temperatures cause spasms of the blood vessels, which leads to reduced blood flow to the area and whitening of the affected skin. This is followed by a blue color (due to less oxygenation of the blood in that area). After the area is warmed and the episode resolves, the skin turns red as the blood flow returns. This cycle usually lasts for a few minutes to several hours, and patients might find that warming measures, such as using mittens or gloves, help to prevent this from happening. Patients might also notice ulcers at the tips of the fingers, which can result from injury to the fingertips from reduced blood supply with Raynaud phenomenon attacks.

Chapter 2: Can Scleroderma Be Identified Early During the Disease?   13

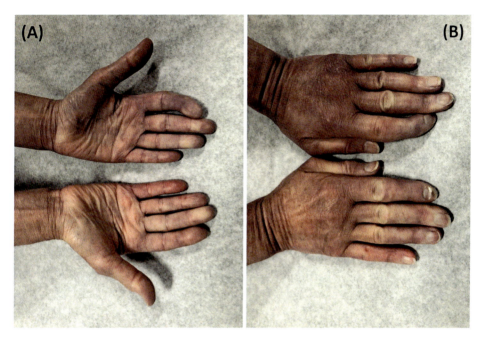

Figure 2-1: (A) Raynaud's phenomenon and (B) puffy hands in a patient with scleroderma.

During your visit, you will also be asked about other signs and symptoms (e.g., fatigue, fevers, weight loss, joint pain or stiffness, muscle aches). These symptoms are not specific to scleroderma, but they can be seen in those with this disease. You will also be asked about symptoms that could point to involvement of any of your internal organs such as your heart and lungs. You might be asked about signs of lung disease (e.g., shortness of breath [especially during activity or exertion] or cough) and signs of heart disease (e.g., shortness of breath, chest pain, *palpitations*). You might be asked about dry mouth or dry eyes (collectively referred to as "*sicca symptoms*") that can occur in people with scleroderma as well as in a related disease, called *Sjogren syndrome*. You will be asked about signs and symptoms of *gastrointestinal* (GI) involvement, such as acid reflux, trouble swallowing (referred to as *dysphagia*), feeling full earlier than normal while eating, or whether you have any blood in the stool or have black stool that could be a sign of bleeding in the GI tract. Scleroderma can also cause a buildup of bacteria in the gut (*small intestinal bacterial overgrowth* (SIBO)) that can result in nausea, vomiting, diarrhea, and poor appetite. To screen for kidney disease, you might be asked whether you have a history of high blood pressure, headaches, a change in your vision, or swelling of your legs, ankles, or feet. You might also be asked about any signs of depression, or *sexual dysfunction*, which can accompany scleroderma as well as many other chronic conditions.

If you already have scleroderma, it will be helpful to know which medications, if any, you have tried and whether you have found them helpful. Some medications are intended to control the underlying activity of scleroderma, whereas others are intended to control symptoms on a day-to-day basis.

In addition to all of these questions, a family history (asking about diseases that run in your family) and a social history (asking about your occupation, living situation, and use of tobacco, alcohol, or other substances) will be obtained. Answers to these questions—such as your occupation and whether your symptoms have affected your ability to work, a history of smoking or alcohol use, and whether there is a family history of scleroderma or an *autoimmune disease*—will be helpful for your doctor to know. Additionally, it will be helpful to know whether you've had age-appropriate cancer screening, which can include a *mammogram*, a *colonoscopy*, *stool blood tests*, or other tests. As with many other *autoimmune diseases*, scleroderma has been associated with several cancers. Whereas several small studies have shown no increased risk of cancer in those with scleroderma, other studies have shown an increased risk of various types of cancer (including cancer of the lungs, breast, bladder, blood, or bone marrow) (Kasifoglu et al, 2016).

Taking a comprehensive history can provide valuable clues to your doctor when deciding on a diagnosis of scleroderma, before ordering blood work or specialized tests.

Why Is the Physical Examination Important?

If scleroderma is suspected, your doctor will perform a thorough physical examination including an exam of your skin, heart, lungs, abdomen, and joints.

Your doctor will evaluate your skin for the presence or absence of findings, some of which are more specific to scleroderma, and some of which can be seen in other conditions. You will be evaluated for puffy fingers or toes, for tightening of your skin, for telangiectasias (i.e., dilated blood vessels near the surface of the skin, commonly referred to as "*spider veins*") and *calcinosis*. Telangiectasias are most commonly noted on the skin of the face, chest, and hands (Figure 2-2). If your Raynaud phenomenon is severe, pitted scars and ulcerations on the tips of the fingers or toes can be seen. Calcinosis, manifested by deposits of calcium-containing material under the skin, can be seen in some people with scleroderma. The calcium deposits (often white or light yellow) can break through the skin and be visible. If your doctor finds calcium deposits, an *X-ray* might be ordered to further evaluate the extent of the calcium deposition. The color or pigmentation of your skin can also change; scleroderma can cause areas of lightening and darkening of the skin, and if these occur together in a similar area, it can create a black and white, or "salt and pepper," pattern to your skin. Your scalp and hair will also be evaluated for hair loss.

Chapter 2: Can Scleroderma Be Identified Early During the Disease? 15

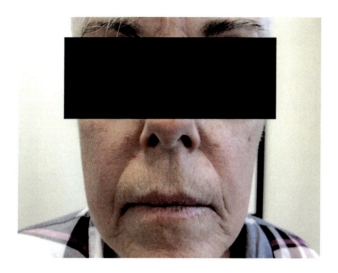

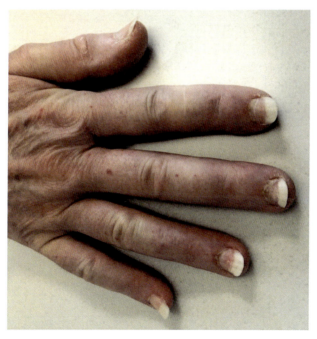

Figure 2-2: Telangiectasias (dilated blood vessels) on the face and hands of a patient with scleroderma.

Your doctor might also perform nailfold capillaroscopy to evaluate for changes in the blood vessels of your fingers, using a small hand-held microscope. This evaluation will look for certain clues that suggest scleroderma; for instance, *capillary dilation*, or enlarged blood vessels, or in the more progressive cases, capillary "drop-out," in which the capillaries disappear and are fewer in number. Bleeding of the small vessels around the cuticles, called *cuticular hemorrhage*, can also be seen with the hand-held magnifying lens.

As part of your skin assessment, your doctor might perform a modified *Rodnan Skin Score* (Figure 2-3). This assessment involves pinching the skin to measure skin thickness or tightening. This score evaluates the involvement of skin in 17 different areas of the body; for example, the face, chest, abdomen, arms, legs, fingers, and feet. A score of 0 (uninvolved), 1 (mild thickening), 2 (moderate thickening), or 3 (severe thickening) is assigned to each area to give a total score representing the degree of skin thickening throughout the body; the highest score is 51. A higher score indicates more severe disease.

The skin exam also helps to determine whether you have the limited or diffuse form of scleroderma. In *limited scleroderma*, the outermost parts of the body (past the elbows and knees) as well as the face, are involved. In *diffuse scleroderma*, the areas closer to the center of the body, such as the chest, abdomen, or trunk, are involved, as well; people with diffuse skin involvement also can have skin thickening of the face. Unfortunately, having less skin involvement does not necessarily signal less internal organ involvement.

Your doctor will also assess whether there is involvement of your joints and muscles. *Flexion contractures* can develop when the joints are locked in a flexed or bent position due to the thickening of the skin on both sides of the joint. Muscle weakness can also develop and an evaluation of the strength of different muscle groups might be performed. *Tendon friction rubs* can be felt as rubber-like cords over tendons when the joint is moved; some individuals with scleroderma or examiners might feel a grinding sensation. When present, they are often found in the tendons of the fingers, wrists, elbows, shoulder, knees, or ankles. Finally, a general exam of the heart, lungs, abdomen, and nervous system will be performed to evaluate for the presence or absence of any organ dysfunction, though this cannot always be detected by the physical exam alone.

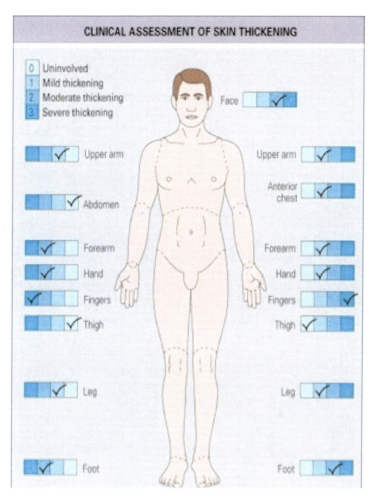

Figure 2-3: Modified Rodnan Skin Score for assessing skin involvement in a patient with scleroderma. (Reprinted from Bolster MB, Silver RM. Clinical features of systemic sclerosis. In: Hochberg MC, Silman AJ, Smolen JS, Weinblatt ME, Weisman MH, eds. *Rheumatology*, 6th edition. Philadelphia: Elsevier Ltd; 2014; 1165-1176. Copyright 2015, with permission from Elsevier.)

How Will My Doctor Know Whether I Have Scleroderma?

Your doctor will make the diagnosis of scleroderma based on your history, physical exam, and associated laboratory testing. Different *autoantibodies* are characteristic of scleroderma and can also help predict your risk of organ involvement. The most common antibodies associated with scleroderma are *anti-centromere antibodies* (ACA) and *anti-Scl-70 antibodies* (the latter is also referred to as *anti-topoisomerase I antibody*). The presence of anti-centromere antibodies is associated with limited scleroderma. Some of the other typical findings seen in those with limited scleroderma include calcinosis, Raynaud phenomenon, swallowing difficulties, *sclerodactyly* (thickening of the skin of the fingers), and telangiectasias. This constellation of findings (calcinosis, Raynaud phenomenon, esophageal dysmotility, sclerodactyly, and telangiectasias) was previously known by the acronym CREST syndrome. The anti-Scl-70 antibody, which is more commonly associated with diffuse scleroderma, is predictive of the development of more widespread thickening of the skin. Unlike the *antinuclear antibodies* (ANA), which can be seen in some people in the general population as well as in other *rheumatic diseases*, anti-Scl-70 antibodies are specific to scleroderma. In general, people with scleroderma might have either an anti-centromere or anti-Scl-70 antibody; however, affected individuals do not usually have both (Ho and Reveille, 2003). Some other antibodies that could be present in those with scleroderma include *anti-PM-Scl, anti-RNA Polymerase III*, and *anti-Th/To antibodies*. The presence of the anti-RNA Polymerase III antibody has an association with diffuse skin involvement, *digital ulcers, gastric antral vascular ectasia* (GAVE), and kidney disease. An increased association with cancer has been found in those with anti-RNA Polymerase III antibodies. In those with a positive anti-RNA Polymerase III antibody, routine cancer screening with your primary care provider is important. Each person with scleroderma does not necessarily have one or more of the autoantibodies; some people might have none. It is not known whether these specific autoantibodies are directly responsible for the disease manifestations in scleroderma; however, they are helpful for the purpose of classifying the disease and predicting certain aspects of the prognosis.

Although there is no single diagnostic test for scleroderma, classification criteria are used to diagnose scleroderma for the purposes of clinical research. The *American College of Rheumatology* (ACR) and *European League Against Rheumatism* (EULAR) developed criteria in 2013 that uses a point system to determine the likelihood of someone having systemic sclerosis. Skin thickening of the fingers that extends past the fingers and onto the hands is sufficient to meet the criteria for scleroderma if it occurs on both hands. Other findings that are included in the criteria include puffy fingers, ulcers on the fingertips, telangiectasias (dilated blood vessels on the surface of the skin), lung disease, abnormal nailfold capillaries (visualized by nailfold capillaroscopy), Raynaud phenomenon (color changes of the fingers induced by cold), and antibody testing indicative of scleroderma. The total score, with higher points indicating more manifestations, is representative of the likelihood of scleroderma (van den Hoogen et al, 2013).

What Are the Different Types of Scleroderma?

We have primarily focused on the *systemic form of scleroderma*, also known as *systemic sclerosis*. Within systemic sclerosis are the limited and diffuse forms, which we discussed earlier in the chapter. Other forms of scleroderma are localized to the skin (without internal organ involvement), and these are mimics of scleroderma that your doctor will help identify.

Localized scleroderma (scleroderma without any systemic manifestations or organ involvement) is limited to the skin; it can present as *morphea, linear scleroderma,* or *scleroderma en coup de sabre*. Morphea presents as plaques on the trunk or extremities that can be red or dark and that can become shiny after an extended period. Linear scleroderma is represented by a streak of hard, waxy skin and often develops on the arms, legs, or forehead; it is more common in children. Scleroderma *en coup de sabre* (named to indicate a saber or sword-like wound) often occurs around the head and neck, characteristically on the forehead, and appears as a long crease.

Other conditions that can mimic scleroderma include *eosinophilic fasciitis, scleromyxedema,* and *scleredema*. Eosinophilic fasciitis can have a *"peau d'orange"* appearance (i.e., looking like an orange peel) of the skin on the extremities and typically spares the fingers; sparing of the fingers helps to differentiate it from scleroderma. Scleromyxedema often involves the muscles and gives a waxy appearance to the skin. Scleredema, a condition that can be associated with *diabetes*, presents with thickening and hardening of the skin, often involving the upper back; it also spares the hands and feet.

What Factors Increase My Risk of Developing Organ Involvement in Scleroderma?

Internal organ manifestations typically develop within the first 2 to 5 years of disease (by 5 years in about 75% of people with scleroderma); thus, there is a critical window for early recognition and either prevention or treatment of organ disease (Jaeger et al, 2016). Even though involvement of the heart, lungs, or kidneys can occur after 5 years, the chances of developing these problems becomes much lower.

It is important to note that the degree of skin thickening does not always correlate with the degree of internal organ disease, although diffuse skin involvement is indeed a risk factor for internal organ involvement. Interestingly, over time, the skin actually softens; thus, in later stages of the disease, the extent of skin involvement is less indicative of the degree of internal organ disease (Khanna, 2019).

Although scleroderma is predominantly seen in women—in a ratio ranging from 5:1 to 10:1—men who develop scleroderma are at greater risk for developing internal organ involvement (Barnes and Mayes, 2012). Men have a higher risk of *renal crisis* as well as impaired lung function. They also tend to develop their first *Raynaud phenomenon symptoms* earlier in the disease course than women (Jaeger et al, 2016).

Race and ethnicity correlate with both the risk of disease and its severity. Certain groups have different prevalence rates of disease. African Americans tend to be younger at the time of their diagnosis and they have more severe lung disease and more severe disease overall (Mayes and Assassi, 2015). The Choctaw Native Americans have the highest prevalence of scleroderma of any group in the country (Bossini-Castillo et al, 2015). This is likely due to several *genes*, including a uniquely Native American gene that serves to regulate immune function (Mayes and Assassi, 2015). There is a much lower risk in those with origins in Japan, Iceland, England, and Greece (Mayes and Assassi, 2015).

Many *autoantibodies* convey an increased risk of developing certain aspects of scleroderma. The *anti-centromere antibody* is associated with limited skin involvement as well as with *pulmonary arterial hypertension* (PAH), whereas anti-Scl-70 antibody is associated with diffuse skin involvement and with the presence of *interstitial lung disease* (ILD; Ho and Reveille, 2003). However, people with limited skin involvement can still develop ILD. Anti-RNA polymerase III antibody is associated with more severe skin disease, ulcers on the fingertips, a condition of blood vessel dilation and bleeding in the stomach (*gastric antral vascular ectasia* [GAVE]), *scleroderma renal crisis* (SRC; severe kidney disease), and an increased risk of cancer (Ho and Reveille, 2003). In general, antibodies that have a better prognosis include anti-centromere, anti-PM-Scl, and *anti-U1-RNP*. Antibodies associated with a worse prognosis include anti-Scl-70, anti-Th/To, and anti-RNA Polymerase III (Ho and Reveille, 2003). Anti-Th/To is associated with limited skin disease but can also be predictive of the development of pulmonary hypertension (Ho and Reveille, 2003).

Multiple studies have looked at environmental factors and their impact either on the development or the severity of disease in people with scleroderma; however, there is no conclusive evidence to show that any factor has a clear role. Smoking, or tobacco use, is not a risk factor for developing scleroderma, but it can contribute to worsening lung disease, increased problems with the blood vessels (particularly Raynaud phenomenon symptoms and fingertip ulcers), and overall disease severity (Marie and Gehanno, 2015). Exposure to silica (from drilling, sanding, coal mining) or certain organic solvents (e.g., white spirit, aromatic solvents, chlorinated solvents, trichloroethylene, ketones) might be associated with scleroderma.

Medications, such as high-dose *corticosteroids* (including *prednisone*) pose some risk for developing SRC (Steen and Medsger, 1998). Thus, use of prednisone in people with scleroderma is often avoided or used only in low doses. There is no evidence to suggest that foods, additives, moderate consumption of alcohol, or other supplements contribute to either scleroderma or to organ involvement.

Can I Pass Scleroderma Along to My Children or Grandchildren?

In scleroderma, as with many conditions, there is a complex interplay of both environmental and *genetic factors* that contribute to the risk of disease. Multiple studies have shown that the presence of a family history of scleroderma is the most significant risk factor for developing the disease (Frech et al, 2010); however, there is no certainty that your children or grandchildren will get scleroderma if you have scleroderma. A first-degree relative of someone with scleroderma has a 13-fold higher risk of developing scleroderma than members of the general population, and this rises to a 15-fold risk if your relative is a sibling (Bossini-Castillo et al, 2015). Unlike other diseases such as *Huntington disease, cystic fibrosis, sickle cell anemia,* or *Tay-Sachs disease*, in which a single gene is often affected and is able to be tested, there are no simple genetic tests to screen for scleroderma. Because scleroderma is quite rare, the absolute risk of developing it for each affected family member is still less than 1% (Frech et al, 2010).

HOW ARE COMPLICATIONS OF SCLERODERMA RECOGNIZED AND TREATED?

Nancy Elorreaga, LCSW and Tracy M. Frech, MD, MS

CHAPTER

In This Chapter

- What Can My Doctor Learn from Talking to Me About My Symptoms?
- What Tests Are Used to Diagnose Scleroderma?
- What Screening Tests Should I Expect My Doctor to Perform?
- Which Screening Tests Will Need to Be Repeated?
- What Is the Role of Preventative Measures for Avoiding Complications?

Appointments with your doctor, whether at his or her office or at a scleroderma center, can be overwhelming, especially when you meet your *rheumatologist* for the first time. The symptoms you are experiencing and how you are feeling and functioning will help to determine whether you are having complications of scleroderma. Scleroderma clinic visits can be complex because your health care team (e.g., physicians, therapists, dietitians, nurses) work to recognize potential complications as well as to provide you with the best treatment available; however, sometimes scleroderma has few symptoms and/or is difficult to diagnose. To receive comprehensive care, you might need to see several providers, including a rheumatologist, a *pulmonologist*, and a *gastroenterologist*, to best recognize and treat the complications of scleroderma. It is important to understand why your symptoms might lead to further testing and whether the results of such testing might lead to a change in treatment.

What Can My Doctor Learn from Talking to Me About My Symptoms?

The symptoms that you experience and your level of functioning can be the most important clues to identifying complications of scleroderma (Bassel et al, 2011). Your physician will ask you questions about your symptoms in a comprehensive yet efficient manner. On occasion, questionnaires, which might also be labeled *patient reported outcome measures* or *health assessment questionnaires*, can assist in identifying symptoms and screening for complications of scleroderma. These questionnaires might be given to you in paper format or electronically; they are often used for research purposes to help physicians and health care systems link symptoms to diseases. These questionnaires can be brief, such as the General Health Assessment Questionnaire, or be more symptom specific, relating to your *gastrointestinal* (GI) tract, to your breathing, or to your mood (e.g., depression). If completing the questionnaire makes you worry about your responses, be sure that you discuss your concerns or worries with members of your health care team during your visit. Your report of how you are feeling and how your symptoms have developed and changed is one of the most important aspects of your visit with your health care provider.

Alternatively, if you are not given a questionnaire at your care visit but have tracked your symptoms either by a diary (such as the *Raynaud's Condition Score*) or online questionnaires (such as the *University of California Los Angeles Gastrointestinal Tract 2.0*), you can bring your diary or log to your office visit and request to have these forms added to your medical record. Questionnaires, particularly those that have been tested or validated in those with scleroderma, can be very helpful for monitoring responses to treatments and guiding your management (Pauling et al, 2017).

What Tests Are Used to Diagnose Scleroderma?

The diagnosis of scleroderma is made by identifying a constellation of symptoms, physical exam findings, laboratory assessments, and *internal organ screening studies*. *Classification criteria* help your physician to make the diagnosis of scleroderma (van den Hoogen et al, 2013). It is important to note that sometimes, especially early in the disease process, you might not meet criteria for scleroderma. If this occurs, close clinical follow-up will be helpful.

The physical exam will be used to assess the degree of skin thickening. This assessment involves the physician pinching the skin of your fingers, hands, upper and lower arms, chest, abdomen, face, thighs, legs, and feet, on both sides of your body; this process is used to calculate the *Modified Rodnan Skin Score* (see Chapter 2) (Kim et al, 2017). Additionally, your physician will examine your hands closely for puffiness, inspect the pads of your fingers for ulcers and scars, and might evaluate your *nailfold capillaries* with a magnification device. The nailfold capillaries are very small blood vessels located at the base of your fingernails; this exam can reveal the presence of dilated loops, hemorrhages, capillary loss, or abnormal vessels that are characteristically seen in people with scleroderma (Cutolo et al, 2006). Your physician will also look for *telangiectasias*. These are visible, dilated, superficial blood vessels that are round, large, and often mat-like; they are commonly found on the hands, the chest, the lips, or the inside of the mouth in those with scleroderma. Although not a part of the classification criteria for scleroderma (but important for identifying potential complications), your physician will also examine your blood pressure, determine your muscle strength (to screen for muscle involvement), and press on your joints and *tendons* looking for signs of *inflammation*. Examination of your heart and lungs helps to ensure that there are not manifestations here of *internal organ involvement*.

What Screening Tests Should I Expect My Doctor to Perform?

Internal organ screening for heart and lung involvement is part of the diagnostic evaluation because these organs generate symptoms that can be quite limiting for people with scleroderma and also contribute importantly to the classification criteria of scleroderma; such screening is often conducted at the time of diagnosis as well as periodically when you are seen in follow-up. This screening includes *pulmonary function tests* (PFTs) *with spirometry and diffusion capacity*, an *echocardiogram*, and a *high-resolution computed tomography* (HRCT) scan of the chest (Molberg and Hoffmann-Vold, 2016; Pope, 2017). The decision to order these studies is based on disease duration as well as skin distribution; assessment might be completed in a step-wise manner. The reason for these screening tests is that *pulmonary arterial hypertension* (PAH; elevated lung pressures) and *interstitial lung disease* (ILD; lung scarring) can occur in people with scleroderma; if either manifestation is identified, it will require specific treatment. Additional studies might be indicated if any one of these screening tests is abnormal. For example, if the echocardiogram reveals elevated *pulmonary pressures*, a *right heart catheterization* (to establish the diagnosis of pulmonary arterial hypertension) will be indicated. If PAH is found, your physician might recommend further screening tests, such as a *sleep study* to assess for *obstructive sleep apnea* (OSA), an infectious disease screen, and possibly further testing for the presence of blood-clotting abnormalities (Rimoldi et al, 2014). It is important to realize that screening tests are used to help guide next steps and that a certain test result might prompt further testing (for diagnostic and treatment purposes).

Additional studies might be indicated, based on findings from your physical exam. For example, if your physical exam identifies that you have tender and swollen joints, your physician might order laboratory screening for an inflammatory arthritis as well as *joint imaging* (such as standard *radiographs*, also known more commonly as *X-rays*, or an *ultrasound*). If you have muscle weakness, your physician might ask that you have blood work to screen for muscle inflammation as well as an *electromyogram* (EMG) *with nerve conduction study* or *magnetic resonance imaging* (MRI) of the muscle(s) that is demonstrating signs of weakness. The results of these screening tests can lead to the decision to perform a *muscle biopsy* (Walker et al, 2017).

During your diagnostic evaluation, screening laboratory tests will look for an *antinuclear antibody* [ANA], *scleroderma-specific antibodies*, and for other *autoimmune conditions*. For example, you might complain of dry eyes and a dry mouth, which will prompt ophthalmologic and dental evaluations, and you might be screened for *Sjogren syndrome* with blood testing that includes an *SSA* and *SSB antibody*. You might also be screened for *diabetes* or *thyroid disease*. The extent of blood work and additional studies obtained will likely be determined by your age, by the duration and extent of your symptoms, and by the consistency of your prior health maintenance. Based on certain disease features (such as the presence of certain autoantibodies), your physician will likely recommend age-appropriate cancer screenings, as well. Of note, the *autoantibody* screens are often only done at the initial visit for diagnostic purposes; these markers do not change with disease activity and thus are typically not repeated at subsequent visits. If these tests have been performed by another laboratory, it is important for you to bring these test results to your initial clinic visit because they can be expensive to perform; if the test results are not readily available, they might need to be repeated. If they have been performed correctly, they will not need to be repeated. However, it is also important to note that some laboratory procedures can be more reliable than others. If your scleroderma diagnosis is in question, your health care provider might request that your test(s) be repeated by their laboratory.

Which Screening Tests Will Need to Be Repeated?

Although disease duration and change of skin thickening can help your health care provider determine the appropriate timing of repeat screening tests, your symptoms and your treatments are the most important determinants of when and how often these tests should be ordered and repeated (Bellando-Randone and Matucci-Cerinic, 2017). If you were diagnosed less than 2 years ago with *diffuse scleroderma* (i.e., having *peripheral* as well as *proximal* skin involvement, involving the skin on your upper arms, chest, abdomen, and thighs [see Chapters 1 and 2]), your diagnosis might require clinic visits and screenings every few months; however, if you have been stable, with *limited scleroderma* (involving only your hands and arms), and have had normal screening test results, you might need only an annual assessment. The standard of care for ongoing assessment of scleroderma of your internal organs includes annual assessment of your PFTs and an echocardiogram. Your physician might use other laboratory tests, including an *electrocardiogram* (EKG) to determine whether an echocardiogram is needed annually.

Nevertheless, each visit with your physician should include a comprehensive interim history, a review of your home blood pressure readings (particularly for people with diffuse scleroderma because blood pressure recordings screen for *scleroderma renal crisis* [SRC]), assessment of your *exercise tolerance*, nutrition, and GI symptoms, as well as a skin exam, focused on whether there have been changes in the thickness of your skin or damage to your skin, and a cardiopulmonary examination.

Treatment of scleroderma (see also Chapter 4) is often thought of in two categories: immune based and *vascular* based. Immune-based medication therapies (e.g., mycophenolate mofetil or cyclophosphamide) are directed at stopping fibrosis of the skin or lungs, or inflammation of the joints and muscles (e.g., methotrexate). These medications require regular laboratory evaluations (blood and urine), which generally are obtained every 1 to 3 months, to ensure that your *bone marrow*, *liver*, and *kidneys* are tolerating the medication. Vascular-based medications are used to target *Raynaud phenomenon*, PAH, and scleroderma renal crisis. Treatment for Raynaud phenomenon includes the use of *calcium channel blockers* (e.g., amlodipine, nifedipine), whereas *phosphodiesterase inhibitors* (e.g., tadalafil, sildenafil), *endothelin receptor antagonists* (ERAs) (e.g., bosentan, macitentan), or *prostacyclin analogs* (e.g., iloprost) are used to address PAH. Angiotensin converting enzyme (ACE) inhibitors (e.g., enalapril, lisinopril) are the cornerstone of treatment for scleroderma renal crisis. Unfortunately, because scleroderma is a rare disease without specific US *Food and Drug Administration* (FDA)–approved therapeutics, receiving authorization for coverage from your insurance company for these medications, to be affordable, may be difficult for your physician to obtain. Fortunately, there are many clinical trials in process, or planned, for people with scleroderma, with a goal of improving treatment options for the complications of scleroderma.

If GI tract symptoms are present, your provider might refer you to a gastroenterologist or order diagnostic procedures to help recognize and diagnose GI tract disease. These treatments are generally targeted to specific GI symptoms rather than toward the *immune system* or *vasculature*. The diagnosis and management of GI symptoms can include allergy testing and implementation of dietary changes. In addition, your physician might recommend that you see a certified dietitian. As previously mentioned, screening questionnaires, such as the University of California Los Angeles Gastrointestinal Tract 2.0, or UCLA GIT 2.0, are excellent methods for identifying GI symptoms in people with scleroderma (Khanna et al, 2013).

The most common GI symptom in someone with scleroderma is *reflux* (*gastroesophageal reflux*; i.e., heartburn). If you have difficulty swallowing or if food is sticking in your throat when you eat, your physician might assess this problem with a *barium esophagram* or *upper endoscopy (esophagogastroduodenoscopy, or EGD)*. The barium swallow can be done in the radiology department with a *speech therapist*, who can simultaneously evaluate you for the risk of *aspiration* (food going into your airway). Alternatively, an EGD is performed by a gastroenterologist or *surgeon* while you are sedated. An EGD is a useful screening tool and can be diagnostic if there is concern for bleeding from the stomach, such as with *gastric antral vascular ectasia* (GAVE or "watermelon stomach"). An EGD can also be used therapeutically to treat certain causes of difficulty with swallowing (such as an *esophageal stricture*) that are common in those with scleroderma. EGDs for GAVE and stricture management might need to be repeated several times each year, depending on the severity or recurrence of symptoms.

Other upper GI tract procedures can be performed if you are having heartburn, such as *pH monitoring with impedance*. Additionally, if you are considering surgery for reflux management, a *motility study* for screening is mandatory. If your physician is concerned about bloating from *small intestinal bacterial overgrowth* (SIBO) due to recurrent diarrhea, a *hydrogen breath test* might be in order. Empiric GI tract symptom treatment and management might include use of reflux medications (to suppress acid production), use of rotating *antibiotics* (for bacterial overgrowth), and *promotility drugs* (for *dysmotility*). These treatment options might be chosen as an alternative to more invasive testing.

Lower GI tract screening is highly recommended in those with scleroderma who are older than age 50, especially if diarrhea or constipation are present. This screening is generally completed with a *colonoscopy*; the timing of having this screening test repeated is determined by the presence of *polyps*. Fecal soilage or spontaneous leakage of stool is a symptom that should be evaluated by a gastroenterologist or by a *colorectal surgeon* to ensure that all necessary screening tests are completed. These additional tests might include *stool studies, rectal manometry,* a *transrectal ultrasound,* and *defecography;* they are used to identify the need for a surgical procedure. These lower-GI studies might need to be completed only once because they are often diagnostic. Even though some topics, such as fecal soilage or anal leakage, might be difficult for you to discuss, they are important topics for your health care providers to know about so that he or she can order appropriate screening tests. Similarly, *sexual dysfunction* can benefit from a referral to a *gynecologist* or *urologist* for more advanced diagnostic testing to improve functioning.

What Is the Role of Preventative Measures for Avoiding Complications?

Two common complaints from people with scleroderma who have completed extensive patient-reported outcomes are the length of the questionnaires and the fear that these questions instill in the person filling them out (e.g., "Am I going to start soiling myself with stool one day?"). As such, people completing extensive scleroderma questionnaires often ask what they can do to stay well.

Symptom management is an essential component of your comprehensive scleroderma care. Although disease management treatments, procedures, and therapies can assist you with a possible overall reduction of disease activity as well as potentially slowing the progression of your scleroderma, your consistent management of symptoms will enhance your level of functioning on a day-to-day basis.

The health care providers you see to treat your scleroderma are specialists who focus solely or primarily on the treatment of scleroderma and scleroderma-related health issues. Other, more general health issues and concerns might arise that are unrelated to scleroderma. As such, a *primary care physician* (PCP) is an important part of your health care team (Saketkoo et al, 2014). The role of your PCP is to allow you to see a provider when you have general and non-scleroderma as well as scleroderma-related health concerns. If you do not have a PCP, it is important for you to select one and to initiate care. It is best for you to select a PCP who not only is close to your home and work, but who is also covered by your insurance plan.

Symptoms of scleroderma can be *acute* or *chronic*. It is important for you to contact your PCP or rheumatologist's office if and when you experience the acute onset of scleroderma-related symptoms. Of note, ongoing communication between your PCP and rheumatologist is helpful in the management and care of your scleroderma symptoms. Recommendations to address various chronic symptoms can be provided to you by your provider(s), particularly by your rheumatologist, during your office visits. To help in the management of the more chronic symptoms, it is important for you to show discipline with any recommended treatment regimens, lifestyle changes, and monitoring. Another vital part to symptom and disease management is to attend your regularly scheduled office visits.

The care you provide for yourself is one of the most important aspects of your scleroderma disease management and can help you achieve and sustain a balance in your life (Shah and Wigley, 2013). Self-care involves caring for your well-being, including your physical health, psychological health, emotional health, spiritual health, relationship health, and workplace and professional health. Creating balance in your life, especially after receiving a diagnosis of scleroderma, is difficult to achieve; however, working toward having this balance will help you to maintain your highest level of health and functioning. The way you approach your self-care to reach your life's balance is personalized; everyone approaches self-care and life balance differently.

Proper nutrition, exercise, sleep, and mental health are the cornerstones to wellness for everyone, but it is especially important for those with scleroderma (see Chapter 9). Often, it is helpful to meet with a *physical therapist* or *occupational therapist* to develop an exercise and stretching plan as well as to learn about *adaptive equipment*. *Pulmonary rehabilitation* and *sleep clinic* can be very helpful for ensuring that *oxygen* delivery is maximized and exercise intensity is appropriate. In addition to the various physical symptoms that can develop with scleroderma, emotional stress can also arise. Many different thoughts and feelings can develop after you have received any diagnosis, particularly a diagnosis of a chronic disease such as scleroderma.

Each person reacts in his or her own way after receiving a scleroderma diagnosis. Common reactions include emotional reactions (such as fear, worry, denial, anger, and sadness), self-blaming, self-defining thoughts, grief, exhaustion, and feeling alone. There are many things that you can do to help and support yourself when you are faced with any of these thoughts and emotions (Kwakkenbos et al, 2015). It is important for you to be kind to yourself, to avoid judging yourself, and to allow yourself to feel, explore, understand, and accept your thoughts and emotions. Pacing your physical and mental activities on a daily basis, effectively managing your stress, and finding as well as utilizing an efficient support system are also critical pieces of your care plan (see Chapter 9). If you have persistent feelings of sadness, hopelessness, or helplessness; if you feel stuck in your grief process or with any other concerns; or you would like more support, it is important for you to seek therapeutic support with a clinic or community provider, such as a *licensed clinical social worker* (LCSW). Support groups, foundations, and organizations for scleroderma can be useful sources of information and support, as well. Even though local support groups can be helpful resources, it is important for you to know that every person with scleroderma is different, and the one person who knows your body and what works best for you is you.

Your physician and health care team should be your partner in your wellness and help explain to you, based on the results of a comprehensive personalized history, physical exam, laboratory, and *ancillary study* evaluation, whether you have complications of scleroderma that require further treatment. You can be proactive in your health by maintaining a healthy weight, knowing your blood pressure, engaging in regular physical activity, addressing GI symptoms, and taking care of your hands, to minimize any complications. You are an important part of your health care team, and by being actively involved in your own care, you will help your providers take the best care of you.

HOW CAN SCLERODERMA AND ITS COMPLICATIONS BE TREATED?

Chase Correia, MD and Monique Hinchcliff, MD, MS

CHAPTER 4

In This Chapter

- Overview
- How Can Skin Thickening Be Treated?
- How Can Raynaud Phenomenon Be Treated?
- How Can the Gastrointestinal Manifestations of Scleroderma Be Treated?
- How Can Pulmonary Complications of Scleroderma Be Treated?
- How Can Renal Complications of Scleroderma Be Treated?
- How Can Muscle and Joint Symptoms of Scleroderma Be Treated?
- Summary

Overview

Scleroderma, a disorder involving *inflammation* and *immune system activation*, can affect many of the body's organs (Hinchcliff and Varga, 2011). When *symptoms* develop, treatment decisions are tailored to your symptoms. Some scleroderma treatments are anti-inflammatory and suppress the *immune system*. Other treatments aim to reverse *fibrosis* (scar tissue) formation, whereas other therapies are designed to increase blood flow to the affected organ to prevent injury and to speed healing. *Immunosuppressive* and *antifibrotic medications* take time to work, and improvement in disease activity is often slow, requiring persistence as well as careful monitoring. *Stem cell transplantation* is a promising therapy for a select group of carefully screened patients with active skin and lung disease (Burt et al, 2011; Farge et al, 2017; Sullivan et al, 2018; van Laar et al, 2014).

A holistic approach to patient care is best because medication for one symptom may worsen another symptom. Take, for instance, the treatment of *Raynaud phenomenon* in which a therapy to improve blood flow to the fingers might worsen heartburn. It is also necessary to plan ahead. Some medications affect fertility or should not be taken during pregnancy. Therefore, careful family planning is required. Another example is the timing of necessary vaccinations. Because an intact immune system is required for *vaccines* to be most effective, vaccines should be administered before an *immune modulator* is started, if at all possible. Scleroderma can affect many different organ systems in the body requiring a team-based approach. Developing a *therapeutic alliance* with your doctor(s) is essential. Your health care providers need to know your goals for the treatment of your disease because scleroderma can affect individuals very differently.

How Can Skin Thickening Be Treated?

Much research is geared toward finding the appropriate treatment for each patient; this is called *precision medicine* (Hinchcliff and Whitfield, 2017). Current medications for skin thickening appear to be effective in some, but not all, individuals. Fortunately, there is a growing list of medications that can be tried. Let's take a look at them.

Cyclophosphamide

Cyclophosphamide was the first medication shown to improve involvement of the skin, lungs, and heart associated with scleroderma (Tashkin et al, 2006; Shah and Kahan, 2012). When given in higher doses, it is a form of *chemotherapy*. For those with scleroderma, it can be given in lower doses as an oral or *intravenous* (IV) medication, and it is dosed low enough to be considered as an anti-inflammatory and *immunosuppressant*. When given intravenously, it is typically administered monthly. Tests for *tuberculosis* and *viral hepatitis* should be checked before starting cyclophosphamide. Additionally, a *complete blood count* (CBC), tests of liver and kidney function, and urine tests should be checked before and during treatment. Dosage adjustments will be made if the *white blood cell* (WBC) count, checked 10 to 14 days after cyclophosphamide administration, is too low. Potential side effects of cyclophosphamide are many and include hair loss, diarrhea, nausea, vomiting, and infections. Sterility and birth defects can also result from starting cyclophosphamide; therefore, a discussion with a *fertility preservation specialist* is of great importance in young individuals who are not receiving cyclophosphamide on an emergency basis. Less common, but serious, side effects of cyclophosphamide include toxicities of the bladder (*hemorrhagic cystitis* [bleeding in the bladder]) heart, liver, and lungs. Any blood in the urine should be immediately reported to your physician. Cancers have also occurred with increased frequency in those treated with cyclophosphamide, but it is difficult to determine whether cancers are directly related to cyclophosphamide administration. Nonetheless, people exposed to cyclophosphamide should undergo regular cancer screening.

Mycophenolic Acid

Two formulations of *mycophenolic acid* (MPA), *mycophenolate mofetil (CellCept®)*, and *mycophenolate sodium (Myfortic®)* are used to treat scleroderma skin thickening. One study showed that skin disease improved in people with active scleroderma who took mycophenolate mofetil for one year (Tashkin et al, 2016). Moreover, those with scleroderma who took mycophenolate mofetil showed improvements in their skin disease that mirrored a decline in a specific cell type that is thought to play a key role in this disease (Hinchcliff et al, 2018). Side effects from MPA include diarrhea (which typically improves over time), low blood counts, and infections. Although increased rates of *lymphoma* have been reported in recipients of *solid organ transplants* who take MPA along with other strong immunosuppressive medications, there are no reports to date of increased rates of lymphoma in people with scleroderma who are prescribed MPA. MPA decreases concentrations of *hormonal contraceptives*; therefore, an alternative form of contraception (e.g., a copper *intrauterine device* [IUD] or barrier method) should be used. You should avoid pregnancy while taking MPA. Studies in individuals with *systemic lupus erythematosus* (SLE) suggest that MPA should be discontinued at least 6 weeks before *conception* (Pisoni and D'Cruz, 2008). There is no available data to make a recommendation for the interval between discontinuing MPA and conception in those with scleroderma, but a delay of at least 6 weeks seems prudent. Tests for tuberculosis and viral hepatitis are typically checked before starting MPA. Blood monitoring is performed on a routine basis with regular tests of kidney and liver function as well as a CBC.

Methotrexate

Methotrexate (MTX), when used at higher dosages, has been used as a chemotherapy drug since the 1980s to treat lymphoma. At much lower dosages, the drug dampens an overactive immune system, and it can be used to treat many rheumatic diseases, including scleroderma. MTX is used in scleroderma to treat skin thickening, particularly when the changes are progressing rapidly or associated with arthritis (van den Hoogen et al, 1996). MTX is taken once weekly in pill form or injected beneath the skin, similar to the way insulin injections are given. Common side effects of MTX include nausea, vomiting, diarrhea, fatigue, hair thinning, and oral ulcers. A low starting dose followed by a slow dosage increase usually prevents side effects. Additionally, *folic acid* (folate, a B-vitamin) can be taken to prevent side effects, such as oral ulcers. The typical over-the-counter folic acid supplement is not as strong as the dosage recommended for people taking MTX. Rare, but dangerous, side effects associated with MTX include low blood cell counts, liver abnormalities, lung toxicity, and infections. Although there is a *black box warning* for lymphoma related to MTX use in those with rheumatoid arthritis, studies have shown that this association disappears when adjusting for other factors that might explain lymphoma risk (Mariette et al, 2002). Tests for tuberculosis and viral hepatitis are typically checked before starting MTX. Blood monitoring is performed on a routine basis with regular tests of CBC, kidney, and liver function. You should report new problems with breathing or infectious symptoms to your doctors. MTX causes fetal death and *congenital abnormalities*; therefore, you must avoid pregnancy while taking MTX. Two forms of contraception are typically recommended in women of childbearing age (https://mothertobaby.org/fact-sheets/methotrexate-pregnancy/). MTX should be stopped by men and women taking this medication before attempting to conceive a child. Men should stop taking MTX for at least 6 months and women for at least 3 months before conception to avoid an increased risk for birth defects.

IV Immunoglobulin

Immunoglobulins bind to overactive immune cells and target them for clearance from the body. Monthly IV immunoglobulin (IVIg) infusions have been studied in those with scleroderma and have been shown to have the potential to improve skin, muscle, and joint symptoms (Sanges et al, 2017; Dourmishev et al, 2018). There are many IVIg formulations, and some have the potential for more side effects than others. IVIg is commonly administered at infusion centers to permit large volumes of fluid to be administered in a monitored setting. Side effects can include mild headache, dizziness, fatigue, back pain, muscle cramps, chest pain, and flushing. In rare circumstances, severe migraine headaches or *blood clots* can occur.

Rituximab

Rituximab is a drug that targets one of the *receptors* (CD20) on a specific type of WBC called *B lymphocytes (B cells)*. When rituximab binds to CD20, the B cell is targeted for destruction by the immune system. B cells play a role in inflammation and produce *antibodies*. Scleroderma is a disease characterized by *autoantibody* formation (blood proteins that target your own tissue), thus *B cell depletion therapy* might be beneficial.

There is limited data to support the use of rituximab for tight skin. A recent review of 88 individuals with scleroderma who received various IV rituximab regimens found skin improvement in those with diffuse cutaneous disease (Thiebaut et al, 2018). Yet, side effects including infections as well as adverse reactions to the medication were reported. Moreover, rituximab is very expensive (approximately to $10,000 per infusion.). The decision to use rituximab to treat tight skin must be carefully considered, weighing the risks, benefits, and cost of treatment.

Autologous Stem Cell Transplantation

Autologous stem cell transplantation (ASCT) is a treatment intended to "re-set" a deregulated immune system in those with scleroderma. There are several treatment protocols for ASCT, and all protocols involve four steps:

1. Careful selection and screening of individuals to identify appropriate candidates
2. Obtaining *stem cells* from the *bone marrow*
3. Using medications to prepare the body to receive the stem cell transplant
4. Post-treatment care (Burt et al, 2011; Sullivan et al, 2018; van Laar et al, 2014)

Screening tests include laboratory and heart and lung studies to ensure that individuals are free of serious kidney, heart, or lung involvement that would increase the risk of poor outcomes. There is a relatively high treatment-associated mortality in those who receive an ASCT related to infection, allergic reaction to transplant medications, and cardiac toxicity, among other complications, occurring even at centers that specialize in ASCT. Thus, it is important to undergo ASCT only if the potential benefits outweigh the risks, and a complete and careful screening process has occurred at an experienced center.

How Can Raynaud Phenomenon Be Treated?

One of the earliest and most common manifestations of scleroderma is *Raynaud* (pronounced "ray-know") *phenomenon* (see Chapter 1). The goal of therapy is to avoid attacks that are precipitated by cold or stress. This is accomplished by keeping the body core (the chest and back) and fingers and toes warm. Dressing in layers and carrying mittens, gloves, or hand warmers at all times is of paramount importance. Methods to reduce stress, including use of mindfulness, prayer, meditation, exercise (walking, yoga, and *tai chi*), can be helpful. You should avoid drugs (*nicotine*, cocaine, tobacco smoke [or vaping], excessive caffeine) and medicines (*methylphenidate [Ritalin]* and *amphetamine/dextroamphetamine [Adderall]*) that increase blood vessel tone and decrease blood flow.

Additionally, medications and supplements can be prescribed for Raynaud phenomenon, including aspirin and vitamin E (to facilitate blood flow to the digits). Calcium channel blockers, *angiotensin receptor blockers* (ARBs), *phosphodiesterase 5 inhibitors*, *nitrates*, *prostacyclin analogues*, and *endothelin receptor blockers* (ERB) can also be used to help the muscles in blood vessel walls to relax and permit greater blood flow (see the section "How Can Pulmonary Complications of Scleroderma Be Treated?") (Herrick, 2017). All medications that act to expand blood vessels can worsen symptoms of *gastroesophageal reflux disease* (GERD), and cause headache, dizziness, flushing, an increased heart rate, and leg swelling. It is important to report any new symptoms to your doctor.

Calcium Channel Blockers

The most frequently used class of medications for Raynaud phenomenon are calcium channel blockers (see Table 4-1). These medications expand blood vessels by blocking the calcium channels in the muscle cells that line blood vessel walls (Rirash et al, 2017). Evidence suggests that these medications can be useful in decreasing the frequency and severity of Raynaud phenomenon attacks. Common side effects include headache, dizziness, nausea, *palpitations*, and ankle edema. With slow dose escalation, calcium channel blockers are usually well tolerated. They can be taken with or without food, but you should avoid grapefruit in all forms because it increases drug levels. Tell your doctor if you are also taking St. John's wort, clarithromycin, or phenytoin because drug interactions can occur. A recent review article suggested that calcium channel blockers might reduce the frequency, duration, severity, pain and disability of Raynaud phenomenon attacks in those with scleroderma-associated Raynaud phenomenon (Rirash et al, 2017).

Angiotensin Receptor Blockers

In those with insufficient benefit from calcium channel blockers, another class of medications, called angiotensin receptor blockers (ARBs) can replace or be added to calcium channel blockers to treat *Raynaud phenomenon symptoms* (Dziadzio et al, 1999). These medicines act to expand blood vessels by blocking a specific angiotensin receptor that increases blood vessel muscle tone; the net effect is blood vessel relaxation. Results of a 1999 study suggest that *losartan* improves the severity and the frequency of Raynaud phenomenon attacks (Dziadzio et al, 1999). A newer ARB, *telmisartan*, looks promising for the treatment of those with Raynaud phenomenon from scleroderma because, in addition to blood vessel dilation, it also decreases scar formation (fibrosis) in laboratory animals with diseases involving fibrosis (Ionica et al, 2016; Shang et al, 2017; Zhang et al, 2017).

Phosphodiesterase 5 Inhibitors

Phosphodiesterase 5 inhibitors can be prescribed in addition to calcium channel blockers and/or ARBs for those with severe symptoms of Raynaud phenomenon (including those who experience painful *digital ulcers*) (Table 4-1). A digital ulcer can appear as a painful circular sore that forms on the fleshy part of the fingertip. Many insurance companies in the United States will not cover the cost of phosphodiesterase 5 inhibitor therapy for those with Raynaud phenomenon despite results of recently published guidelines that support their use (Kowal-Bielecka et al, 2017). If needed, your doctor might be able to participate in an appeal process to try to gain insurance company approval of your medication. Phosphodiesterase 5 inhibitors can improve the frequency, severity, and duration of Raynaud phenomenon attacks and improve digital ulcer healing (Kowal-Bielecka et al, 2017). It is not known whether phosphodiesterase 5 inhibitors are useful for preventing digital ulcers. You can take phosphodiesterase 5 inhibitors with or without food, but you should avoid grapefruit in all forms because it increases drug levels. These medications should not be taken with oral or topical nitrates, because the combination can cause dangerous drops in blood pressure. *Priapism*, a painful *penile erection* that can last longer than six hours, can occur in men taking these medications and warrants emergency care.

Table 4-1: Treatments for Raynaud Phenomenon

Calcium Channel Blockers
nifedipine
amlodipine
felodipine
isradipine
Angiotensin Receptor Blockers
losartan
telmisartan
valsartan
Phosphodiesterase 5 Inhibitors
sildenafil
tadalafil
Nitrate Formulations
nitroglycerin
glyceryl trinitrate

Nitrates

Topical nitrates are another option if a phosphodiesterase 5 inhibitor cannot be used or is ineffective (Chung et al, 2009). There are a variety of forms of nitrates (including *transdermal patches*, creams, gels, and ointments). Some common names are listed in Table 4-1. Liquid formulations must be applied carefully, using gloves to avoid vessel expansion in unintended blood vessels. Topical nitrates should be avoided in those with low blood pressure, heart failure, or *pulmonary hypertension*. They should not be taken in combination with sildenafil, tadalafil, or vardenafil due to the risk of developing a dangerously low blood pressure. Common side effects include headache and flushing.

Selective Serotonin Re-Uptake Inhibitors

Fluoxetine, a *selective serotonin re-uptake inhibitor* (SSRI), can reduce the severity of Raynaud phenomenon attacks (Khouri et al, 2017). However, because of the small number of patients with scleroderma studied to date, it is unclear whether fluoxetine should be widely prescribed for Raynaud phenomenon, and there have been calls for larger trials (Khouri et al, 2017). This medicine is commonly prescribed for the treatment of major depression, and thus clinicians have a lot of experience treating people with fluoxetine.

Endothelin Receptor Blocker

In those with multiple digital ulcers from severe Raynaud phenomenon, bosentan, an endothelin receptor blocker (ERB), can be added to existing therapy. Results of two studies "RAPIDS-1 and RAPIDS-2" showed a reduction in the number of new ulcers in those with scleroderma with multiple digital ulcers treated with bosentan compared to those who were untreated (Korn et al, 2004; Matucci-Cernic et al, 2011). However, no improvement in the healing of existing ulcers was noted. Because bosentan therapy is associated with liver injury, can cause birth defects in animals exposed to the drug, and decreases the effectiveness of birth control pills, careful consideration must be given to the decision to use bosentan in those with Raynaud phenomenon and digital ulcers.

Severe Raynaud Phenomenon Attack

Blood flow to one or more fingers (or toes) can be drastically reduced or stopped entirely in those with Raynaud phenomenon. The digits will appear white for a prolonged period and this resultant *ischemia* can cause tissue damage that can lead to *gangrene*. If untreated, loss of a digit or digits can occur. In the instance of prolonged ischemic change (or white discoloration) that does not return to pink or normal, you should go to the emergency department for evaluation. Evaluation will likely include *vascular* studies to assess for a blood clot in an *artery* that might need aggressive treatment. Pain, a potent inducer of blood vessel narrowing, must be aggressively controlled. Some insurance companies will approve administration of IV prostacyclin analogs (Wigley et al, 1994). Examples of prostacyclin analogs are shown in Table 4-1. These medications are typically administered in US hospitals, but in Europe, you can receive them at an outpatient infusion center.

How Can the Gastrointestinal Manifestations of Scleroderma Be Treated?

Gastroesophageal Reflux Disease

There are many *gastrointestinal* (GI) manifestations of scleroderma (See Chapter 1). Gastroesophageal reflux disease (GERD) can manifest as heartburn, shortness of breath, worsened lung function, hoarse voice, sore throat, frequent throat clearing, increased bad breath, gum disease, tooth decay, or nasal symptoms. Lifestyle modifications, including elevating the head of the bed, is of paramount importance in addition to attaining/maintaining ideal body weight and avoiding late evening meals (Jacobson et al, 2006). Many individuals with scleroderma note improvement in GERD symptoms with lifestyle modifications alone. If these measures are ineffective, *proton pump inhibitors* (PPIs) (Table 4-2) are started as initial therapy (Carlson et al, 2015). H_2 *blockers* can be combined with PPIs for additional symptomatic relief, but they offer little protection against *esophageal ulcerations*. It is important to treat reflux symptoms aggressively to prevent chronic GERD complications that include esophageal ulcerations, *esophageal strictures*, and *Barrett's esophagus*. Barrett's esophagus, or a precancerous lesion in the esophagus, occurs from chronic esophageal exposure to stomach acid. Inadequate treatment can lead to esophageal cancer; fortunately, the progression to cancer is slow leaving ample time for diagnosis, treatment, and cure. Table 4-2 shows the common treatments available for GERD and Barrett's esophagus.

Table 4-2: Medications for GERD

Proton Pump Inhibitors
Standard Therapy
omeprazole (Prilosec®)
pantoprazole (Protonix®)
lansoprazole (Prevacid®)
High-Potency Therapy
dexlansoprazole (Dexilant®)
rabeprazole (Aciphex®)
esomeprazole (Nexium®)
H_2 Blockers
ranitidine (Zantac®)
famotidine (Pepcid®)
cimetidine (Tagamet®)

Proton pump inhibitors (PPIs) are most effective when taken on an empty stomach, preferably 30 minutes before the largest meal of the day. Side effects can include flatulence, constipation, headaches, and dizziness, but usually the medications are well tolerated. Rare side effects include an infectious diarrhea caused by *Clostridium difficile (C. diff)*, *drug-induced lupus*, and kidney disease. H_2 receptor blockers are typically taken on an empty stomach 10 to 60 minutes before eating. Typical H_2 receptor blocker side effects include headache and diarrhea. Rare side effects include *gynecomastia* (breast tissue enlargement) and liver injury.

Small Intestinal Bacterial Overgrowth

Small intestinal bacterial overgrowth (SIBO) results when the small and large bowels are not moving waste products through the digestive system adequately. Lifestyle and diet modulation are first-line therapies. Cooked (rather than raw) vegetables, a low-residue diet (more on this shortly) and regular consumption of caffeine, adequate intake of water, and participation in regular exercise, can improve *intestinal motility* in many people with scleroderma. When these measures are insufficient, addition of medications (including *laxatives*, *antibiotics*, and/or *promotility agents*) are warranted. Treatment should be individualized and a *multidisciplinary* approach involving a rheumatologist, dietitian, and gastroenterologist with knowledge of scleroderma is optimal.

There are three types of laxatives: fiber, water-attracting, and propulsive. *Fiber laxatives* (such as *psyllium husk* and *wheat dextrin [Metamucil and Benefiber]*) increase stool bulk to help facilitate bowel movements. Sometimes, they worsen constipation. Some laxatives can increase water in the stool (e.g., milk of magnesia [Phillips Milk of Magnesia] and *polyethylene glycol* [Miralax®]). Another type of laxative, (*bisacodyl and senna*), increases rhythmic gut contractions that helps to propel stool through the bowels. In more severe cases of delayed intestinal transit, pro-motility agents (including *cisapride, domperidone,* or *octreotide*) can be used. These medications require expertise in their proper administration and monitoring.

A *low-residue diet* means limiting the amount of fiber in the diet to help intestinal motility. Cooked (versus raw) vegetables are easier to digest. Fruits such as bananas, cantaloupe, honeydew, and watermelon, are preferred, whereas fruits with skin or seeds generally should be avoided. White bread and crackers, compared to whole wheat bread, are easier to digest. Sources of protein should include chicken, fish, and eggs, as opposed to beef. Drinking plenty of water and having a caffeinated beverage prior to taking a morning walk can help those with scleroderma have regular bowel movements. If these conservative measures fail, an intermittent course of an antibiotic can restore balance in some people. *Metronidazole, ciprofloxacin,* and *xifaxan* antibiotics are often prescribed to kill the intestinal bacterial overgrowth that results from sluggish motility. In some people, regularly rotating courses of these three antibiotics are necessary.

Many individuals ask about the usefulness of *probiotics*. Only small studies have been conducted that show that probiotics (*Bifidobacterium infantis* or *Lactobacillus*) might help to restore the presence of healthy gut flora especially after a course of antibiotics (Showalter et al, 2018). However, it is important to note that probiotics are bacteria. Too much gut bacteria can cause symptoms of bloating and belching.

Diarrhea, Constipation, and Rectal Incontinence

Having rectal *incontinence* is understandably distressing. It is important to seek the advice of a *gastroenterologist, physiatrist,* or *physical therapist* who specializes in rectal incontinence and pelvic floor muscle dysfunction to optimize management. Causes of rectal incontinence in people with scleroderma include diarrhea and constipation that result from the inability of the gut musculature to propel stool through the bowel. It seems counterintuitive to think that constipation can cause rectal incontinence. Severe and persistent constipation causes the natural release of potent gut stimulators that can result in "overflow" diarrhea. Thus, aggressive treatment of constipation with stool-bulking agents, laxatives, and pro-motility agents combined with physical therapy to improve pelvic floor muscular tone can improve symptoms.

How Can Pulmonary Complications of Scleroderma Be Treated?

Scleroderma lung disease, the leading cause of death associated with scleroderma, has two main forms: *interstitial lung disease* (ILD) (a blood vessel problem in the lungs), and *pulmonary arterial hypertension* (PAH) (a lung inflammation and scarring problem).

Interstitial Lung Disease

Interstitial lung disease (ILD) is another manifestation of scleroderma caused by inflammation of lung tissue, followed by scar tissue formation (fibrosis) that impairs normal breathing (see Chapter 1). Medications used to block inflammation or to reverse fibrosis include mycophenolic acid (MPA), cyclophosphamide, *nintedanib*, and rituximab; people diagnosed with ILD will receive one or more of these medications during the course of their illness. If these medicines are not helpful, autologous stem cell transplantation (ASCT) can be pursued at a specialized center.

Cyclophosphamide

The results of the Scleroderma Lung Study I showed a slight improvement in *pulmonary function tests* in those with active scleroderma who took cyclophosphamide as compared to a group that took a *placebo* for one year. The benefit was modest; however, this result is important because lung function is expected to decline in those with scleroderma with early active disease (Tashkin et al, 2006). Whether taken daily as a pill or monthly IV, cyclophosphamide is a medication with lots of potential side effects, including infertility and the early induction of menopause in menstruating women.

Mycophenolate Mofetil

Since 2016, mycophenolate mofetil has become the *gold standard* for scleroderma ILD treatment. The results of the Scleroderma Lung Study II showed that mycophenolate mofetil was as effective as cyclophosphamide in promoting lung health, and it had far fewer serious side effects (Tashkin et al, 2016). For more information, refer to the discussion of administration, risks, and benefits of mycophenolate mofetil (mycophenolic acid), in the section "How Can Skin Thickening Be Treated?" earlier in this chapter.

Nintedanib

Nintedanib, approved by the FDA in 2019, is a treatment for scleroderma-associated interstitial lung disease that works by reducing fibrosis. It has been shown to slow the rate of decline in pulmonary function in those with scleroderma taking this medication. Nintedanib did not however demonstrate effectiveness for other disease manifestations such as skin thickening. It can be safely taken in combination with mycophenolate mofetil. The most common side effect in those taking nintedanib is diarrhea (Distler et al, 2019).

Rituximab

In 2006, the first report stating that rituximab might be helpful for those with scleroderma was published. Rituximab was shown to improve skin disease in those with a skin disease, called sclerodermatous chronic graft-versus-host disease, similar to scleroderma (Okamoto et al, 2006). Since that time, several studies have been conducted aimed at those with scleroderma to determine whether rituximab (usually given as two IV infusions two weeks apart and repeated at 6-month intervals) improves skin, lung, and skeletal muscle disease that might occur (Daoussis et al, 2010; Lafyatis et al, 2009; Smith et al, 2010; Melsens et al, 2018; Mohammed AGA, et al, 2017; Sari et al, 2017; Daoussis et al, 2012; Daoussis et al, 2017; Bosello et al, 2010; Bosello et al, 2015; Thiebaut et al, 2018; Lepri et al, 2016; Vilela et al, 2016; Giuggioli et al, 2015; Jordan et al, 2015). These studies suggest that skin disease and pulmonary function tests improve in some people who receive rituximab. In addition to these larger and more formal studies, *case reports* have been published suggesting that rituximab might benefit those with scleroderma and ILD, *calcinosis cutis* (calcium pebbles under the skin), PAH, and/or digital ulcers (Ebata et al, 2017; Khor et al, 2014; Numajiri et al, 2017; Dubos et al, 2016), but the results are mixed (Hurabielle et al, 2014; Nakamura et al, 2016; Poormoghim et al, 2016). The uncertainty of its benefits coupled with the high cost of therapy, frequent insurance company denials, risk for a rare neurological side effect (*progressive multifocal leukoencephalopathy* [PML]), and an increased risk for infection during treatment limit its widespread use (Toussirot and Bereau, 2014). Fortunately, as of this writing, a large clinical trial is underway in the United Kingdom that will provide useful information for patients and their doctors (Saunders et al, 2017).

Autologous Stem Cell Transplant

The benefits in carefully selected patients with scleroderma who underwent autologous stem cell transplantation (ASCT) as part of three clinical studies have been published (Burt et al, 2011; Sullivan et al, 2018; van Laar et al, 2014). Overall, the results are promising in terms of improvement or stabilization of lung function and skin disease. However, care should be taken in considering this therapy, particularly for those at increased risk for developing *scleroderma renal crisis* (SRC) because high doses of *steroids* are administered during the third phase of ASCT; high dose steroids are known to increase the risk for developing *normotensive scleroderma renal crisis*. ASCT is useful therapy and should be considered in those who do not achieve an adequate response to more traditional therapy.

Pulmonary Arterial Hypertension

Over the past 30 years, a therapeutic revolution has occurred; there are now many medications that effectively treat pulmonary arterial hypertension (PAH). The goal of therapy for PAH is to increase blood flow through the lung's blood vessels and decrease stress on the heart as it pumps blood to the lungs. Dilation of blood vessels improves blood flow through blood vessels. Blood vessel dilation occurs in response to specific substances that dilate blood vessels or from substances that block or inhibit the constriction (narrowing) of blood vessels.

Body substances that *dilate* blood vessels include *nitric oxide* and *prostacyclin*. Thus, medications that increase nitric oxide, including phosphodiesterase 5 inhibitors and *prostacyclin analogs*, cause blood vessel dilation and improve blood flow. Another drug, *riociguat*, has a slightly different mechanism of action, though it also works through nitric oxide, and results in pulmonary blood vessel dilation.

Several substances cause blood vessels to become constricted, thus reducing blood flow; these include *angiotensin, endothelin,* and *serotonin.* Thus, medications that block endothelin (endothelin receptor blockers [ERB]), and *serotonin receptors* (SSRIs), result in improved blood flow. Lastly, many people with PAH are prescribed *diuretics* that decrease *water retention,* to reduce the amount of fluid that the heart must pump. Any medication that expands or dilates blood vessels can lead to headache, flushing, dizziness, runny nose, an increased heart rate, leg swelling, and worsened symptoms of GERD.

Prostacyclin Analogs

Epoprostenol (Table 4-3) was the first PAH medication to be US *Food and Drug Administration* (FDA) approved; thus, clinicians who treat PAH are very experienced with its use. Data supports the use of IV epoprostenol, as it has been shown to improve function in those with scleroderma-associated PAH (Sobanski et al, 2016). However, epoprostenol therapy is complex; it must be started in the hospital, be administered through a *central line* (a special IV into a large vein), and the proper dose must be identified after slow dosage adjustments *(titration).* Individuals receiving this treatment must wear a refrigerated pump that needs to be refilled at regular intervals to permit continuous infusion of chilled epoprostenol. Malfunction of the battery or the pump is a medical emergency as IV epoprostenol's therapeutic effect lasts only 6 minutes. Highly-trained nurses work diligently to teach patients the skills they need to care for their central line and to maintain and refill the pump. In addition to side effects common to medications that dilate blood vessels, those who take epoprostenol also report jaw pain, muscle aches, nausea, vomiting, and diarrhea. An increased risk of bleeding is also a concern. Newer prostacyclin analogs (Table 4-3) include *subcutaneous* (SC), oral, and inhaled formulations, but their usefulness in those with scleroderma-associated PAH is less established (Sobanski et al, 2016). Whichever formulation is used, prostacyclin analog therapy necessitates careful monitoring of blood tests and symptoms as well as a highly motivated patient.

Table 4-3: Medications Used to Treat Scleroderma Lung Disease

Generic Name (Brand Names)
sildenafil (Revatio®, Viagra®)
tadalafil (Adcirca®, Cialis®)
bosentan (Tracleer®)
ambrisentan (Letairis®)
macitentan (Opsumit®)
riociguat (Adempas®)
epoprostenol (Flolan®, Veletri®)
iloprost (Ventavis®)
treprostinil IV, SC (Remodulin®)

continued

Generic Name (Brand Names)
treprostinil inhaled (Tyvaso®)
treprostinil oral (Orenitram®)
selexipeg (Uptravi®)
mycophenolic acid (CellCept®, Myfortic®)
cyclophosphamide (Cytoxan®)
nintedanib (Ofev®)
rituximab (Rituxan®)

Phosphodiesterase 5 Inhibitors

Phosphodiesterase 5 inhibitors (PD5-I) (Table 4-3) can improve breathing and physical function in those with scleroderma who have PAH (Sobanski et al, 2018). Phosphodiesterase 5 inhibitors induce blood vessels to relax, resulting in *vasodilation*. The FDA has approved this class of drugs for treatment of PAH; thus, most insurance companies will cover the cost. Although initially developed as a drug for blood vessel expansion and for high blood pressure, *sildenafil* was found to cause potent penile erections. Priapism, a painful penile erection that lasts longer than six hours, can occur in men taking these medications. These medications should not be taken with oral or topical *nitrates*, because the combination (with PD5-Is) can cause dangerous drops in blood pressure. Cases of liver toxicity have been reported in people taking sildenafil and *tadalafil*; therefore, regular monitoring is needed during therapy.

Endothelin Receptor Blockers

Endothelin receptor blockers (ERBs) improve physical function and survival in scleroderma-associated PAH (Sobanski et al, 2018). They are classified based upon which endothelin receptor (A and B [non-selective drugs] or just A receptors [selective drugs]) they inhibit. Examples of the non-selective blockers include bosentan and macitentan, whereas the selective blocker, targeting only the type A receptor, is ambrisentan (Galie et al, 2008). These medications are taken orally and result in vasodilation of the blood vessels in the lungs and elsewhere. Common side effects of the non-selective and selective endothelin antagonists are similar and include increased frequency of respiratory tract infections, headaches, leg swelling, and runny nose. Liver toxicity is a concern, and blood tests to measure liver function are performed regularly. These medicines are known to cause birth defects, and pregnancy in those with PAH is high risk to the mother and fetus; thus, birth control is required. The list of medications that should be avoided while taking ERBs is extensive and includes many drugs that treat infectious hepatitis as well as cyclosporine, glyburide, and ranolazine. You should discuss your current medications and any potential drug interactions with your doctor. For some people, medications with differing mechanisms of action are combined in the treatment of scleroderma-associated PAH. For example, PD5-I and ERBs are frequently combined to provide increased benefit (Coghlan et al, 2017).

Riociguat

Riociguat dilates blood vessels by binding to and *upregulating* an *enzyme* in the bloodstream that causes relaxation of blood vessels. Individuals taking riociguat note improved *exercise tolerance* and function. Low-dose riociguat is taken by mouth three times each day, and the dose is slowly increased. Riociguat cannot be combined with a PD5-I or nitrates (that are sometimes prescribed for Raynaud phenomenon). Like prostacyclin analogs, an increased risk of bleeding is concerning.

How Can Renal Complications of Scleroderma Be Treated?

Scleroderma renal crisis (SRC; see Chapter 1) is an important disease manifestation in those with scleroderma that can be effectively treated, particularly if it is recognized early. There are no known drugs that prevent SRC from developing. The heralding sign of SRC is the development of elevated blood pressure. Individuals with scleroderma need to monitor and know their normal blood pressure range. People with diffuse scleroderma are much more likely to develop SRC; thus, these individuals should most closely monitor their blood pressure. When detected and treated early, those who develop SRC can do well. If there is concern for SRC, blood and urine tests should be checked; these tests are part of the routine monitoring that you will have as part of your disease monitoring by your doctor. If the diagnosis of SRC is confirmed, you will be admitted to the hospital where your blood pressure can be continuously monitored and high blood pressure values can be aggressively treated.

Prednisone use has been associated with SRC, especially in those with a positive RNA polymerase III autoantibody in the blood. There is an entity known as normotensive scleroderma renal crisis (normotensive SRC) in which people with scleroderma develop SRC with blood pressure readings that are normal. Normotensive SRC has been associated with prednisone use at doses of 15 mg/day or greater. Because blood pressure elevations are a marker of SRC, the occurrence of normotensive SRC can be much more difficult to detect, and the diagnosis is based on laboratory abnormalities.

Aggressive Control of Blood Pressure

Captopril is the first *angiotensin converting enzyme* (ACE) *inhibitor* to be developed for the purpose of lowering blood pressure. Although captopril has been shown to target the mechanism that is active in SRC and improve survival in those with scleroderma who develop SRC, it is the rapid control of blood pressure that is most important (Langevitz et al, 1991). Captopril is the backbone of SRC therapy because of its short onset of action, permitting frequent dosage adjustments and enabling more rapid attainment of tight blood pressure control. Typically, captopril is initially prescribed, and the dosage is escalated until the maximum dosage is reached or blood pressure control is achieved. If the blood pressure is difficult to control despite high dosages of captopril, other blood pressure–lowering medications can, and should, be added until the blood pressure returns to the normal range for that person. Thus, it is critically important for those with scleroderma to know their normal blood pressure range. After the blood pressure is controlled, captopril can be converted to longer-acting formulations such as *enalapril* or *lisinopril* (Penn et al, 2007). Typical side effects of ACE inhibitors include low blood pressure, dizziness, headache, and cough. Sudden onset of shortness of breath (air hunger), trouble breathing, or weird sensations around the mouth or in the throat after taking an ACE inhibitor should be immediately reported to medical staff because allergies to ACE inhibitors are potentially very serious.

How Can Muscle and Joint Symptoms of Scleroderma Be Treated?

Myositis

When *myositis* (muscle cell inflammation and breakdown) occurs with scleroderma, *glucocorticoids*, typically prednisone, are the first-line treatment. High dosages (roughly 60–80 mg/day) are necessary to rapidly decrease muscle inflammation, but steroids are tapered as quickly as possible to prevent harmful side effects that can include SRC, elevated blood pressure, elevated blood sugars, elevated *intraocular pressure (glaucoma)* and *cataracts*, fluid retention, GI discomfort, *osteoporosis*, localized bone death (*osteonecrosis* or *avascular necrosis*), euphoria or *psychosis*, trouble sleeping, body fat redistribution, skin thinning, *purple striae*, infections, and muscle weakness from steroids themselves (Curtis et al, 2006). Prednisone (at 20 mg/day or higher) for more than one month should be accompanied by daily calcium and vitamin D supplements and might require initiation of prescription medicines *(bisphosphonates)* to protect the bones. Your physician might also prescribe an antibiotic (e.g., *trimethoprim-sulfamethoxazole, dapsone, atovaquone*, or *aerosolized pentamidine*) to prevent a lung infection called *pneumocystis carinii pneumonia* or *pneumocystis jiroveci pneumonia* that can occur in those taking immunosuppressing medications. You might also need to take a PPI to protect the stomach against ulcers. You will also be monitored closely for any signs of possible normotensive SRC, given that this has been associated with the use of prednisone doses 15 mg daily or higher.

If you have active myositis you should not exercise rigorously until the inflammation in the muscles is under control. After blood tests reveal normal muscle enzyme levels, you can resume exercise. Often, it is useful to exercise under the direction of a physical therapist who can guide the level of intensity to prevent muscle and joint injury.

Arthralgias/Arthritis

Those who have scleroderma often experience joint pain from true joint disease or in response to thickened skin and *tendon* sheaths overlying joints. Physical activity after consultation with a physical therapist or *occupational therapist* should be pursued. Carefully designed exercise programs that can include simple range of motion exercises, swimming in heated pools, yoga, and aerobic exercise can be designed to permit people with scleroderma to maintain or regain joint range of motion, improve strength and balance, and decrease joint and soft-tissue pain. If these measures fail, acetaminophen and *non-steroidal anti-inflammatory drugs* (NSAIDs) can be tried. Some people with painful ulcers overlying joints benefit from opioid analgesics that improve pain but might worsen constipation.

Summary

Scleroderma is a complex, but treatable, condition. Many targeted treatments are available, and vital research is underway to improve skin thickening, Raynaud phenomenon, lung disease, cardiac involvement, GI involvement, and arthritis. Although there is not one medication that improves all of the symptoms of scleroderma, lifestyle management and medications are available to help ease the burden of disease. Routine screening for organ involvement permits early detection of complications and initiation of lifestyle modification and/or medication treatment. A team-based approach to patient care is often helpful because the symptoms of scleroderma are broad. A strong therapeutic alliance between you and your care team goes a long way to help you live with scleroderma.

WHAT SHOULD I CONSIDER IF I WANT TO BECOME PREGNANT?

Jessica L. Sheingold, MD and Virginia Steen, MD

CHAPTER 5

In This Chapter

- Will I Be Able to Have Children?
- What Are the Risks to My Health If I Become Pregnant?
- What Are the Risks to My Baby If I Have Scleroderma?
- Which Medications Are Safe, and Which Should Be Avoided If I Want to Become Pregnant?
- Will I Be Able to Breastfeed?
- Is My Child at Risk of Developing Scleroderma?

Will I Be Able to Have Children?

Most women with scleroderma have normal pregnancies and deliver healthy babies, but scleroderma is a disease that affects each person differently. Whereas some people with scleroderma have problems that are limited to their skin, others develop difficulties with their heart, lungs, and kidneys. Women with major involvement of their internal *organs* might not be able to become pregnant without placing their own health, as well as the health of their baby, at serious risk, but this varies greatly from person to person. Additionally, some medications can affect male and female *fertility* or be *toxic* to a developing *fetus*. Any person, male or female, who plans to have a family should consult with their *rheumatologist* before *conceiving*. Setting up a *preconception counseling* appointment with your doctor will allow him or her to assess whether it is safe for you to become pregnant, discuss the risks that might be involved, and make any medication changes that are necessary. Additionally, women with scleroderma should plan to see an *obstetrician* who specializes in *maternal fetal medicine* (MFM), because these specialists have added training in *high-risk pregnancies* that are complicated by a chronic disease. MFM obstetricians will also meet with parents-to-be for preconception counseling appointments to discuss your risks and to answer your questions.

Physical features of scleroderma can make sexual intercourse challenging and uncomfortable for some people. Women with *diffuse skin disease* might have thickening of the skin around their genitals or other skin changes that limit joint mobility. It is not uncommon for women with scleroderma to complain of pain during sexual intercourse related to vaginal dryness; this *symptom* might improve with the use of topical lubricants. Pain related to arthritis, *digital ulcers*, *Raynaud phenomenon*, and *heartburn* can all make sexual activity difficult and uncomfortable, but this varies from person to person. Any concerns or obstacles should be discussed with a rheumatologist or obstetrician/gynecologist.

A common source of worry among people with scleroderma is how their fertility might be affected by scleroderma. In the past, researchers noted that women with scleroderma had fewer pregnancies; however, there were many factors that likely accounted for this observation. Unfortunately, it was not understood how the disease might affect the pregnancy or how the pregnancy might influence the course of scleroderma itself. Many physicians recommended against becoming pregnant even with insufficient data. Moreover, the average age of onset of scleroderma is 43 years. In prior generations, most women would have completed their childbearing before their scleroderma developed; thus, there would have been fewer pregnancies in women after the diagnosis of scleroderma. Physical aspects of scleroderma also influenced a woman's decision to refrain from becoming pregnant. Fortunately, recent studies suggest that fertility is not significantly affected by scleroderma. A study comparing healthy women, women with scleroderma, and women with *rheumatoid arthritis* found that only 2% to 5% of women in each group were unable to become pregnant, despite trying (Steen and Medsger, 1999). The percentage of women who had not conceived after 1 year was similar across the three groups (12%–15%). In those women who were evaluated for infertility by a physician, no specific trend or universal cause was common to all women. Overall, women with scleroderma who had a bout of infertility were eventually able to conceive at rates similar to those of healthy women and women with rheumatoid arthritis.

Some medications used to treat the manifestations of scleroderma can adversely affect fertility. *Cyclophosphamide*, a powerful *immune suppressing medication*, reduces the fertility of both men and women. Rheumatologists should discuss the risk of infertility and ways to minimize it in any person who plans to receive this medication. Other more commonly used medications to treat scleroderma (including *methotrexate, mycophenolate mofetil*, and *leflunomide*) do not affect fertility or the ability to become pregnant; however, these medications are toxic to the developing fetus and should be stopped well before *conception* occurs. Discontinuation of any medication should be done only under the guidance of a physician.

What Are the Risks to My Health If I Become Pregnant?

Overall, studies have shown that scleroderma generally does not worsen when a woman becomes pregnant, although there are a few notable exceptions. Each woman should discuss her individual risk of pregnancy with her rheumatologist before becoming pregnant. A survey of 133 women with scleroderma examined the symptoms of Raynaud phenomenon, digital ulcers, joint pain, and skin thickening during prior pregnancies. Researchers found that 7% of people worsened, 5% improved, and 88% experienced no significant change (Steen et al, 1989). The limitation of this study was that it surveyed women after their pregnancy; therefore, participants might not have recalled their symptoms accurately. The researchers then followed a group of women *prospectively* through their pregnancies to obtain a more accurate assessment. They found that 18% became worse, 16% improved, and 63% had stable symptoms (Steen, 1999). The finding that most women have stable disease throughout pregnancy was further supported by a study of 42 pregnancies in Brazil (72% with stable disease, 14% with improvement, and 14% with worsening) (Sampios-Barros et al, 2000). A large Italian study, called the *IMPRESS study*, similarly found overall stability of scleroderma-related symptoms by evaluating 109 pregnancies (Taraborelli et al, 2012). Most studies have noted that heartburn tended to worsen, although this occurs in many women, with or without scleroderma, during pregnancy. The IMPRESS study also found that Raynaud phenomenon improved in 32% of pregnancies, and finger ulcers improved in 20%, although symptoms recurred after delivery.

The trends observed in these studies should be reassuring for women who primarily have skin disease and Raynaud phenomenon; most of these studies did not include women who had more serious internal organ involvement. During pregnancy, the body changes naturally to support the growing baby. Women who have compromised function of their organs might not be able to adapt without putting their own health at risk. For example, the amount of blood in the body increases by 50% during pregnancy, whereas the blood pressure and resistance within the blood vessels drops. This change can improve symptoms of Raynaud phenomenon, but it can cause problems for women with lung, heart, and kidney involvement who cannot process the excess blood volume. For women with *pulmonary hypertension* or advanced *chronic kidney disease*, this change is particularly dangerous; physicians often advise people with these conditions that pregnancy is too dangerous for them. The heart rate naturally increases by about 20%, and the heart increases its output by 30% to 50% during pregnancy. The lungs see an increase in the *minute ventilation* (or the amount of air inhaled and exhaled in a minute); pregnant women need to take in 20% more oxygen. Because of this change and a reduction in the *functional residual capacity* of the lungs, even healthy women can find themselves short of breath during pregnancy as early as the end of the first trimester. Respiratory symptoms are thus more likely in women with scleroderma-associated *interstitial lung disease* (ILD) because these women already have baseline breathing problems or require supplemental oxygen (Sobanski et al, 2016). Specific *pulmonary function tests* (PFTs) and assessment of *oxygen saturation* are necessary before becoming pregnant. It is essential to speak with your rheumatologist and obstetrician about your individual health risks before becoming pregnant.

Scleroderma Renal Crisis

Several situations can be particularly dangerous to a pregnant woman with scleroderma. Women who have had or are at high risk of developing *scleroderma renal crisis* (SRC) face several challenges. SRC is a condition in which the blood pressure rapidly rises, in part due to changes in the kidney's blood vessels. This is a life-threatening condition that, without treatment, leads to *renal failure* and, potentially, death. Fortunately, if recognized early, it is usually treated successfully with a class of blood pressure medications called *angiotensin converting enzyme* (ACE) *inhibitors*.

Several major points are worth noting regarding the diagnosis and treatment of SRC in pregnancy. First, the signs and symptoms are similar to those of *preeclampsia*, but the treatments are very different. If new *hypertension* develops during your pregnancy when you have scleroderma, it should be considered a medical emergency, and both the rheumatologist and obstetrician must determine the best course of action. You will be admitted to the hospital for testing, monitoring, and treatment. It might be necessary to perform a biopsy of your kidney to establish the correct diagnosis.

Another major challenge in the treatment of SRC is that this condition requires the aforementioned ACE inhibitors. These drugs are *teratogenic*, meaning that they can cause damage to your unborn child, particularly when they are taken during the second and third trimesters of pregnancy. Despite this fact, these medications must be used during pregnancy if a renal crisis occurs; without them, this condition could be rapidly fatal for both you and your child. Those who are at highest risk for developing SRC are those with early-onset disease, diffuse skin disease, and those who have *RNA polymerase III antibodies*. Women with long-standing limited skin disease and *anti-centromere antibodies* rarely develop this complication. It was once thought that pregnancy itself could increase the risk of developing renal crisis, but more recent studies have suggested that this is not true. About 10% to 20% of women with early, diffuse scleroderma will develop renal crisis, regardless of whether they become pregnant (Steen, 2007). For this reason, it is advisable to delay pregnancy if you have had diffuse skin disease for less than 5 years. After that point, your overall risk for developing renal crisis decreases, and there is lower risk that renal crisis will develop during pregnancy. If you have previously suffered from SRC, you will be put on an ACE inhibitor indefinitely, and, if you desire to become pregnant, the risks and benefits of discontinuing the ACE inhibitor would need to be discussed with your rheumatologist and obstetrician. If you have suffered from permanent kidney damage (called chronic kidney disease) as a result of SRC, the normal changes of pregnancy can be overwhelming to your already strained system and cause kidney function to worsen (Williams and Davidson, 2008). The individual risk to each person varies significantly, and a preconception counseling appointment is essential.

Pulmonary Hypertension

Pulmonary hypertension is a complication of scleroderma that is likely to worsen during pregnancy. Fortunately, when this scleroderma-related complication occurs, it usually develops in women older than age 50 (beyond their childbearing potential), although it can occur in younger women, such as those with antibodies to *U1RNP* (Sobanski, Giovanelli, et al, 2016). Pregnancy naturally increases the volume of circulating blood, and the heart increases its output to accommodate this change. For those who have pulmonary hypertension, their heart and lungs often cannot adapt to this change; this places them at risk for life-threatening *heart failure*. Before the advent of modern medications, most women with pulmonary hypertension of any cause (not only those with scleroderma) died during pregnancy. Newer treatments for pulmonary hypertension have dramatically improved the course of this manifestation of scleroderma, and use of these new agents has resulted in some successful pregnancies in milder cases (Jais, 2012). Overall, pulmonary hypertension is still associated with a high risk of complications, including maternal and fetal death during pregnancy. Any person with scleroderma who has pulmonary hypertension must carefully discuss her specific illness with a pulmonary hypertension specialist before becoming pregnant.

Interstitial Lung Disease

Interstitial lung disease (ILD), or *pulmonary fibrosis*, is a common complication of scleroderma with a wide range of severity. Unfortunately, few studies report on how women with ILD due to scleroderma fare during pregnancy. A small study of 15 pregnant women with ILD (of any cause) was mostly reassuring; overall these women did quite well, although there was an increase in rates of *premature births* (Lapinsky, 2014). No definitive evidence shows that pregnancy causes a worsening of ILD. However, the normal changes of pregnancy can make women feel more short of breath and require some women to temporarily use oxygen. It is generally recommended that women avoid becoming pregnant if they have a *forced vital capacity* of less than 50% on pulmonary function testing, although the evidence to support this number is lacking (Sobanski, Launay, et al, 2016). Pulmonary function tests and oxygen saturation should be performed on women with scleroderma before becoming pregnant.

Cardiac Disease

The heart is not usually the major site of severe involvement in scleroderma, although people might have cardiac abnormalities. Risk factors for pregnancy complications are the same as for those who have other causes of heart disease, including prior cardiac events (such as a heart attack or stroke), *arrhythmias*, and heart failure (especially those with a reduced *left ventricular ejection fraction* of less than 40%). People with these risk factors are often advised against becoming pregnant by their physician. Again, a pre-pregnancy evaluation by your rheumatologist and a *cardiologist* is critical for understanding your individual risks during pregnancy.

What Are the Risks to My Baby If I Have Scleroderma?

Most women with scleroderma who become pregnant deliver healthy babies. Each woman and child is unique; just as pregnancy might worsen or improve aspects of a woman's scleroderma, the disease might also affect her pregnancy. Researchers and physicians have sought to understand this relationship and to learn how scleroderma might affect the risk of *miscarriage*, premature birth, low birth weight, and infant death.

Miscarriage

When considering the rates of miscarriage, we must consider the age of the women being studied. The average miscarriage rate in the general population is about 12% to 15% of all pregnancies, but this varies significantly by age. Women between the ages of 20 and 30 years have a miscarriage rate as low as 9%, but this number climbs to a staggering 80% of all pregnancies in women older than age 45 (Sobanski, Launey, et al, 2016). Scleroderma is a disease that typically develops during the fifth decade of life or later; by the time a woman develops scleroderma she is likely to have a higher-than-average miscarriage risk based on her age alone.

Several studies have carefully compared miscarriage rates in pregnant women with scleroderma to similarly aged healthy pregnant women. Many of these studies demonstrated that women with scleroderma have more miscarriages; however, there are other factors that play a role, such as differences in socioeconomic status (Steen et al, 2007). Interestingly, some researchers have noted an increased rate of miscarriage in women who later developed scleroderma but who had not yet developed scleroderma at the time of the pregnancy. This observation led to the theory that the miscarried pregnancy itself might have contributed to the future development of scleroderma. It was suspected that the fetal cells that cross into the maternal circulation might be *immunogenic* and lead to the development of an *autoimmune disease* (Englert, 1992). More recent studies, however, have failed to replicate this finding, and demonstrate similar rates of miscarriage between women who go on to develop scleroderma and women in the general population (Steen and Medsger, 1999).

Larger observational studies have reassuringly found that the rate of miscarriage in women with scleroderma is similar to that in the average female population. When miscarriage rates in healthy women were compared to the rates in women with scleroderma and women with rheumatoid arthritis, there was no difference; there was a miscarriage rate of about 12% to 13% in each of the three groups (Steen and Medsger, 1999). Importantly, a large review of multiple studies reported a consensus that miscarriage rates are similar before and after the development of scleroderma and that it is similar to that of the general population (Sobanski, Launay, et al, 2016).

Premature Births

Scleroderma is a disease that affects the blood vessels, leading to symptoms of Raynaud phenomenon as well as less common but more serious *vascular* complications (including SRC, pulmonary hypertension, and/or digital ulcers). From the second trimester on, the developing fetus depends on an adequate blood supply from the mother for nutrition. Scientists have found abnormalities in the *placental blood vessels* in women with scleroderma, which raises concerns of restricted blood flow leading to smaller babies (termed *small for gestational age* [SGA]) and premature births, occurring before 37 weeks of gestation.

Several studies have found an increased rate of premature births in women with scleroderma. One study found that before the onset of scleroderma, women had a similar rate of *preterm births* as compared to those in the general population, at about 8% of all pregnancies. After the onset of scleroderma, however, this rate jumped to 15% (Steen and Medsger, 1999). However, this rate was similar to the rate in women with rheumatoid arthritis (14%), who would not have been expected to have the same type of blood vessel abnormalities. A second study by the same group of researchers found that preterm births occurred in 28% of scleroderma pregnancies, although reassuringly, all but one baby survived. Of these premature births, more than half were born between 36 and 37 weeks' gestation, just before becoming "full term." Of these nearly full term deliveries, most were induced by physicians for "non-medical reasons" and might have otherwise made it to term (Steen, 1999).

An important observation of this study was that preterm births were more common in women with severe lung and *gastrointestinal* (GI) involvement related to their scleroderma. Women with early diffuse skin disease also had markedly elevated rates of premature delivery, at 65% of pregnancies (Steen, 1999). This finding further supports the important recommendation that women with early diffuse scleroderma delay becoming pregnant until their disease has stabilized.

The consensus of several observational studies is that women with scleroderma are probably more likely to have premature deliveries than those in the general population, but these deliveries are usually close to term and their infants tend to do well.

Small for Gestational Age and Intrauterine Growth Retardation

Just as abnormal blood vessels in the *placenta* are suspected to contribute to increased preterm delivery rates, they are also implicated in the observation that women with scleroderma tend to have smaller-than-average babies in some studies. An infant is defined as "small for gestational age" (SGA) when the infant's weight is below the tenth percentile for his or her gestational age. One possible cause of a SGA infant is *intrauterine growth retardation* (IUGR), meaning that the unborn baby is growing more slowly than expected when measured throughout the pregnancy. IUGR could be the downstream effect of restricted blood flow, which can occur in scleroderma. From the available studies, it is not clear whether women with scleroderma truly have SGA infants more often. Several researchers have noted a trend toward women with scleroderma having smaller babies than the general population, but this difference was small and might not be significant. However, the IMPRESS study did find that some of the women with scleroderma who had SGA infants had extremely small babies, termed *"very low birth weight"* (less than 1,500 grams [3.3 lbs]) infants. Although it is rare for a woman with scleroderma to have a very low birth weight infant, this does happen more often than in the general population, occurring in 5% of scleroderma pregnancies versus only in 1% of healthy pregnancies.

Similarly, it is unclear whether IUGR occurs more often in scleroderma than in the general population; the findings of different studies have been inconsistent. Overall, it seems that IUGR and SGA infants are uncommon in women with scleroderma, although occasionally more severe cases have occurred. Rheumatologists and obstetricians who care for women with scleroderma will monitor for this on ultrasound exams. All pregnancies in women with scleroderma should be managed as "high-risk pregnancies" and followed closely by a maternal fetal medicine physician.

Neonatal Death

Fortunately, there is much less debate about the rate of *neonatal death* and *stillbirth* in women with scleroderma. In the Steen study, there were similar rates of neonatal death in women with scleroderma, women with rheumatoid arthritis, and healthy women (Steen and Medsger, 1999). The IMPRESS study found a rate of 2%, similar to the rate in the general population (Taraborelli et al, 2012).

Overall, women with scleroderma tend to have healthy babies. Although there might be an increased rate of premature delivery in women with scleroderma, their infants overall do as well as average newborns. Miscarriage rates do not appear to be significantly increased, and there is conflicting data on whether infants born to mothers with scleroderma tend to be SGA. Most studies agree that even if the overall pregnancy complication rate is slightly increased, the severity of these complications is not so severe that pregnancy should be discouraged in most women.

Which Medications Are Safe, and Which Should Be Avoided If I Want to Become Pregnant?

Scleroderma varies greatly from person to person. Whereas some women with scleroderma will not require treatment, others must take medications to control serious internal organ involvement. Some medications are "safe" to take during pregnancy and breastfeeding, but others can harm the unborn or nursing child. Table 5-1 provides a summary of medications and their safety information during pregnancy and breastfeeding. Several medications are described in greater detail below; however, most of these medications have not been formally tested in pregnant women. Much of what we know about medication safety during pregnancy comes from observational studies, and the data is modest at best. Many medications should not be discontinued abruptly without consulting a rheumatologist; a preconception counseling appointment will include a detailed discussion of how best to manage medications through pregnancy and after delivery.

NSAIDs

Non-steroidal anti-inflammatory drugs (NSAIDs) are medications commonly used to treat pain and arthritis. NSAIDs cross the placenta, and it is well established that use after 30 weeks of gestation can be harmful to the baby's circulatory system and kidneys. Additionally, use of NSAIDs can be associated with an increased risk of bleeding. More recent reports have raised concerns of reduced fertility, and that even use in early pregnancy might be associated with birth defects (Antonucci et al, 2012). Although not all studies agree, the safest choice is to avoid NSAIDs throughout pregnancy, particularly in the third trimester, and to use an alternative pain medication such as acetaminophen.

Prednisone

Prednisone is a relatively safe medication to use during pregnancy, and it is the treatment of choice for flares of autoimmune disease in pregnant women. It is less commonly used in women with scleroderma because high doses of prednisone increase the risk for SRC in susceptible people. However, for women who have features of another *autoimmune disorder* such as rheumatoid arthritis or *systemic lupus erythematosus* (SLE), prednisone might be needed during pregnancy. Less than 10% of the prednisone dose crosses the placenta, and there is minimal risk to the baby unless the mother is on a high dose for an extended time (Mitchell et al, 2010). The primary risk is due to prednisone's effects on the mother, such as an increased risk of infection and *gestational diabetes*.

Table 5-1: Medications and Their Safety in Pregnancy and Breastfeeding

	Pregnancy	Breastfeeding
NSAIDs	Avoid throughout pregnancy; should not be used at all during the third trimester.	Safe for use.
Prednisone	Safe for intermittent use in low doses.	Safe for use; excreted in breast milk. Timed feedings and pumping can reduce the baby's exposure.
Hydroxychloroquine	Safe for use.	Safe for use.
Methotrexate	Cannot be used during pregnancy. Must use birth control while taking. Should be discontinued 3 months before conceiving.	Cannot be used during breastfeeding.
Leflunomide	Cannot be used during pregnancy. Must use birth control while taking. After discontinuation, a course of cholestyramine should be completed to bind up any medication that remains in the body.	Unknown if excreted into breast milk and therefore should not be used.
Azathioprine	Safe for use.	Safe for use.
Mycophenolate mofetil	Cannot be used during pregnancy. Must use birth control while taking.	Cannot be used during breastfeeding.
Cyclophosphamide	Cannot be used during pregnancy.	Cannot be used during breastfeeding.
Calcium channel blockers (amlodipine, nifedipine)	Safe for use.	Safe for use.
Phosphodiesterase type 5 inhibitors (sildenafil, tadalafil)	Very limited data suggests safety of sildenafil.	Unknown safety.
Endothelin receptor antagonists (ERAs) (bosentan, ambrisentan)	Cannot be used during pregnancy.	Unknown safety.
Prostacyclin analogs (epoprostenol, iloprost)	Very limited data suggests safety.	Unknown safety; excreted in breast milk

Hydroxychloroquine

Hydroxychloroquine is a commonly used *disease-modifying antirheumatic drug* (DMARD) that treats arthritis and systemic lupus erythematosus. It is occasionally used in people with scleroderma who have arthritis. This medication has a well-established track record of safety in pregnancy and in breastfeeding. Patients with lupus are even started on this medication before conception (if they are not already on it) due to its ability to prevent lupus flares during pregnancy.

Methotrexate

Methotrexate is another DMARD medication that is occasionally used to treat arthritis and skin thickening. This medication is known to be dangerous to the unborn child, causing high rates of miscarriage (Mitchell et al, 2010). All women of child-bearing age who are taking methotrexate should use appropriate birth control to prevent pregnancy. Patients should discuss with their rheumatologist discontinuation of this medication at least three months before attempting to conceive. If a woman takes methotrexate unknowingly while she is pregnant and does not have a miscarriage, the rate of birth defects is relatively low (Soh and Nelson-Piercy, 2015).

Leflunomide

Leflunomide is a drug that is similar to methotrexate; it is used to treat inflammatory arthritis. It is also thought to be dangerous to the unborn child, as studies in animals showed that birth defects occurred even at very low doses of the medication (Mitchell et al, 2010). Again, women on leflunomide must use a reliable birth control method and must discuss how to discontinue their leflunomide before becoming pregnant. Leflunomide remains in your body for up to 2 years; although this can be helpful when treating arthritis, it can be dangerous to the fetus if you do become pregnant. If a woman on leflunomide desires to become pregnant, her rheumatologist will prescribe a medication called *cholestyramine*, which will bind the leflunomide that has been stored and help clear it from her body (Soh and Nelson-Piercy, 2015).

Azathioprine

Azathioprine is a DMARD that can be used to treat a variety of autoimmune diseases, and it has a good safety profile in pregnancy. For this reason, rheumatologists might switch a woman with arthritis who has been on methotrexate or leflunomide, or a woman with ILD who has been on mycophenolate mofetil, to this medication for the duration of pregnancy and breastfeeding. There have not been any *randomized controlled trials* (RCTs) testing this medication in pregnancy, but it has not been associated with harm to the baby throughout many pregnancies in women with rheumatic diseases (Soh, 2015).

Mycophenolate Mofetil

Mycophenolate mofetil is often used to treat ILD in scleroderma. It is associated with specific birth defects and must be discontinued before pregnancy (Soh and Nelson-Piercy, 2015). Depending on the extent and stability of the ILD, it might not be safe to discontinue this medication without starting an alternative treatment. In many cases, the rheumatologist will switch a woman to a safer medication, such as azathioprine or prednisone.

Cyclophosphamide

Cyclophosphamide is a strong immune suppressing medication that is used in a variety of severe rheumatic diseases. Although other medications with fewer side effects are generally preferred, cyclophosphamide is still occasionally used in people with scleroderma. Cyclophosphamide can significantly reduce both male and female fertility and is associated with high rates of miscarriage if taken during pregnancy. If the baby survives the pregnancy, there is a low risk for long-term effects on the infant (Soh and Nelson-Piercy, 2015). Because of this, cyclophosphamide is not used during the first trimester, but it has been successfully used in extreme and life-threatening cases later in pregnancy. Such situations are fortunately rare in scleroderma.

Calcium Channel Blockers

Calcium channel blockers such as amlodipine and nifedipine are commonly used to treat Raynaud phenomenon. Some studies have found that Raynaud phenomenon improves during pregnancy, and thus ongoing use of calcium channel blockers might not be required. Calcium channel blockers can be used safely during pregnancy, if needed (Khan et al, 2010). They are commonly used to treat preeclampsia and hypertension during pregnancy and have been used to help counter preterm labor.

Phosphodiesterase Type 5 Inhibitors

Medications such as *sildenafil* and *tadalafil* are potent *vasodilators*; they are used to treat more severe Raynaud phenomenon, digital ulcers, and pulmonary hypertension. Women with pulmonary hypertension, in general, should avoid becoming pregnant because this condition in pregnancy is associated with high rates of maternal death. For women taking sildenafil for less severe manifestations, there is very limited data suggesting that it might be safe in pregnancy. A review of case reports demonstrated no increase in severe side effects in either the mother or the baby (Dunn et al, 2017). There is even less data regarding tadalafil in pregnancy.

Endothelin Receptor Antagonists

Endothelin receptor antagonists (ERAs) include medications such as *bosentan* and *ambrisentan*, among others. They are used to treat pulmonary hypertension, which is a dangerous condition for pregnant women; those with pulmonary hypertension should use contraception and avoid pregnancy altogether. If a pregnancy does occur, the endothelin receptor antagonist must be discontinued because these agents are known to be harmful to the unborn baby (Olsson and Channick, 2016).

Prostacyclin Analogs

Prostacyclin analogs such as *epoprostenol* and *iloprost* are also used to treat pulmonary hypertension. In most cases, it not safe for women with pulmonary hypertension to become pregnant. If a pregnancy does occur, case reports have demonstrated that use of prostacyclin analogs during pregnancy does not harm the mother or the child, although this has not been formally studied (Olsson and Channick, 2016).

Will I Be Able to Breastfeed?

No studies have evaluated breastfeeding in women with scleroderma; however, most women should not have difficulty. Women with diffuse skin disease who have thickening of the skin across the chest might have more discomfort associated with the increase in breast size. No studies have been done to determine whether such women struggle with a reduction in breast milk production as a result of skin tightness and thickening across the chest.

Many medications used in scleroderma are safe to take while breastfeeding, whereas others are not (see Table 5-1). This data is limited and based on observational and animal studies. Further information on specific drug levels in breast milk and any adverse effects can be found in the National Institutes of Health (NIH) online toxicology database, "LactMed," at www.toxnet.nlm.nih.gov/newtoxnet/lactmed.

NSAIDs are generally safe to use during breastfeeding. Many of these medications can be used to treat pain and fevers in infants. *Ibuprofen*, for example, is transferred in extremely low levels in breast milk, with levels much lower than the dose that would be used in the infant to treat fever (Walter and Dilger, 1997). Ibuprofen is the drug of choice in this class of medications, should a woman need to take an NSAID while breastfeeding. Other NSAIDs such as naproxen and diclofenac are also likely to be safe, but there is much less data available for these and other NSAIDs. *Naproxen* and *diclofenac* levels in breast milk are extremely low, but because these are longer-lasting medications than ibuprofen, they could remain around longer in the infant's circulation. No adverse effects have been conclusively linked to exposure to NSAIDs in breast milk.

Prednisone is also safe to take during breastfeeding. The amount transferred into the breast milk is only a very small fraction of the mother's dose, and it has not been associated with any adverse effects in infants. If high doses of prednisone are needed over a prolonged period, the dose received by the infant could be higher. In such cases, use of prednisolone rather than prednisone and avoiding breastfeeding in the 4 hours after the dose is taken will help minimize the infant's exposure (Ryu et al, 2018). There have also been reports that high doses of maternal steroids, including those given in joint injections, can cause a temporary drop in milk production. Fortunately, women with scleroderma are rarely given high doses of prednisone, making this situation unlikely.

Hydroxychloroquine and azathioprine both have limited transfer into the breast milk and are considered safe to take while breastfeeding. Hydroxychloroquine has no known adverse effects on the child or on the mother's milk production. It is commonly used in women with systemic lupus erythematosus throughout pregnancy and *lactation*. Azathioprine can also be used during pregnancy. The amount entering breast milk is extremely small, and if breastfeeding is avoided for 4 hours after taking the dose, the infant exposure is almost zero (Bar-Gil et al, 2016).

Methotrexate, leflunomide, mycophenolate mofetil, and cyclophosphamide are generally avoided during lactation, and alternative agents are used. Low-dose weekly methotrexate (such as is used for arthritis) is excreted in small amounts in breast milk. Some researchers have argued that this does not likely pose a significant risk to the infant, especially if breastfeeding is withheld for 24 hours after the dose (Delaney et al, 2017). It is true that there have not been any cases of reported adverse effects, but in most situations a woman will have already been switched to an alternative agent during her pregnancy. Leflunomide and mycophenolate mofetil have not been studied, and thus should be avoided during breastfeeding. It is not known to what extent cyclophosphamide is excreted into breast milk, but its use in the mother has been linked to extremely low blood counts in breastfed infants (Wiernik and Duncan, 1971).

Is My Child at Risk of Developing Scleroderma?

The cause of scleroderma is not known, and there are likely multiple factors that play a role. Scleroderma in the mother or father does not predict that the child will go on to develop the disease. Inherited *genes* play a role in part, but how these genes are expressed and the environment also play a significant role, making it nearly impossible to know who will go on to develop the disease.

Certain genes might somewhat increase the risk of developing scleroderma. The genes that carry the code for certain types of *"HLA molecules"* in the *immune system* have been shown to play a role, as they do in many autoimmune diseases. The HLA molecules are responsible for detecting foreign substances in the body. In autoimmune diseases, the body mistakenly identifies something within the person as foreign, thus activating the immune system inappropriately. Inheriting certain types of HLA molecules might be more likely to contribute to the development of autoimmune disease. This might be why different types of autoimmune diseases tend to cluster in families, and why having one autoimmune disease increases your risk of having a second. For example, one study showed that 36% of patients with scleroderma have a *first-degree relative* with at least one autoimmune disease, most commonly rheumatoid arthritis or *autoimmune thyroid disease* (Hudson et al, 2008).

Reassuringly, inheriting a risk-increasing gene is not enough to cause scleroderma. Studies have shown that perhaps the more important contributor is not the genes themselves, but how those genes are expressed. This is the focus of the field of *epigenetics*. Whether a gene is "turned on," "turned off," or somewhere in between is the result of complicated molecular interactions. These epigenetic mechanisms that modify the genes are also inherited from parent to child (Salazar and Mayes, 2016).

Despite inheriting multiple risk factors for the development of scleroderma, most children of parents with this disease do not go on to develop scleroderma. It is thought that there must be some environmental trigger that eventually leads to the development of scleroderma in individuals with an underlying inherited, or genetic, risk. Potential triggers for autoimmune disease that have been the focus of recent research include various viruses and changes in the *microbiome*, or the bacterial species that normally live on and within the body (Pattanaik et al, 2015).

Overall, scleroderma in a parent does increase the risk that the child might one day develop an autoimmune disease, but this will not be the case for the majority of children. Risk factors and triggers for the development of scleroderma is an area of ongoing research; physicians might, at some point, be able to better predict who will develop this disease.

HOW AM I LIKELY TO FEEL WHEN I LEARN THAT I HAVE SCLERODERMA?

Daniel J. Daunis, Jr., MD; Christopher M. Celano, MD; and Marcy B. Bolster, MD

CHAPTER

In This Chapter

- Should I Blame Myself for Developing Scleroderma?
- What Can I Do If I Feel Depressed, Angry, or Scared?
- Are My Feelings of Depression Normal?
- How Long Will It Take Me to Regain My Emotional Equilibrium?
- Should I Tell Others About the Diagnosis and the Prognosis?
- What Should I Tell Others About My Condition?
- How Can I Manage My Fear of Having a Complication from Scleroderma?
- How Can I Learn to Be Less Stressed and More Hopeful and Optimistic?

Should I Blame Myself for Developing Scleroderma?

Although some people might blame themselves for developing scleroderma, this is unwarranted. The cause of scleroderma has not been clearly established, but it is likely triggered by a combination of *genetic* and *environmental factors*, and these interactions are not under your control. Rather than focusing on why you developed scleroderma, it is more important to focus on those things that you can change to improve your care of this disease such as your joint stiffness, *Raynaud phenomenon*, *fingertip ulcers*, and swallowing difficulties. For example, being more active improves your physical strength, makes you less prone to limitations of your mobility and flexibility, and reduces the risk of joint stiffness and pain. Importantly, if you smoke cigarettes, it is essential that you quit smoking to improve your *circulation*, decrease *symptoms* related to Raynaud phenomenon, and reduce your risk of developing fingertip ulcers. Changing your diet can improve your general health and might reduce the likelihood that you will need to take medications for scleroderma. Finally, medications are often necessary to prevent and to treat many of the symptoms and complications of scleroderma, such as problems with your heart, lungs, *gastrointestinal* (GI) tract, or kidneys. It is important for you to take your medications for scleroderma as prescribed to improve your circulation, reduce pain, and prevent potentially serious problems related to the impact of scleroderma on different organ systems.

What Can I Do If I Feel Depressed, Angry, or Scared?

When first diagnosed with scleroderma, it is not uncommon for you to feel sad, down, frustrated, or angry. And this makes sense. Receiving a new medical diagnosis can be overwhelming, and having scleroderma often requires that you make significant changes in your lifestyle, such as changing your diet, becoming more physically active, or taking new medications. For some people, these feelings are completely normal. However, other people experience more intense feelings of sadness that last for longer periods and can be accompanied by changes in interest level, energy, concentration, and appetite. These symptoms can become so severe that they affect your daily functioning. If this occurs, these feelings might represent an illness such as *major depressive disorder* (MDD), which is known more commonly as *"depression."*

Identifying MDD, if you have it, is very important. Even though there is no clear evidence to suggest that scleroderma causes depression, some evidence suggests that those with depression have more difficulty adjusting to scleroderma and have more difficulty with physical function (Benrud-larson, 2002). Ultimately, suffering from MDD can decrease your adherence to important treatments for scleroderma and, as a result, decrease your overall quality of life.

How can you know whether you have MDD? The easiest way is to ask yourself, "Have I been feeling depressed or had trouble enjoying things as I normally would for the past two weeks?" If so, and if you have experienced feelings of guilt or worthlessness, and had a reduction in your interests, low energy, poor concentration, been feeling either restless or slowed down, had changes in the amount of your sleep (too much or too little), had changes in your appetite (too much or too little), or had thoughts of suicide, you might be suffering from MDD (American Psychiatric Association, 2013).

If you believe that you are suffering from MDD, it is critical that you speak with your doctor. There are a variety of treatment options, including use of medications and/or psychotherapy, that are safe and effective for treating depression. However, it can be very difficult for your doctor to know whether you are depressed during the course of a routine check-up. Therefore, if you are experiencing these symptoms, it is very important for you to bring it up with your doctor. Talking with your doctor will give you the opportunity to engage in treatment that can help improve your health and function and help you be better able to take care of yourself and your scleroderma.

Are My Feelings of Depression Normal?

As just described in the previous section, some feelings of depression can be a normal part of coping with your diagnosis of scleroderma. Many people with scleroderma feel anxious or nervous regarding the possible progression of their illness, decreased mobility, change in appearance, and treatments for scleroderma. For example, starting an exercise or physical activity program can be overwhelming. This is understandable. If you are having any of these feelings, it can be helpful to share your feelings with family members, friends, or other people you trust. Your family and friends can support you and help you to come up with a plan for how to safely engage in healthy behaviors. Alternatively, in-person and online *support groups*, which consist of other people with scleroderma, are available to help you cope. Members of a support group can help by sharing their experiences with scleroderma, answering questions that you might have about what the disease means and what you can do to treat it successfully. Members also can help by pointing you in the right direction for getting the resources you need to help treat your disease. Of course, you need to remember that scleroderma can affect different people in different ways, so the experiences of others with scleroderma might differ from your own.

If you are experiencing feelings of depression more intensely or notice that these feelings are affecting how you function, call your doctor. There are safe and effective treatments for depression and other psychiatric problems. These treatments can include taking a medication, engaging in therapy, or combining both. Your *primary care provider* (PCP) or *rheumatologist* will be able to help you get the assistance you need.

How Long Will It Take Me to Regain My Emotional Equilibrium?

When you are first diagnosed with scleroderma, you might feel overwhelmed and even worry that things will never get better. However, it is important to recognize that although some aspects of your life might be different, the way you feel emotionally should return to normal. How long it takes to get back to normal varies from person to person. One way to estimate how long it will take for you to feel better is to think about how you have dealt with other stressful events in your life. If you usually adjust quickly, your emotions will likely feel normal again soon. If it takes you longer to feel better, it might be helpful to recognize this as soon as you can and give yourself more time to adjust. If you find that you are having trouble coping with the symptoms of scleroderma, or if you are having feelings of depression or *anxiety* that are affecting your daily functioning, you should talk with your doctor or another member of your treatment team. They can help to determine how best to manage those feelings and whether further evaluation is needed.

Should I Tell Others About the Diagnosis and the Prognosis?

When you are first diagnosed with scleroderma, it is common to wonder whether you should talk about your diagnosis with others. As we have discussed, sharing a new diagnosis of scleroderma with others can be difficult, especially if you are experiencing anger, frustration, or shame about the diagnosis. Further, you might worry that by sharing details of your diagnosis, you might unintentionally increase the worry of others. These types of concerns often lead people to hide their illness from others.

Although this is understandable, there are several benefits of sharing your diagnosis, the symptoms you are experiencing, and the expected disease course with people in whom you trust. For many people, feelings of depression or anxiety decrease after discussing their diagnosis and expected effects of scleroderma with their family and friends. Furthermore, research studies have found that talking about the experience of your illness with family or friends or in support groups often decreases the amount of distress experienced when you first learn of the diagnosis. Thus, sharing your experience with others can help you to more easily adjust to the diagnosis of scleroderma.

There might be a variety of people in your life with whom you can both share your diagnosis and find support. For example, friends or family are often great sources of emotional support and can help you to cope with your illness. Further, close friends and family can often provide more practical types of support. You might find that you are better able to adhere to a healthy diet, medications, or an exercise plan through teaming up with a friend. Also, simply doing things that you regularly enjoy with family and friends can be a great way to relax and to reduce stress.

Support groups, which are composed of other people diagnosed with scleroderma, provide another great resource and a way to talk to others about your diagnosis (Figure 6-1). In addition to emotional support, these groups can provide you with ideas and strategies to better cope with your symptoms as well as support you in adhering to your treatment plan.

It is likely that you will meet others who can share their experiences with certain symptoms, medications, and complications. It is important to remember that everyone's experience will differ somewhat; thus, everything you hear in a support group might not apply to you or work for you.

Figure 6-1: A support group helping a patient diagnosed with scleroderma.

What Should I Tell Others About My Condition?

After you have decided to talk with friends or family about your diagnosis, the next question is, "What do I say?" Knowing what to say and how much to say can be overwhelming, but it is very important to consider. A likely best first step is to talk about your emotions surrounding your new diagnosis rather than the details of the illness itself. This can be as simple as talking about the emotions you experienced when you were first told of the diagnosis. You might consider talking about emotions, such as fear and worry, regarding your disease and how your diagnosis and these feelings might affect you. In this way, you might find much needed emotional support from close friends and family.

You should also consider talking about a few more practical considerations regarding scleroderma—specifically, increased care around mobility, gastrointestinal symptoms, breathing, and ability to do everyday tasks and activities. For example, you might notice that scleroderma affects how comfortable you feel eating in one sitting, how you swallow and digest food, or how often you need to use the restroom. Letting your family members or friends know about some of your symptoms and ways to manage them can help greatly in making plans. Family members and friends also might be grateful to know how they can be most helpful for you, and this can help to strengthen your relationships with them.

You might consider talking to your employers or supervisors about your diagnosis if it directly affects your work. For example, you might require special access or accommodations if you have *limitations in mobility*, or you might benefit from adjusting the temperature in your office to be a few degrees warmer to avoid any circulation problems due to your Raynaud phenomenon. It might also be helpful to make *ergonomic* adjustments to your workstation to make you more comfortable and avoid complications such as *carpal tunnel syndrome*. Even though you should discuss only those things about which you feel comfortable talking, it might be important to make some small changes to help you function better and to maintain your *productivity* in your workplace.

How Can I Manage My Fear of Having a Complication from Scleroderma?

As we have discussed, when you are diagnosed with scleroderma, it can be normal for you to experience concern, worry, or fear regarding your disease and its potential manifestations and complications. There are, however, several things you can do to manage your fear of experiencing a complication. You might begin by educating yourself about the actual risks of developing complications. Talking to your doctor about the risks of certain complications and, importantly, the steps you can take to reduce those risks can help you to gain a sense of control over your illness and to help reduce your fear. This is an important time to work closely with your doctor and health care team to undergo appropriate *screening tests* to provide early detection of internal organ involvement, should it occur, and to begin treatment early, if needed. From a practical standpoint, focusing on the things that you can control (e.g., diet changes, *tobacco cessation*, exercising, stretching, taking medications) is often more helpful than worrying about things outside of your control (e.g., how your symptoms might change over time). Ultimately, if you are making sufficient changes to your lifestyle and are adhering to your treatment, you should experience comfort in knowing that you are doing all that you can to decrease your risk of complications.

How Can I Learn to Be Less Stressed and More Hopeful and Optimistic?

Several different psychological interventions aim to reduce stress and increase hopefulness and optimism. Some of these focus on helping people learn how to relax or *meditate*, whereas others focus on performing exercises such as writing a letter of gratitude or using a strength in a new way, to increase positive feelings. Although these treatment programs are effective at reducing stress or increasing well-being, they have not been studied widely in people with scleroderma.

Despite limited study in people with scleroderma, these interventions provide practical steps to reduce your stress and improve your mood. First, it is important to set aside time to relax. You could meditate, perform *yoga*, or use a resource such as an online resource that guides you through a series of *progressive muscle relaxation* (PMR) exercises. Second, it is very important to focus on the positive aspects of your life. This could include thinking of things for which you are grateful, taking time out of your day to do something enjoyable or meaningful, or spending time with family and close friends. Ultimately, taking time to make sure that you are feeling well, psychologically, is critical. *Psychological health* and *physical health* go hand in hand, and feeling well psychologically will help you to take care of your medical problems and find fulfillment in your daily life as you pursue healthy living.

HOW CAN I LEARN MORE ABOUT SCLERODERMA?

Maria C. Prom, MD and Chris Derk, MD

CHAPTER 7

In This Chapter

- Where Can I Turn for More Information About Scleroderma?
- Should I Seek a Second Opinion?
- Should I Obtain Professional Counseling or Psychiatric Care?
- Should I Seek Care at a Specialized Center for My Scleroderma?
- How Can My Local Library or the Internet Be of Assistance to Me?
- What Are the Most Reliable Internet Resources for Me to Use for Information?
- What Local, Regional, or National Organizations Provide Useful Information About Scleroderma and Its Complications?
- What Articles or Videos Offer Sound Advice or Information?
- Would It Be Helpful for Me to Speak with Someone Who Has a Similar Condition?
- What Is the Role of Social Media in Learning About Scleroderma?
- Summary

Where Can I Turn for More Information About Scleroderma?

In the age of technology, it is easy to quickly become overwhelmed by the amount of information available about scleroderma. There is no shortage of information available to help understand the diagnosis, *symptoms*, monitoring, treatment, and even the latest research in scleroderma care. However, it can be difficult to know where to begin and what information is correct, up-to-date, and trustworthy. In this chapter, we provide a guide to reliable resources for information about scleroderma. We also provide advice about who to ask or how to determine what information is accurate and trustworthy. Readily available resources for information include medical professionals; patient pamphlets and handouts; books; the internet; educational courses; medical societies and organizations; and articles from news sources, magazines, and medical journals.

Often, the first person for you to turn to is your medical provider, who has diagnosed or who treats your scleroderma; this is often a *rheumatologist*. He or she might be able to provide pamphlets, handouts, or even books to provide recommendations about where to learn more based on your specific needs. Medical providers can also help with referrals to other medical professionals, when needed, who can provide specialized care for scleroderma.

Additional reliable resources are medical societies and organizations that provide information about scleroderma to both patients and care providers. We discuss these groups and provide information about how to access them later in this chapter. The internet or local library are also good places to obtain information. Libraries provide access to resources (such as books, videos, magazines, newspapers, journals, and even the internet) and they offer assistance from a librarian who is specially trained to help find information that is reliable, up-to-date, and best fits your needs and interests. We discuss these resources in more detail later in this chapter.

Should I Seek a Second Opinion?

After receiving a new diagnosis of a lifelong illness like scleroderma, it is common to wonder whether you need a second opinion, either for the diagnosis itself or for the treatment that has been recommended. Scleroderma is a rare disease and *primary care providers* (PCPs), and even some rheumatologists, are less familiar with its diagnosis and treatment as compared to more common diseases. Like many *rheumatic disorders*, it is difficult to diagnose scleroderma because it can look different in each individual, it can have similarities to other illnesses, and there is no specific blood test that is diagnostic for the condition. As such, it might be worthwhile to seek a second opinion. A scleroderma specialty center can be helpful in providing a second opinion and can also be beneficial in working with your local rheumatologist to manage your disease. We discuss specialized centers in more detail later.

Scientists continue to learn more about scleroderma all the time, but because there is no blood test that definitively makes the diagnosis, the diagnosis of scleroderma is currently based on the patient's description, a physical exam, and several blood and other medical tests. To make a diagnosis, your PCP will take all of this information and compare it to a set of agreed-upon criteria that doctors and other medical professionals have come together to create, called *classification criteria*. Classification criteria are based on specific symptoms, physical exam findings, and blood and other medical tests (as described in Chapters 1, 2, and 3). Additionally, there are specific recommendations, called *clinical practice guidelines*, on how medical providers should be monitoring and treating diseases such as scleroderma. This includes things such as which blood tests and exams should be completed at regular visits to your doctor's office or with a specialist, and what people should be doing at home to monitor and care for their scleroderma. There are also recommendations about when and what medications should be given to treat scleroderma based on the results of your medical exams, blood tests, and the presence of complications or other medical conditions that you might have. Patients and their families can learn more about whether they are receiving the usual recommendations through the resources provided in this book or through medical organizations dedicated to the management of scleroderma, such as the *American College of Rheumatology* (ACR).

Before seeking a second opinion, consider the following questions: "Does the diagnosis and/or treatment fit with the general recommendations?" "What specific questions do you have about the diagnosis and/or treatment?" "What is it about the diagnosis or recommendation that is concerning?" "Is there difficulty managing scleroderma despite following the medical provider's recommendations?" In finding a physician who can provide a second opinion, it is best to ask your current scleroderma provider or another trusted provider for a referral and consider finding either a rheumatologist who specializes in scleroderma or a specialized center for scleroderma. This chapter provides online resources for finding specialized scleroderma providers and centers.

Should I Obtain Professional Counseling or Psychiatric Care?

At times, it can be helpful for people with scleroderma to consider seeking mental health support. It is very common to feel overwhelmed or distressed over the diagnosis and management of scleroderma. Individuals with scleroderma frequently feel distressed by the complexity and unpredictable nature of their illness, feel fearful of future complications and the progression of illness, feel hopeless, struggle with self-image and self-esteem, and report worsened quality of life. Seeking additional support when these feelings arise can be very beneficial and can help make treatment for scleroderma more successful. If you have scleroderma, you are not alone; there are professionals who can help you and your family members cope with and overcome these thoughts and emotions. Even if you are not having these emotional concerns or thoughts, counselors or therapists can help you to overcome challenges in understanding and managing scleroderma by helping to make changes in habits or behaviors that are getting in the way of successful self-management.

It is important to be aware that these thoughts and feelings can sometimes be a sign of more significant mental health problems. If you have scleroderma, you are at a much higher risk of developing *depression* and *anxiety*. In fact, *depressive symptoms* and anxiety are quite common in scleroderma: it is estimated that approximately 50% of people with *systemic sclerosis* will have depression and at least 20% will have anxiety. Depressive symptoms are often related to chronic fatigue and pain, *gastrointestinal* (GI) involvement, severe disease, inadequate social support, fear of complications and progression of disease, sexual dysfunction, poor coping skills, and lower self-esteem related to physical appearance.

Research has shown that depression in those who have chronic medical conditions is related to poorer self-care and disease management (such as not taking medications reliably), more complications, and worse outcomes of the disease. Therefore, it is very important to be screened for these symptoms and to reach out for help and to engage in treatment when experiencing symptoms, such as sadness, loss of interest, and isolation. Depression and anxiety can be treated successfully in scleroderma, and treatment might then help to improve scleroderma self-management. When experiencing symptoms of depression or anxiety, individuals with scleroderma should reach out to their PCP or scleroderma specialty provider for help with treatment. Treatment can begin with getting a referral to a mental health provider who can make recommendations for medications or can provide one-on-one or group counseling. There are even mental health providers dedicated specifically to helping treat the mental health of those who have chronic illnesses such as scleroderma. Health insurance companies can also provide a list of local mental health providers.

Should I Seek Care at a Specialized Center for My Scleroderma?

Given the complicated diagnosis and management, lifelong challenges, and other medical complications of scleroderma, specialized centers have been developed for the treatment of this rare disease. So, what exactly is a specialized center? A *specialized scleroderma center* is a medical clinic designed to provide comprehensive care specifically to people with scleroderma. These centers have medical providers from a variety of disciplines who specialize in scleroderma care; they offer diagnostic evaluations and treatment of the disease and its complications. The services offered by a scleroderma center can differ depending on the center and available resources from other specialists. Services might include doctors who are specialized in scleroderma care (rheumatologists), patient-care coordinators and nurses specialized in scleroderma care and patient education, *physical therapists, occupational therapists, pain specialists,* digestive system doctors *(gastroenterologists),* skin doctors *(dermatologists),* lung doctors *(pulmonologists),* kidney doctors *(nephrologists),* heart doctors *(cardiologists),* and *surgeons.* Centers might also have their own laboratory, scleroderma education courses, patient registries, and *research studies.*

Because scleroderma is a complex disease, specialized centers can be useful for anyone suffering from the disease, not just those with a severe or complicated illness. Scleroderma centers are not, however, intended to replace a local rheumatologist. Instead, they work with that provider to take care of the person's scleroderma-related needs over time. These centers are frequently located in larger cities or in large medical centers, and they thus might not be easily accessible for everyone. As such, many people see their local provider more frequently and go to specialized centers less frequently to receive additional recommendations or care for a complicated aspect of their disease that they can then complete with their local doctor. The decision to seek care and how often people visit a specialized center will depend on several things, including one's medical history, manifestations of scleroderma, challenges of treatment, resources available at your primary treatment office, and even health insurance coverage. The first step in making this decision is to have this discussion with the medical provider currently managing your scleroderma because he or she will best understand your specific needs. The health care provider will also be able to help make referrals to local specialized centers if this is the next best step. It is especially important to be seen at a specialized center when there are difficulties in managing scleroderma with typical treatments and complications requiring other types of specialty doctors (such as heart or lung doctors, as listed earlier). Specialty centers also might offer the advantage of additional treatment options and participation in research studies for treatments still being studied.

How Can My Local Library or the Internet Be of Assistance to Me?

The local library and internet are great places to learn more about scleroderma. Libraries can be particularly helpful for those who could use the assistance of a librarian to find more information as well as for those who prefer books or other printed information. Public libraries offer free access to resources (such as books, videos, magazines, newspapers, the internet, and even medical journals). Librarians can be tremendously helpful; they are knowledgeable about what resources are available and are specially trained to help find information that is reliable, up-to-date, and tailored to your needs and interests. Additionally, if a book or other resources are not available at your local library, a librarian can retrieve them from other libraries. One thing to keep in mind when using books is that although they can be a great place to start, our knowledge about scleroderma increases every day, and older books might contain information that is no longer accurate. As such, it is important to check the year that the book was published and be aware that more recently published books will have more current information.

When looking for the most up-to-date information, the internet is often the best place to begin. The internet can be an easy, quick, and reliable source of information, but it can also make you feel like there is too much information available. A quick search of scleroderma on the internet will identify news and magazine articles, informational websites, professional organization websites, government-sponsored websites, health and wellness websites, websites selling supplements, pharmaceutical-sponsored medication websites, professional journal articles, blogs and personal websites, social media (e.g., forums, message boards, and interest groups), videos, and even fake-news humor websites. With so much material available, it can be difficult to know where to begin or what information to trust. Anyone can publish anything on the internet without it having to be true or validated, and many websites do not have doctors or medical professionals checking to ensure that the information supplied is correct. Fortunately, there are several websites created by medical professionals, medical centers, and rheumatology and scleroderma organizations that provide reliable patient information based on the latest scientific research and recommendations from professional associations, which we explore in the next section.

What Are the Most Reliable Internet Resources for Me to Use for Information?

Websites created by medical professionals, medical centers, and rheumatology and scleroderma organizations provide the most reliable and up-to-date information. Table 7-1 provides an alphabetical list of some of them that includes what types of resources are available through their websites, as of this writing. We discuss specific medical societies and organizations in more detail later in this chapter, and Table 7-2 provides information on how to access these groups.

Table 7-1: Websites Supported by Medical Professionals and Organizations

Organization	Internet Address	Resources Available
Arthritis Foundation	www.arthritis.org/about-arthritis/types/scleroderma/	• Advocacy • Blogs and forums • Newsletter • Patient information • Provider finder • Resources • Support groups
Cleveland Clinic	https://my.clevelandclinic.org/health/diseases/8979-scleroderma-an-overview	• Patient information • Resources
Mayo Clinic	www.mayoclinic.org/diseases-conditions/scleroderma	• Articles • Patient information
Medline	https://medlineplus.gov/scleroderma.html	• Articles • Patient information • Resources
National Organization of Rare Disorders (NORD)	https://rarediseases.org/rare-diseases/scleroderma/	• Advocacy • Clinical trials resources • Patient information • Resources
Pulmonary Hypertension Association	https://phassociation.org/	• Advocacy • Articles • Patient information • Videos • Support Groups

Organization	Internet Address	Resources Available
Scleroderma Foundation	www.scleroderma.org	• Advocacy • Articles • Education courses • Forums • Meetings and events • Newsletter • Rheumatologist finder • Patient information • Resources • Support groups • Videos
Scleroderma International Network	https://sclero.org/	• Advocacy • Blogs and forums • Patient information • Patient stories • Resources • Rheumatologist finder • Support groups • Videos
Scleroderma Research Foundation	www.srfcure.org	• Advocacy • News articles • Patient information • Research information • Scleroderma center list • Resource list • Webinars
WebMD	www.webmd.com/scleroderma	• Articles • Ask a medical professional • Patient information

Websites created and reviewed by medical professionals cover only a small portion of what is available on the internet; therefore, it is important to learn how to determine which websites and articles you should trust. One way to research this is to look at the background, education, and training of the authors or sponsors of the website or article; those with medical certifications or training, and particularly specialty training in rheumatology or scleroderma, will in general be more reliable than those written by non-medical professionals or by patients. Additionally, it can be helpful to know from where the information on the website is coming; indications of more reliable information are listings of specific scientific studies or articles from professional medical journals or information published by *professional medical societies* (of which we provide a list later in this chapter). It is also important to notice the difference between information provided by a website and by advertisements from private companies that might help sponsor the website. Overall, it is best to ask your medical provider to confirm whether information from the internet is accurate and whether it applies to your particular situation. Most important, you should not stop or change your scleroderma management or order medications, natural supplements, or medical devices based on online information unless it is recommended by or first discussed with your medical provider, especially given that such an action could interfere with current treatments.

What Local, Regional, or National Organizations Provide Useful Information About Scleroderma and Its Complications?

There are several medical societies and organizations dedicated to providing education, support, and resources regarding scleroderma and its complications to both patients and medical providers, including recommendations on patient care, patient resources, patient education tools, advocacy, and referrals. These societies and organizations are run by medical professionals and provide the most up-to-date and reliable information. These groups have their own websites online, and sometimes they have other forms of access, such as local offices, email, or phone numbers to call with specific questions. Table 7-2 presents some of these medical societies and organizations, how to access their patient information websites, and what types of resources are available through their websites, as of this writing.

Table 7-2: Professional Medical Societies and Organizations for Scleroderma

Organization	Website or Other Access Information	Resources Available
American Academy of Dermatology	www.aad.org/public/diseases/painful-skin-joints/scleroderma	• Advocacy • Dermatologist finder • News articles • Patient information • Resources
American College of Rheumatology (ACR)	www.rheumatology.org/I-Am-A/Patient-Caregiver/Diseases-Conditions/Scleroderma	• Advocacy • News articles • Patient information • Patient stories • Resources • Rheumatologist finder • Social media connections • Videos
National Institute of Arthritis and *Musculoskeletal* and Skin Diseases (NIAMS)	www.niams.nih.gov/health-topics/scleroderma	• Clinical trial finder • Patient information • Resources

What Articles or Videos Offer Sound Advice or Information?

Articles and videos can be a great source of information about scleroderma and its complications. They can provide the newest information about the diagnosis, biology, management, and treatment of scleroderma and its complications, as well as how to support your care and well-being. Videos can be particularly helpful for visual learners and those who prefer videos to reading. They can be a good way to learn to care for yourself and how to keep an eye out for signs of complications. Videos can also be a way to hear the experiences of others who have scleroderma.

When looking for specific articles and videos about scleroderma, medical providers, including specialty providers (such as rheumatologists), might be able to provide specific suggestions about information that best fits each individual's needs. When searching for articles or videos, keep in mind the previous discussion of general recommendations on how and where to find more information about scleroderma and how to know what information is trustworthy. To review, resources include the local library (including the librarian) and the internet, while paying attention to the date when the information was written, the author, and the source of the information provided. Generally, articles and videos provided or approved by medical societies and organizations, medical centers, and medical professionals will be the most reliable. The websites provided in Tables 7-1 and 7-2 are a good place to begin. Additionally, medical journal articles can provide more in-depth information but can often be difficult for the general reader to interpret.

Newspapers and magazines frequently publish articles about scleroderma and the latest research. Although these are usually more reliable sources than some internet websites, you should still be cautious about how the writers of these articles interpret the information. Generally, the authors and publishers of newspaper and magazine articles are not medical professionals, and they can misinterpret the latest research or exaggerate or put an emphasis on the information that they find is most interesting or that will draw the most attention from readers. If possible, it can be helpful to find out from where the information in the article came and read the original source of the information. If that is not possible, medical providers can help answer questions or provide more information.

Would It Be Helpful for Me to Speak with Someone Who Has a Similar Condition?

Although family, friends, and medical professionals can provide support and understanding, they might not be able to understand fully the challenges of managing scleroderma. For many people, it can be helpful to speak with someone who has the same condition. Support groups and social media outlets (such as online forums, message boards, and interest groups) created for individuals with scleroderma or other rheumatic diseases are a common way for individuals to share their experiences and struggles, get peer support or advice, and can even help individuals stay motivated and engaged in treatment and healthy decision making. Isolation and not having strong social support have been related to people with scleroderma having mental health issues, and seeking social support can help to address these challenges. These groups and networks can also be a good way to find out about other local and internet resources and about experiences other people have had with those resources.

When considering joining a *support group*, there are a lot of options, including where the group meets (in-person or online), who leads the group (an outside facilitator or a peer), how the group runs (group discussions or invited speakers), how often the group meets (weekly or less often), and whether the groups have a specific focus (couples, caregivers, women, or type of illness). Online support groups are often better for those who do not live near in-person groups, are not comfortable speaking in front of others, are younger, or have difficult schedules and cannot get to an in-person group regularly (online groups often have 24/7 access). Keep in mind that support groups are not *therapy groups* (which is another option) but are groups where individuals with illness come together to discuss and share their experiences with the illness.

When you are unsure which group or online social network is the best fit for you, or if you are in need of help finding one, a good place to begin is speaking to medical providers, checking with local medical centers, or checking out the websites listed in Tables 7-1 and 7-2 or those provided in Table 7-3. Before picking a group, you should think about what would make you feel most comfortable, what you would want to get from the group, and what aspects would make it easier to get to the group. If you are still unsure, it is always okay to attend a meeting or two to see whether it is a good fit for you.

When engaging in a support group or online social networks, it is always important that you keep in mind that you might not know the background of others with whom you are speaking, and you should think carefully about the advice provided by others because it might not always be correct, reliable, applicable, or right for you. As we discussed previously, it is always best to ask your medical providers about information that you find online. Your medical providers have the training and education to determine whether the information is accurate or the right choice for your specific situation.

Table 7-3: Recommended Resources for Support Through Groups and Social Media

Organization	Website or Other Access Information
American College of Rheumatology (ACR)	simpletasks.org
Arthritis Foundation	www.arthritis.org
Scleroderma Foundation	www.scleroderma.org
Scleroderma International Network	https://sclero.org/

What Is the Role of Social Media in Learning About Scleroderma?

As technology changes, there are more and more opportunities to not only connect with others and find support online, but also to learn more about scleroderma through social media outlets. However, as discussed earlier, it is important to be careful about the reliability of this information, whether it is coming from an individual or a news source. Keep in mind that articles and information found on social media sites might not be written by medical professionals, and the writers might exaggerate, misinterpret, or over-emphasize information to draw attention. It is always best to seek social media sources supported by medical organizations or groups, such as the groups listed in the tables in this chapter, many of which share information on multiple social media outlets. Additionally, it is important to ask your medical providers about information found through social media, given that your medical providers, who know you well, can determine whether the information is accurate or the right choice for your specific situation.

Summary

People with scleroderma are not alone when trying to understand and manage their scleroderma. There is a wealth of information available to learn more about scleroderma (e.g., from medical professionals, patient pamphlets and handouts, books, the internet, educational courses, medical societies, and organizations, as well as articles from news sources, magazines, and medical journals). This chapter provided specific reliable resources for more information and support as well as guidance to distinguish information that is likely to be accurate and trustworthy.

HOW CAN MEMBERS OF MY HEALTH CARE TEAM HELP ME MANAGE MY SCLERODERMA?

Mark A. Matza, MD, MBA and Vivien Hsu, MD

CHAPTER

In This Chapter

- What Role Will My Primary Care Provider Play in Helping to Take Care of Me and My Scleroderma?
- What Role Will My Rheumatologist Play in Taking Care of Me?
- What Role Might Other Subspecialists Play in Taking Care of Me?
- How Can Occupational Therapy and Physical Therapy Help Me with My Scleroderma?
- How Can Other Members of My Health Team Improve My Function and Help Me Cope?
- Summary

What Role Will My Primary Care Provider Play in Helping to Take Care of Me and My Scleroderma?

Scleroderma is a complex disease (Gabrielli et al, 2009) that affects your body in many ways; your health care team, composed of multiple doctors and other professionals, will help manage this with you.

Your *primary care provider* (PCP) will play an integral part in the daily management of your scleroderma and will help coordinate any additional care that you might need (Mayes and Ho, 2018) along with your *rheumatologist* and other *subspecialists*. It is crucial to have someone help to coordinate your care with different providers, a "quarterback" or "point person," so to speak. Often, this will be your PCP, your rheumatologist, or both. Your PCP will continue to address important health care needs with you, in terms of health maintenance and treatment of your other health conditions.

Frequently, your PCP is the first to recognize the development of your scleroderma, either due to skin thickening, hand swelling, onset of *Raynaud phenomenon*, or abnormalities in your blood work. He or she might refer you to a rheumatologist who has experience and expertise in confirming and managing your scleroderma. However, your PCP remains an important provider whom you should continue to see regularly. Your PCP will help to address persistent scleroderma-related symptoms despite treatment as well as other unrelated conditions (e.g., a viral illness). Your PCP should be the first person to determine what tests or intervention you might need to address your symptom(s).

Your PCP will help you to navigate the health care system and ensure that you are staying up-to-date with your general health care, including vaccinations, cancer screening, as well as visiting with your subspecialist providers in a timely fashion. These subspecialists should communicate with your PCP, who will review notes and treatment plans, and help to ensure that all your medications are working for you. Your PCP might contact your other care providers when questions arise. Regular communication among your providers is essential and can take the form of email messages; faxed office notes and laboratory results; physician letters; and phone conversations among your rheumatologist, your PCP, and one or more of your other subspecialists.

Aside from managing your general care and ensuring referrals, your PCP should assist in the initial evaluation of new *symptoms* such as persistent cough, fever, or recurring diarrhea. This evaluation can be done in collaboration with your other care providers, including your rheumatologist. Most people with scleroderma experience Raynaud phenomenon and *gastroesophageal reflux disease* (GERD). Your PCP might prescribe a treatment while you await your appointment with a subspecialist, or he or she might implement the recommendations from the subspecialist. Additionally, your PCP might adjust the dosages of your medications that were started by the subspecialist, such as *proton pump inhibitors* (PPI) to better control your reflux, or calcium channel blockers for Raynaud phenomenon. If necessary, your PCP will also monitor your blood pressure on a more frequent basis to ensure that it is in the normal range, and will adjust your blood pressure medications as needed. Likewise, your PCP can ensure timely laboratory testing (such as kidney and liver function or blood counts) be completed to monitor for internal organ involvement as well as to arrange other tests to monitor your scleroderma. It is essential to have good communication among your caregivers, including your PCP and your subspecialists, to facilitate and enhance the management of your scleroderma.

Routine screening tests (including screening for high cholesterol levels, anemia, or common cancers) are often necessary. Scleroderma can be associated with cancer (Shah and Wigley, 2013), and your PCP will ensure that you are up-to-date with age-appropriate cancer screenings. Depending on your age and gender, this can include cervical cancer screening (with a Pap smear), breast cancer screening (with a mammogram), and *gastrointestinal* (GI) cancer screening (with a colonoscopy or an *upper endoscopy*). Other tests can be obtained depending on your symptoms and medical history. Almost all people with scleroderma will require yearly *pulmonary function tests* (PFTs) and an *echocardiogram* (an ultrasound of the heart), and your PCP might assist with arranging for these tests, including any authorization needed by your health insurance plan.

What Role Will My Rheumatologist Play in Taking Care of Me?

The Initial Evaluation

Your rheumatologist is the person who is most familiar with all aspects of evaluating and managing your scleroderma. This subspecialist is specifically trained to manage common scleroderma symptoms and to look for hidden complications of this disease. Your visit with your rheumatologist will begin by taking a thorough history of your disease, and this will involve a discussion of your symptoms. Because scleroderma can affect many different parts of your body, your rheumatologist will ask you about your skin (e.g., has there been thickening, discoloration, or ulceration of your skin?), your joints (e.g., have you had joint pains, joint swelling, or difficulty with your hand function?), your GI tract (e.g., have you experienced GI symptoms, such as, gastroesophageal reflux, nausea, vomiting, difficulty swallowing, or changes in your bowel habits?), any breathing or pulmonary problems (e.g., have you had shortness of breath or a persistent cough?), as well as problems with your circulation (e.g., have you had blood flow problems to your fingertips that might have contributed to fingertip ulceration? or had Raynaud phenomenon [a painful discoloration of the fingertips from cold exposure]?). These are a sampling of questions that you might be asked.

Your rheumatologist has been trained to perform a comprehensive physical exam, which should include a thorough evaluation of your skin, joints, lungs, heart, and abdomen; in addition, your rheumatologist should also arrange for initial testing to confirm the nature and severity of your scleroderma. This will include blood tests to confirm your *antibodies* (such as the *antinuclear antibody* [ANA] as well as more specific scleroderma antibodies such as the *anti-centromere, anti-Scl-70* and *anti-RNA polymerase III antibodies*). Other tests such as pulmonary function tests (PFT) and an echocardiogram study are necessary in the initial screening to assess whether your scleroderma has affected your lungs or heart. In addition, a computerized tomography (CT) scan of your chest might be performed.

Follow-Up Visits with Your Rheumatologist or "Scleroderma Doctor"

These visits will be important for you because your rheumatologist will monitor you and your scleroderma as it changes over time (Morrisroe et al, 2016; Lee and Pope, 2016). A well-trained rheumatologist will monitor your skin for improvement or worsening and recommend appropriate treatments as needed. Your management might include *physical therapy* and/or *occupational therapy* especially if you have problems with joint mobility or *joint contractures* early on (Bonji et al, 2009; Young et al, 2016). Some people also have *arthritis* or *inflammatory muscle disease* that will require treatment, and your rheumatologist will recognize this while monitoring you closely. Your rheumatologist will initiate treatment for your Raynaud phenomenon and recommend appropriate wound care if fingertip ulcers develop (Bonji et al, 2009). Local wound care is crucial to ensure that your fingertip ulcers heal in a timely fashion. Some rheumatologists who consider themselves "scleroderma experts" are trained to manage other complications, including scleroderma-related lung disease. However, many rheumatologists prefer to work with their pulmonary and cardiology colleagues to best manage your lung and heart complications.

Close evaluation of changes in your condition and intervening early if you are getting worse, especially in the early years of your disease, will offer you the best chances for recovery and improvement in your quality of life.

Your rheumatologist will also ensure that appropriate monitoring is being performed as part of your ongoing care. These tests are crucial to guide your management. Your PCP can also be helpful in ensuring that your scleroderma monitoring is being conducted. These monitoring tests might differ from time to time and from patient to patient. For instance, your blood pressure and blood work including *complete blood counts*, *kidney function*, and urine tests might need closer monitoring. Although the antibodies might not need repeating after the initial evaluation, other tests should be followed yearly to ensure there is no decline over time. These will include some blood work, pulmonary function tests, an echocardiogram, and sometimes a chest CT scan. Your rheumatologist will ensure that all testing is being completed. Your rheumatologist can ensure that everything is being accomplished at appropriate intervals and that you are improving with treatment. Your rheumatologist should review the test results with you and adjust any medications or therapy, as needed. In addition, your rheumatologist might advise other subspecialists to participate and help manage a specific problem that has arisen. Thus, communication among your rheumatologist, your PCP, and any other subspecialists is a crucial part in managing your scleroderma.

What Role Might Other Subspecialists Play in Taking Care of Me?

In addition to your rheumatologist, other subspecialists might play a role in the management of your scleroderma. While following you closely, your PCP or rheumatologist might identify a new or worsening *symptom* or *sign* of organ involvement that might need additional attention and recommend other subspecialists to help with your care. Two of the most common organs affected by scleroderma are the GI tract and the lungs; however, there might be a role for other subspecialists (besides *gastroenterologists* and *pulmonologists*, respectively) in the management of your scleroderma.

Gastrointestinal Tract

The bowels are affected in more than 95% of people with scleroderma. Dysfunction can involve the entire GI tract (including your mouth, esophagus [or food pipe], intestines, *colon*, and anus). Heartburn (or chest burning), painful or difficulty swallowing, erosive reflux (or heartburn) are common symptoms from untreated or undertreated *gastroesophageal reflux*. Additionally, scleroderma can involve the intestines and colon and cause changes in bowel habits. Symptoms of impaired bowel function often include recurrent abdominal pain, bloating, diarrhea, constipation, and unintentional weight loss from *small intestinal bacterial overgrowth* (SIBO) or from malabsorption of important nutrients. Stool *incontinence* occurs in roughly 25% or more of people who have scleroderma bowel involvement (Morrisoe et al, 2016; Richard et al, 2017). Depending on the severity of your symptoms, your PCP or rheumatologist might suggest obtaining a consultation from a GI doctor (or gastroenterologist) who might need to perform an *endoscopy*, a colonoscopy, or another important procedure to confirm the cause or severity of your condition. With prolonged gastroesophageal reflux, some individuals develop scarring of the esophagus, termed a *stricture*, and this can lead to difficulties in swallowing food, particularly solids, such as meat or bread. If a stricture develops, an *esophageal dilation* that stretches the esophagus by means of a balloon inserted through an *endoscope*, might help to alleviate these symptoms. Unexpected bleeding from the GI tract might require an urgent intervention by a GI specialist to establish the source of bleeding that might relate to *telangiectasias*, also termed *arteriovenous malformations* (AVMs), or other abnormalities in the GI tract. The gastroenterologist might become a regular member of your treatment team or you might see this specialist on an as-needed basis.

Lungs

A *pulmonologist* (pulmonary or lung) doctor might be involved to evaluate you for lung involvement and help you manage your lung involvement, most likely from *interstitial lung disease* (ILD; fibrosis of the lungs) or *pulmonary artery hypertension* (PAH; elevated pressures in the blood vessels of the lungs). At times, a *cardiologist* (or heart specialist) might be needed to evaluate you for PAH.

Before recommending treatment, a complete evaluation by the pulmonologist will involve a review of all your pulmonary function tests, *chest CT scans*, echocardiograms, and any exercise testing results before making recommendations; the lung doctor will work in collaboration with your rheumatologist to develop the best treatment plan for your scleroderma lung disease.

Kidneys

Less commonly (in 5–10% of those diagnosed with diffuse scleroderma), your kidneys can also be affected by scleroderma. *Scleroderma renal crisis* (SRC) can cause unexpected high blood pressure and, if left untreated, can lead to *kidney failure*. Although this complication might be first recognized by your PCP or rheumatologist, the kidney doctor (*nephrologist*) might be called in to manage your blood pressure and follow your kidney function to ensure that you are improving. Often, however, scleroderma kidney involvement is managed by your rheumatologist and PCP without the need for consultation with a nephrologist. As with other specialist involvement, communication between your nephrologist (if included), your PCP, and your rheumatologist is crucial.

Hands

The hands are affected in a number of ways in almost all people with scleroderma (Young et al, 2016). Common problems arise from painful or frequent episodes of Raynaud phenomenon, finger or hand puffiness, skin thickening *(sclerodactyly)*, *contractures* resulting in reduced range of motion of the finger joints, joint inflammation or arthritis, painful *tendon friction rubs*, skin or fingertip ulcers, and *calcinosis* (or calcium deposits under the skin). The management of these varied hand manifestations will differ depending on your current symptoms and will differ from person to person over time. Your rheumatologist will determine whether physical or occupational therapy is needed, or oversee proper wound care for any painful fingertip ulcers.

Coping

More than half of those who have scleroderma report symptoms of depression or anxiety (Nguyen et al, 2014; Faezi et al, 2017; Milette et al, 2018; Morrisroe et al, 2018). This can be due to fear and mood disturbances resulting from having a chronic illness, or due to chronic pain or fatigue (see Chapter 6 for a more detailed discussion). Medications can also contribute to mood changes or anxiety. Changes in the physical appearance of your face or hands (e.g., skin thickening or pigmentation) can contribute to your feeling depressed or anxious. Additionally, hand contractures, arthritis, and painful fingertip ulcers often lead to difficulty in performing daily activities and job-related functions. These difficulties contribute to feelings of frustration and certainly add to the experience of anxiety and depression.

Your PCP and rheumatologist might be the first to recognize your anxiety and depression and will address these symptoms; intervention is important, and the sooner it is recognized, the better. Interventions might include counseling as well as medication. Your PCP or rheumatologist might begin an antidepressant or pain medication, though a *psychiatrist* is trained specifically to evaluate you for anxiety or depression and to prescribe these medications to help you. A *psychologist* is best trained to provide counseling, which can be as important as the medication prescribed by the psychiatrist. Counseling can include developing coping strategies, use of biofeedback and other relaxation techniques, and education of you and your caregiver(s) about your needs (see Chapters 6 and 10).

Sexual Dysfunction

Sexual dysfunction can occur in both men and women. In men, sexual dysfunction can develop (Jaeger and Walker, 2016) either as a consequence of fibrosis or from damage to blood vessels within the penis; this can be evaluated by a *urologist*, who might also assist in this management. In women, vaginal dryness can be evaluated and managed by a *gynecologist*. *Musculoskeletal* difficulties (including joint pains, joint contractures, skin tightening, calcinosis deposits in the pelvic or hip areas), and depression can contribute to sexual dysfunction in women. The rheumatologist will need to evaluate you and make recommendations depending on your difficulties.

Skin

The *dermatologist* (or skin doctor) might be the first doctor to recognize that you have scleroderma. This specialist will usually refer you to a rheumatologist for the comprehensive care of your scleroderma, given that the skin is not the only organ to be affected by scleroderma. However, the dermatologist might help with some scleroderma manifestations affecting your skin, including troublesome calcinosis, fingertip ulcers, as well as laser therapy to remove telangiectasias (or red spots) from the skin. Laser therapy is not a cure for these spots, because these telangiectasias will often recur. Dermatologists are well qualified to evaluate and manage persistent or recurrent rashes that you might develop, regardless of whether they are related to your scleroderma. A rash can be the initial presentation of a new disease or can develop as a side effect from a medication you are taking.

Surgery

Depending on its location, painful or troublesome calcinosis can be surgically removed by an experienced hand or *orthopedic surgeon*. Hand surgery might be the last resort to correct fixed contractures of the hands that did not fully correct with physical therapy or occupational therapy. This is often considered in those who have recurrent painful knuckle ulcers on their hands. Despite medical intervention, occasionally a persistent fingertip or toe ulcer might be due to scarring of a larger blood vessel leading to the hand or foot; in this case, a *vascular surgeon* might perform bypass surgery and/or a *digital sympathectomy* (a procedure in which the hand surgeon cuts the tiny nerves to the smaller arteries in the fingers) in hopes of improving blood flow and hastening the healing of the ulcer.

Eyes

Dry eyes due to scarring of the tear glands affects the majority of people with scleroderma, most commonly in their later years. Sometimes, *Sjogren syndrome* (an autoimmune disease affecting the salivary and tear glands) might co-exist with your scleroderma, and the rheumatologist can confirm whether this autoimmune disease is also present. The management often requires an *ophthalmologist* to examine your eyes and confirm that dryness exists before making recommendations to optimize and maintain tear production for your dry eyes.

Mouth

Dryness of the mouth (Poole et al, 2005; Yuen et al, 2011; Pischon et al, 2016; Poole et al, 2010) is a complaint expressed by more than half of people with scleroderma due to reduced blood flow as well as scarring of the salivary glands that results in less saliva production. Additionally, medications can contribute to dryness of the mouth. Other problems such as chronic gastroesophageal reflux can promote more rapid tooth decay, with acid contributing to erosion of the teeth while you are sleeping, especially if you are not sleeping with your head and chest sufficiently elevated, or if your esophageal reflux is not adequately controlled. These problems often lead to dental cavities, gum disease, tooth decay, and ultimately, loss of teeth. The *dentist* will confirm whether you have sufficient dryness to require closer follow-up, more frequent dental cleaning, and might recommend additional *periodontal care* as a preventive measure. The dentist might recommend a specific toothbrush (powered or not) for those who have hand or mouth deformities.

How Can Occupational Therapy and Physical Therapy Help Me with My Scleroderma?

Occupational therapy (OT) and *physical therapy* (PT) play important roles in the treatment of musculoskeletal (e.g., of the skin, joints, and muscles) difficulties resulting from your scleroderma. For instance, skin tightness and joint pains can affect joint range of motion and flexibility, leading to joint contractures. Muscle weakness is another common musculoskeletal manifestation of scleroderma. In addition to medical management, both PT and OT are vital to regain and maintain joint range of motion and restore strength and flexibility. Physical therapy often focuses on stretching, strengthening, and range of motion exercises of the upper and lower extremity joints, whereas the occupational therapist is best trained to work with your hands, to improve mobility and strengthening, and find ways to help you carry out your activities of daily living (see Chapters 4 and 9).

How Can Other Members of My Health Team Improve My Function and Help Me Cope?

Registered dietitians will make dietary recommendations to help you gain or lose weight depending on your circumstances or GI symptoms. Dietitians can tailor your diet for symptoms of gastroesophageal reflux, swallowing difficulty, diarrhea, or constipation due to motility abnormalities affecting the small bowel.

Other members of your health care team might include *nurse practitioners* (NPs), who might be part of your medical team at the PCP or rheumatologist's office. An NP can be the first person to evaluate you during an urgent visit to your doctor or before you see your physician at a routine appointment. Trained NPs are extremely helpful and can spend the extra time needed to educate you or provide you with the additional care you need. This can include wound care for your finger ulcers or even helping with managing your pulmonary hypertension.

The *pharmacist* is another important source of information about your medications and their side effects, the best time to take your medications (with or without food), as well as important drug interactions among your medications. The pharmacist often will alert you when you need medication refills and might alert your prescribing doctor about important drug interactions and side effects.

If you are hospitalized, the *case manager* or *social worker* is trained to assist you with the application process for disability as well as any other continued care needs after your hospital discharge. This can include specialized nursing care or administering and monitoring of intravenous *antibiotics* at home. The case manager or social worker will arrange for inpatient or outpatient rehabilitation as well as equipment (such as home oxygen, hospital bed) that you might need after you go home.

Summary

Scleroderma is a chronic and complex disorder affecting many organs; the management is different for every individual diagnosed with scleroderma. Your scleroderma manifestations can change over time; to address your needs effectively, close follow-up and collaboration between your PCP, rheumatologist, other subspecialists, and health professionals are needed.

HOW CAN I REDUCE MY RISK OF SCLERODERMA AND ITS COMPLICATIONS?

Karen L. Smarr, PhD and Zsuzsanna H. McMahan, MD, MHS

CHAPTER 9

In This Chapter

- Can Exercise, Dieting, Quitting Smoking, or Reducing Stress Prevent Scleroderma or Improve Its Treatment?
- What Role Does My Diet Play in How I Am Feeling? Can Dietary Modifications Improve My Health?
- What Can I Do to Change My Exercise Habits?
- Can I Make Lasting Changes on My Own or Will I Need the Help of Others?
- Should I Build a Support System?

Can Exercise, Dieting, Quitting Smoking, or Reducing Stress Prevent Scleroderma or Improve Its Treatment?

Although there is no data that supports a specific management strategy (e.g., a dietary or lifestyle modification for preventing scleroderma), management strategies exist that might help to control *symptoms* and reduce the likelihood of scleroderma-related complications. Several types of scleroderma exist, but the focus of this chapter is on *systemic sclerosis* ("scleroderma"), not on *localized scleroderma* (i.e., *morphea*), a rare condition that causes painless, discolored, often thickened patches on your skin.

Identifying modifiable *risk factors* for those with scleroderma is important to maximize quality of life. People with scleroderma are at increased risk for *atherosclerotic coronary artery disease* (CAD, also called *atherosclerotic cardiovascular disease*, ASCVD) as are people with other *rheumatic diseases* (Shah et al, 2013). You can reduce these risks by making lifestyle modifications. In the early 1990s, Dr. Dean Ornish and colleagues provided early evidence of the benefits of making comprehensive lifestyle changes (e.g., beginning to exercise, quitting smoking, making dietary changes) in those with CAD. Health and quality of life improvements were seen in the group that made comprehensive lifestyle changes, reducing the risks associated with cardiovascular disease. Every person determines their readiness for change and their level of motivation for lifestyle change.

Research indicates that there are several crucial steps to enable a change in behaviors and routines. In the book called *Changing for Good*, investigators discuss the *Transtheoretical Approach* or *Stages of Change* theory (Prochaska et al, 1994). Table 9-1 lists and describes the specific stages involved in change theory.

Table 9-1: Stages of Change Theory and Description

Pre-contemplation	When you have not yet considered making a lifestyle change.
Contemplation	When you are considering making a behavior change (like quitting smoking, starting to exercise, or modifying your diet).
Preparation	When you are planning and making contingency plans for at-risk times, setting a change date, and investigating ways to accomplish the goal.
Action	When you change the behavior on your change date and pursue strategies to accomplish your goal for the first 6 months.
Maintenance	When you have successfully changed the behavior for 6 months to 5 years.
Relapse	When you return to a behavior that you are working to change for a brief or longer period. This will require you to return to an earlier step to implement additional strategies to help prevent another relapse.

Moving through these stages of change is important when modifying your lifestyle to reduce clinical risks.

Exercise

If you have scleroderma, sustaining a regular level of physical activity (as tolerated) is important for you to maintain strength, balance, flexibility, and cardiopulmonary health (*American Heart Association* [AHA], 2018; Mosca et al, 2011). *Occupational therapists* (OT) and *physical therapists* (PT) encourage exercise and provide personalized recommendations as to the level of activity that is appropriate for you. Significant data demonstrates that regular exercise is associated with improved outcomes with regard to long-term health; for example, reductions in muscle weakness and stress, and improvements in muscle mass, cardiovascular health, overall physical function, blood flow/circulation, and muscle/skin tone (AHA, 2018; Mosca et al, 2011). In the absence of regular exercise, you should begin exercising slowly *and* increase your activities gradually. The development of a practical and sustainable exercise routine is essential. If you have scleroderma, you should exercise in moderation to minimize the risk of injury and pain that might culminate in a setback. Remember to pace yourself, to avoid painful activities, and to obtain adequate rest at night to allow for post-exercise recovery. Weight-bearing exercises build strength and improve overall physical health and function. Some individuals hire an *American College of Sports Medicine* (ACSM) *certified exercise physiologist* (CEP) to recommend safe exercises and to provide personalized exercises, until they become comfortable with an independent exercise routine. Many physical activities exist that do not require the CEP's expertise. At a minimum, you should perform daily range of motion and stretching exercises to maintain optimal *musculoskeletal* function, to reduce your risk of *joint contractures*, and to allow ease of movement, without pain. Walking, biking, swimming, and water aerobics (pool activities should take place in a warm pool) are all reasonable options for those with scleroderma. Regular walking (especially after eating) will serve to stimulate the bowels, and it might ease *constipation* by promoting the movement of food through the *gastrointestinal* (GI) tract. Incorporating exercise into your daily life can take preparation. Planning and taking action are often challenging steps. When you begin exercising (however slowly) you will begin reaping its benefits.

Diet

Limited data exists to support specific dietary modifications for the management of those with scleroderma. There is no specific dietary recommendation to prevent the complications of scleroderma, although diet has a role in the management of symptoms, particularly GI tract symptoms. A healthy, well-balanced, diet is important when managing and living well with scleroderma. *Gastroesophageal reflux disease* (GERD), *gastroparesis, small bowel dysmotility, small intestinal bacterial overgrowth* (SIBO), and *malnutrition* related to inadequate calories and *malabsorption* can occur in scleroderma; therefore, tailoring your diet to meet your needs is critical (Nagaraja et al, 2015). *Dietitians* typically rely on evidence from general nutrition recommendations and symptom management to help guide their approach to patients with scleroderma.

Most people with scleroderma develop some GI symptoms such as heartburn, swallowing problems, early fullness, nausea, diarrhea, constipation, stool *incontinence*, and other digestion problems (Nagaraja et al, 2015). *Lactose malabsorption* is more prevalent among people with scleroderma who have GI symptoms than it is in healthy people with GI symptoms (Marie et al, 2016). Lactose malabsorption is associated with more GI symptoms, independent of SIBO; the implementation of a lactose-free diet might reduce GI complaints in those with scleroderma. This suggests that eliminating lactose from your diet (i.e., dairy products) might offer some symptomatic relief in those with GI symptoms. Though there is no data in scleroderma, other food sensitivities, such as a sensitivity to *gluten*, could be managed by eliminating gluten for a while to see whether your symptoms improve. Shifts in diet and lifestyle can be challenging, although they can be important in the management of the GI symptoms of scleroderma. Stages of change apply to making these types of dietary changes, and the belief in your ability to succeed at changing a behavior and avoiding relapse when in a high-risk situation is key to making successful changes.

The *Academy of Nutrition and Dietetics* (Melina et al, 2016) recommends a diet containing fiber and water for optimal GI function, thereby speeding bowel movements and managing constipation. Fiber is sometimes used to treat constipation in scleroderma (Gyger and Barron, 2015). However, if you have early fullness, and there is evidence of delayed emptying of the stomach (i.e., gastroparesis) you might benefit from a diet low in fiber and fat, such as the *FODMAP diet*, though data in this area is lacking (Nagaraja et al, 2015). High-fiber diets should be used with caution if you have *colonic hypomotility* because these agents bulk the stool but might not lead to sufficient colonic stimulation. As a result, bloating might worsen and distention can occur. Moreover, if you have bloating and distention, you might benefit from *probiotics* (Frech et al, 2011). If you do have colonic hypomotility, increasing your water consumption also might help you to manage your symptoms, provided that you do not also have gastroparesis. Modifying dietary habits to address specific symptoms might help improve your quality of life. Consultation with a dietitian can be helpful.

Smoking

Smoking can complicate the management of scleroderma-associated *interstitial lung disease* (ILD). If you have smoking-related *chronic obstructive pulmonary disease* (COPD) and develop ILD, you are more likely to develop reduced lung function and capacity, experience more symptoms and exacerbations, and suffer worse overall function (Hudson et al, 2011; McMahan et al, 2013).

Smoking is also associated with *vascular disease*, which is a significant problem in people with scleroderma (Hudson et al, 2011). Many individuals with scleroderma often experience *Raynaud phenomenon* as an initial symptom of the disease. Raynaud phenomenon involves the constriction of blood vessels in response to cold and to stress, which reduces blood flow to the finger tips. As a result, affected individuals, particularly those who smoke, are at increased risk of poorly healing sores on their fingertips or even of losing their fingers and toes (Harrison et al, 2002). *Nicotine*, contained in all tobacco products and e-cigarettes, acts in the body by restricting the flow of blood, and thereby aggravates symptoms related to Raynaud phenomenon. In addition, those with scleroderma might experience a progressive *vasculopathy*, which can result in *peripheral vascular disease* (PVD), *cardiovascular disease*, and *erectile dysfunction* (ED) (Walker et al, 2009). These complications are made more likely by smoking. Smokeless tobacco products are no safer than cigarettes, because they contain many hazardous chemicals, some known to cause cancer. In fact, more than 4,000 chemicals are contained in tobacco smoke, with 70 of these known to cause or promote cancer (The *Centers for Disease Control* (CDC), 2018). E-cigarette vapor or aerosol has been reported to contain fewer chemicals than cigarettes, although they contain hazardous chemicals (e.g., nicotine), heavy metals (e.g., lead), and cancer-causing agents. The Centers for Disease Control and Prevention (CDC) has reported that e-cigarettes or "vaping" is no safer than smoking. Although smoking cessation will not prevent scleroderma from developing, it can reduce the complications of scleroderma and its health risks. As a result, it is recommended that people with scleroderma should stop smoking (Leask, 2011).

Reducing the risk of developing a life-threatening condition seems like a very good reason to quit smoking; however, the commitment to stop requires considerable effort to initiate and to maintain change. Your likelihood of success will be improved by enlisting the assistance and support of a non-smoking family member or friend who can help with accountability and support. Identifying potential triggers for relapse and eliminating exposure to triggers can also help with smoking cessation.

A gradual reduction in the number of cigarettes smoked is usually a good first step (Fiore et al, 2008). Unfortunately, the abrupt cessation of smoking is generally associated with symptoms of *nicotine withdrawal* (e.g., cravings that last about 15–20 minutes, problems with sleeping, restlessness, mood changes [e.g., irritability, sadness]) that are worst in the first few days to weeks of smoking cessation. Due to the stress associated with nicotine withdrawal and its frequent weight gain, most people who stop smoking abruptly relapse and require additional assistance to remain smoke-free.

You should not become discouraged if you relapse, even if it happens multiple times, because this is common (CDC, 2018; Prochaska et al, 1994). It can be very difficult to stop smoking; therefore, a combination of approaches might be needed to quit completely. Doctor(s) might recommend using *nicotine replacement therapy* (NRT) products, a medication, smoking cessation counseling, or a combination of these to quit. For example, heavy smokers might need to use two different NRT products at the same time (e.g., a long-acting patch, supplemented by a fast-acting nasal spray or gum to ease symptoms of withdrawal). Smoking cessation classes can teach you strategies to help you quit and to prevent relapse. Some NRT products are available in drug stores or grocery stores, whereas others require a doctor's prescription. Check with your employer or health insurance company's smoking cessation benefit programs (e.g., classes, NRT, and other methods at no cost or for a nominal fee). There is also a free telephone service available to help you quit and to stay tobacco-free, which you can call at 1-800-QUIT-NOW or 1-800-784-8669. Alternative treatments such as *acupuncture* and *hypnosis* can help some people quit smoking who have a strong desire to quit; these should be considered after use of NRT products and after other smoking cessation approaches have failed. E-cigarettes are not considered to be an approved smoking-cessation strategy. Maintaining your status as a non-smoker requires your commitment to change your daily behaviors and to create new routines. For example, avoiding locations that might trigger your cravings, choosing to spend time with non-smoker friends, determining which products to place in your mouth or hand as replacements, and learning how to cope with daily stressors and challenges can help you to successfully commit to give up smoking. Finding ways to motivate you to change, to take action, and to enhance your inner fortitude to work through relapses, will be your keys to success.

Stress

Receiving a diagnosis of scleroderma is often overwhelming, and it can be a difficult diagnosis to accept. It is often a significant life stressor, and it can compound other major life events (e.g., job loss, the birth of a new baby, coping with loss of loved ones, moving, divorce). Daily stressors combined with the stress of dealing with scleroderma can be emotionally and physically exhausting (Hui et al, 2009). Each person responds to and copes with stress differently. The chronic, ongoing stressors of managing scleroderma can also affect your physical health. For example, because there is a brain–gut connection, stress can negatively affect your GI system and function.

Stress can also aggravate symptoms of Raynaud phenomenon because stress stimulates the constriction of blood vessels, further reducing blood flow to the fingers. As a result, physicians encourage stress reduction (through exercise, *meditation*, and support groups). Individuals might vary in the stress management strategies that they find most effective. Research in the rheumatic diseases suggests that gentle stretching and moving (e.g., *tai chi* and *yoga*), are effective strategies in the management of stress and anxiety (Bartlett et al, 2013; Wang, 2012). These interventions ease muscle tightness and tension and allow the mental focus to be on breathing, which can be extremely relaxing. Listening to calming music creates a relaxed environment. The CALM app on a phone or computer, which uses guided imagery for sleep and meditation, can be helpful. There are other apps that offer *progressive muscle relaxation* (PMR) that teach relaxation by creating tension in certain muscles and then relaxing that muscle, noticing the different states of tension and relaxation. The tense–relax technique progresses throughout the body until all the muscles have become relaxed. Progressive muscle relaxation, taught by professionals, can be applied to those with rheumatic diseases (Parker et al, 1995; Greco et al, 2004). Another well-studied stress management technique is *mindfulness-based stress reduction* (MBSR; Kabat-Zinn, 2005). Though not studied in scleroderma, this has been studied and found to be helpful in those with *multiple sclerosis* who often suffer from psychological distress. MBSR can help reduce stress, anxiety, pain levels, and can improve overall psychological well-being. Apps can be purchased online to allow home practice or you can join an MBSR class or local meditation group, or attend a retreat for more in-depth teaching.

Biofeedback is a non-invasive approach in which electrodes or probes are placed on the body (e.g., finger, forehead, or other muscles) while sitting relaxed, watching the visual display or "feedback" about biological measures ("bio"), such as muscle tension, skin temperature, skin moisture, and blood flow. Research supports biofeedback as an effective stress management approach (Greco et al, 2013). Biofeedback promotes a relaxed physiological state and treats pain and stress by relaxing muscles, warming skin, and improving blood flow. Biofeedback is efficacious in persons with chronic pain conditions, including rheumatic diseases (Frank et al, 2010). *Raynaud phenomenon symptoms* associated with scleroderma might be helped by biofeedback, though studies are conflicting (Sporbeck et al, 2012; Yocum et al, 1985; Freedman et al, 1984). One study supports biofeedback for fecal incontinence in scleroderma (Collins et al, 2016). Multiple biofeedback sessions will be required to learn and practice the skills. Ask for a referral to a psychologist or other biofeedback-trained professional if this interests you.

Although data in scleroderma is lacking, practicing some simple breathing exercises, like *diaphragmatic breathing,* described at https://my.clevelandclinic.org/health/articles/9445-diaphragmatic-breathing or *4-7-8 breathing,* might help to relax and calm the mind. No equipment is needed. After you've learned them, these techniques can be practiced anywhere; for example, in the car, at home, when visiting friends, grandchildren. These techniques shift the mind and body toward the relaxed state of the *parasympathetic nervous system* and away from the *adrenaline*-based and rushed state of the *sympathetic nervous system*. The practice of 4-7-8 breathing takes about 30 seconds to complete a series of four 4-7-8 breathing exercises. Step-by-step instructions to complete the 4-7-8 breathing exercise are as follows:

- Perform exercise in any position. When seated, have both feet are on the ground. Sit with upright posture with back straight.
- Throughout the entire exercise, place your tongue on the roof of your mouth just behind your front teeth.
- Begin by blowing all the air out of your mouth.
- Close your mouth.
- Breathe in air through your nose quietly and hold quietly for a count of 4.
- Hold your breath for a count of 7.
- Blow the air out forcibly through your mouth making a blowing sound or whooshing sound for a count of 8.
- Repeat for four breath cycles that take about 30 seconds.

In addition to managing stress and taking the medications your doctors prescribe, protect your fingers and toes to avoid Raynaud phenomenon symptoms and its serious complications (e.g., *digital ulcers, digital pits,* or *gangrene*). Avoid physiological stress by minimizing cold exposure and following these Raynaud phenomenon precautions, as listed in Table 9-2.

Table 9-2: Precautions to Minimize Raynaud Phenomenon

• Do not allow your body to become cold. Always protect your body from cold by dressing warmly. Wear a coat and hat to maintain your body temperature so that blood from the fingers and toes is not needed to keep the vital organs warm and supported. Wearing layers to keep your core body warm will help dilate the blood vessels to your arms and legs. This provides improved blood flow to your fingers and toes. Overdress and remove layers as needed rather than underdressing.
• Avoid exposure to extremely cold weather and temperatures and always avoid extended cold exposure.
• Plan ahead by having gloves, coats, hats, and other clothing readily available for layering, as needed. Have these items available in the car for an emergency. Keep an emergency bag packed and ready to take when traveling.
• Dress appropriately in your home during the winter months (e.g., layering clothes, using warm slippers). Maintain air conditioning in the house at a temperature to stay warm or wear layers inside to ensure maintenance of a warm body. Avoid blowing air conditioning and be prepared to layer your clothing to keep the body warm even in summer climates.
• Be careful when reaching into a freezer. Protect your hands with warm gloves or mittens that are stored near the freezer for your convenience.
• Use kitchen items like grippers, silicone gloves, pot holders, or lightweight gloves to avoid touching refrigerated foods and containers that might act as a trigger.
• Use HotHands (single use, long-lasting, air-activated heat packs) or other similar products. You can pack these with emergency items to allow your hands and feet to be warm when you are out in the cold. Battery-powered gloves will also keep your hands warm.
• Use heating devices (e.g., space heaters, electric blankets) as needed to ensure the maintenance of a warm body temperature during all seasons.
• Call your doctor if you are developing an ulcer or skin sore, to avoid infection and other complications.
• Minimize your stress by using the previously described methods, exercise, or other approaches that work for you.

Sleep disturbances are common in scleroderma (Prado et al, 2002). Practicing good sleep hygiene is important to promote restful sleep (Irish et al, 2015). General health-promoting sleep habits from the *American Academy of Sleep Medicine* (AASM) (2018) and other organizations that specialize in sleep should reduce stress and help with emotional responses to daily challenges (see Table 9-3).

Table 9-3: Strategies to Reduce Stress and Promote Restful Sleep

• Create a predictable sleep schedule with a set bedtime and time to rise; your body responds best to routines. Aim to sleep for no less than 7 to 8 hours per night to ease tension and stress. This will help you develop times to awaken naturally.
• Avoid daytime sleeping to promote good nighttime sleep.
• Avoid the use of electronic devices (e.g., phones, laptops) and TVs at least 1 hour before bedtime. The blue light emitted from these devices can interfere with melatonin levels, negatively affecting sleep. Glasses that help block out blue light can be used, if preferred.

- Avoid caffeine after noon due to its stimulant effects.
- Avoid smoking and drinking alcohol because these adversely affect sleep quality.
- Develop a relaxing bedtime routine (such as taking a hot shower or bath, meditating, or reading a book before going to sleep). Allow the evening darkness to indicate that it is time to begin your bedtime routine. Sleeping and intimacy should be the only activities associated with bed.
- Exercise regularly (such as daily walking and stretching, strength training three times per week). Avoid evening or late afternoon exercise due to its stimulant effects.
- If you are awakened during the night and it is difficult to quickly fall back to sleep (e.g., due to your mind racing), get up and rest quietly in the dark; avoid stimulating activities like smoking, use of electronic devices, or watching TV. Return to bed as soon as you are feeling sleepy.
- Sleep in a dark, quiet, cool room. Consider using a fan or other device to produce white noise. Use an eye mask or other light-blocking methods to ensure darkness when you are sleeping. Use ear plugs to avoid being awakened by a partner's snoring or by hearing sleep-disturbing sounds.
- Practice gastroesophageal reflux disease (GERD) precautions (more on this shortly) to avoid reflux and to promote good sleep.

What Role Does My Diet Play in How I Am Feeling? Can Dietary Modifications Improve My Health?

Unfortunately, data on diet in scleroderma is lacking; however, the importance of a balanced diet in the general population, and in patients with scleroderma, cannot be over-emphasized. A healthy diet can reduce risk factors and potential complications of illness. Dehydration can adversely affect several bodily functions, including digestion and constipation. Be sure to consume water throughout the day, especially when you are thirsty. If you have delayed gastric emptying (gastroparesis), be more conservative in your water intake because too much water intake could make your symptoms worse (Nagaraja et al, 2015). Listen to your body to determine the ideal amount of daily water intake. When you are constipated, with normal gastric function, be sure to drink plenty of water to promote optimal hydration because this can also support more regular bowel movements. Daily physical activity, as tolerated, including walking after meals, is also helpful to manage your symptoms of constipation. Use the color of your urine as a gauge to determine whether you are adequately hydrated. Urine should be pale yellow or straw colored to medium-yellow colored. To stay well hydrated, avoid caffeinated drinks (e.g., coffee, tea) and alcohol, given that these are *diuretics*, and they induce increased urination.

Regular use of spices and herbs (e.g., ginger, turmeric, curry, basil, rosemary) and certain foods (e.g., dark cherries) are promoted as anti-inflammatory and inhibiting pain *prostaglandin* production (Scleroderma Foundation, 2018a), though there is no data supporting their use in people with scleroderma. Some data suggests that the FODMAP diet can be effective for treatment of those with *irritable bowel syndrome* (IBS), as FODMAPs are thought to induce symptoms in individuals with IBS due to *luminal distention* and *visceral hypersensitivity* (Magge and Lembo, 2012). People with scleroderma and symptoms of IBS may try the FODMAP diet to see if it is helpful in eliminating symptoms (Nagaraja et al, 2015). The Scleroderma Foundation suggests that the first step could be a trial of eliminating gluten (all wheat, barley, and rye products), and additional data supports a trial of lactose elimination (e.g., dairy) to assess symptomatic improvements (Marie, et al, 2016). These shifts in dietary patterns require a major adjustment of foods you typically eat as well as close examination of ingredient labels to improve your overall GI health. The stages of changes apply, so don't be discouraged if you relapse occasionally; you can quickly get back into your new routine.

A low FODMAP diet eliminates certain foods; therefore, seeing a dietitian is highly recommended to ensure that this diet is adequate to meet all of your nutritional needs. Ask your doctor for a referral to a trusted dietitian. Vitamin supplementation is appropriate if blood tests determine that deficiencies exist. Although scientists continue to learn about the *microbiome*, doctors recommend taking probiotics for bloating or stomach distention (Frech et al, 2011; Gyger et al, 2015; Nagaraja et al, 2015).

Table 9-4 lists steps that you can take to relieve symptoms of gastroesophageal reflux (Sandhu and Fas, 2018).

Table 9-4: Steps to Take to Minimize Symptoms of Gastroesophageal Reflux

• Avoid or minimize the intake of foods that aggravate heartburn or promote gas and belching, like spicy and acidic foods (e.g., hot spices, tomato or citrus-based products, fruit juices, raw onions, radishes, chocolate, peppermint) and any other problematic foods, particularly if they cause you to be symptomatic.
• Avoid or minimize your intake of coffee (caffeinated and decaffeinated) and carbonated drinks, particularly if they make you feel symptomatic.
• Stop smoking and drinking alcohol.
• Avoid eating late at night and having large heavy meals as the last meal before bedtime. Try to eat the last meal of the day at least three to four hours before bed which will allow digestion to occur when you are upright and not lying down.
• Try eating small meals more frequently during the day, rather than eating three larger meals, and then evaluate whether your symptoms improve.
• If you are eating three meals a day, ensure that your breakfast and midday meal are your largest meals of the day to allow plenty of time to digest your food before bed.
• Many people find relief by elevating the head of the bed by about 6 inches to allow gravity to help keep stomach acids from backing up into the *esophagus*. This ensures that your head and upper body are elevated while sleeping. You can purchase bed risers to do this, which are typically sold in sets of four. Wedge pillows that elevate your waist, chest, neck, and head might help to control your symptoms.

What Can I Do to Change My Exercise Habits?

If you are not already involved in an exercise program, develop a regular exercise routine with the focus on strength, endurance, and stretching. Areas of pain, stiffness, and decreased flexibility can serve to guide your area of focus. An occupational therapy or physical therapy referral might be indicated for improving your flexibility before beginning to exercise independently, particularly if you have joint contractures or musculoskeletal limitations (Horváth, et al, 2017; Stefanatoni et al, 2016). Early in the disease course, you might experience weakness, stiffness, or difficulty with flexibility; thus, physical therapy is recommended. The frequency of physical therapy can be determined after an evaluation by the physical therapist with the goals to help prevent further loss of function and to improve your reduced range of motion. If you have ILD, *pulmonary rehabilitation* might be a good option, particularly if you have severe ILD (Dowman et al, 2014). A *pulmonologist* can help guide which pulmonary rehabilitation is right for you. If you have early diffuse cutaneous disease you are at a high risk for renal crisis in the first 4 to 6 years after your diagnosis (McMahan and Hummers, 2013). Doctors recommend monitoring your blood pressure at home several times weekly because high blood pressure can indicate involvement of your kidneys.

The *Arthritis Foundation* offers tips for exercising safely when arthritis is associated with scleroderma. For toning and strengthening your arms and legs, the Arthritis Foundation's "Weight Training 101" at https://www.arthritis.org/living-with-arthritis/exercise/how-to/weight-training-for-beginners.php discusses how to identify appropriate use of free weights and references the *American College of Rheumatology* (ACR) and *American Council on Exercise* (ACE) recommendations that support completing one set of 8 to 12 repetitions as tolerated, "working the muscle to the point of fatigue by the last few reps of each set."

An extensive array of exercise tips is available through the Arthritis Foundation website. These include a personalized online tool at https://www.arthritis.org/living-with-arthritis/tools-resources/your-exercise-solution/index.php, which helps design an exercise program to allow exercising comfortably with arthritis without pain. Other Arthritis Foundation online tip sheets include: "A New Way to Stretch" at https://www.arthritis.org/living-with-arthritis/exercise/how-to/stretching-benefits.php, which discusses the importance of doing dynamic stretching as a pre-exercise work-out; "7 Dynamic Warm Ups" at https://www.arthritis.org/living-with-arthritis/exercise/workouts/simple-routines/dynamic-stretching.php?_ga=2.173382886.493862312.1529848779-1004891772.1528604627, which provides specific dynamic stretches to move the body while stretching to help avoid injury and improve flexibility; and "Exercise: How Much is Enough?" at https://www.arthritis.org/living-with-arthritis/exercise/how-to/how-much-is-enough.php, which explains the Office of Disease Prevention and Health Promotion's Physical Activity Guidelines for Americans related to exercise frequency, intensity, time, and types.

For many people with scleroderma, following the American Heart Association (AHA) (2018) general guidelines regarding exercise might also be helpful. The AHA defines regular exercise for healthy adults as at least 2.5 hours per week of moderate exercise or 1.25 hours of vigorous exercise per week, or a combination of both moderate and vigorous exercise (Mosca, et al, 2011; AHA, 2018). Spreading out smaller episodes of exercise throughout the week is encouraged; you can try performing 10 minutes of exercise (e.g., walking) three times a day. These activities should be easy to integrate into your schedule and to perform without being out of breath. Frequent smaller segments of exercise lead to much larger health benefits, as the exercise accumulates day after day. There are even greater cardiovascular benefits when exercise increases up to 5 hours per week of moderate intensity level or

2.5 hours per week of vigorous intensity or a combination of both. Strength training is also recommended for two or more days per week. Consult with your doctor and follow these guidelines, as tolerated, to improve your overall health and reduce your health risks.

Everyone with scleroderma can benefit from exercising, as tolerated. Start exercising today to begin accruing benefits. Making lifestyle goals and indicated changes for your health and well-being are important and achievable by preparing and taking action and by working hard to continue to maintain an exercise routine. Each time you relapse, you might find it difficult to begin again without more motivation. Keep the scale tipped toward including exercise in your daily routine to reap its health benefits while maintaining your motivation to improve your health.

Can I Make Lasting Changes on My Own or Will I Need the Help of Others?

Lasting changes in your behavior require adequate preparation, determination to achieve the change benefits, belief in goal attainment, and the motivation to make the change. Although the support of friends and family is important, your own commitment to change is critical in attaining and sustaining your goal. Your belief that you can make changes is an important component of the Stages of Change theory (Prochaska et al, 1994). Learning occurs with each relapse, and following the relapse, you will need to plan ahead when facing the next challenge.

At each stage of change, you must weigh the pros and cons to decide whether your behavioral change is truly desired and worth pursuing (Prochaska et al, 1994). When the scale is tipped against making a change, many people stay in the pre-contemplation and contemplation stages. However, when the scale is tipped in favor of making a change you will move into preparation and action stages. Progression through the stages occurs at a variable pace after completing certain activities. You might consistently progress from stage to stage or, in some cases, repeat one or more of the earlier stages. Relapse is common and expected, particularly given that these are usually long-term, well-ingrained habits. The occurrence of a relapse simply means that the investment of additional work is required to make longer-lasting behavior changes. It becomes important to continue to work on making the requisite changes to attain the desired goal. Relapse rates drop significantly after maintaining a behavior change for at least 5 years (Fiore et al, 2008).

Ongoing support from family and friends is also important for success. Emotional and physical health are interconnected, with physical health directly affecting mental health, and vice versa. When living with and managing scleroderma, it is important to acknowledge your emotional responses. A psychologist, licensed counselor, or other mental health provider can offer potentially beneficial services, including *behavior therapy*, *relaxation techniques*, biofeedback, and *cognitive-behavioral therapy* (CBT) to learn and practice more adaptive coping skills when managing a chronic disease.

Should I Build a Support System?

It is important to recognize that many people with scleroderma remain in the workforce, and stay active and engaged in life. Research on patients with rheumatic diseases shows that building a support network enhances your quality of life (Savelkoul et al, 2000; Revenson et al, 1991). An individual's perception of available support is considered an important component in preventing stress and depression and in making a healthy adaptation to stressful situations. People can also benefit from a positive focus on upcoming life events, hobbies, and social activities with family and friends, and a reduced focus on scleroderma and other negative stressors. Mental and physical engagement in daily life can help in maintaining positive thoughts (e.g., family activities, children, grandchildren, an upcoming vacation, changes in the garden, future plans, short- and long-term goals), rather than on the unpredictable nature of scleroderma.

It is strategically important to regularly engage in social activities and to continue involvement in hobbies to maintain support and to reduce feelings of isolation, depression, and anxiety. Some might turn to the internet for social and emotional support (Khanna et al, in press). You should consider joining a community group, volunteering, or becoming more involved in a group for which you are passionate. For example, you might join a bird-watching group to spend time outside and to enjoy nature. Your church or other community organizations might offer classes of interest. Take up a new hobby. Each of these activities will offer opportunities to meet new people with similar interests, to regain confidence, and to enrich your skill set. Group exercise offers health benefits and serves to keep your mental focus on physical fitness goals. Such classes also offer a great environment for making friends and for finding additional social support. Local YMCAs and health clubs offer group classes (e.g., water aerobics, yoga, tai chi, meditation) that will also facilitate social interactions.

Prior to engaging in new activities, it is important to establish clear boundaries and to take into consideration any physical limitations, if present. Don't be afraid to ask others for help. Remember to pace yourself and to rest as needed. Don't accept more responsibilities than you feel capable of taking on at any given time. Be prepared to set limits on requests for time and attention; be empowered to control your life. Decide what activities offer enjoyment and will be pursued. Say "no" to invitations when the requests ask for too much. Reduce or eliminate activities that do not offer you enjoyment and instead find other activities that will help you to successfully manage your mental and physical health.

HOW DO FAMILY MEMBERS RESPOND TO A FAMILY MEMBER WITH SCLERODERMA?

Maria C. Prom, MD and Kevin M. McKown, MD

CHAPTER 10

In This Chapter

- Should I Talk to Family and Friends About the Changes My Body Is Experiencing?
- Who in My Family and Circle of Friends Is at Risk for Becoming Stressed?
- What Are Some Indicators That a Family Member Is Not Coping Well?
- What Are Some Ways to Improve Coping in Family Members?
- Are Support Groups Available to Family Members?
- Summary

Should I Talk to Family and Friends About the Changes My Body Is Experiencing?

The decision as to whether and how much to discuss your illness and the changes your body is experiencing is one that each person must make for him or herself. This decision might be different depending on the friend or family member and might be affected by worry about how friends and family members will react.

Family members might react to your diagnosis in different ways, but common reactions to learning about a family member having a chronic illness include feelings of sadness, anger, shock, surprise, fear, grief, regret, worry, and/or stress (Jewett et al, 2016). Some family members feel afraid because of what the diagnosis means for your long-term health, for your life, and for the life you had planned looking forward. They can be fearful about potential complications or progression of the disease or worry that new medications will cause unwanted side effects. Family members might also worry about, or be fearful of, receiving the diagnosis themselves or of other *autoimmune disorders*, given that autoimmune disorders often run in families. However, these reactions do not mean that family members or friends will not also be understanding and supportive.

When making the decision about discussing your illness and the changes your body is experiencing, it is important to keep in mind the impact the disease will have on those around you. It is especially important to keep in mind their level of desire to understand what you are going through and how to best support you. In fact, as we discuss later in this chapter, a shared understanding of the disease and good communication with family and friends are incredibly important to improve the management of your scleroderma and coping for everyone involved.

Who in My Family and Circle of Friends Is at Risk for Becoming Stressed?

Receiving a diagnosis of scleroderma can be stressful and overwhelming for both you and for those around you (including your caregivers, partner, children, parents, siblings, and friends). A diagnosis of scleroderma often requires that you make many changes to your life (such as taking new medications, scheduling and attending more doctor visits, changing your daily routine, and monitoring for and managing complications of scleroderma). It could also mean adapting to changes in how you feel physically and emotionally, how you might look, what you might be able to do each day, and how much you want to be around other people. These changes can be even more stressful because they are not easy to predict due to the disease being very different for every person. Although these changes certainly affect you, they also affect the people around you, especially those who are closest to you.

The changes to lifestyle, medical management, and the potential disabilities that can come with scleroderma can be particularly stressful for family members and friends. Those who live in the same home with you or who spend a lot of time with you can also be affected, particularly those who provide care for you or who depend on you. The risk of family and friends becoming stressed is often affected by their emotional reactions to the diagnosis and management of scleroderma (as just discussed), the lifestyle changes associated with scleroderma, and the time and financial challenges associated with scleroderma treatment.

Necessary lifestyle changes such as taking medications every day, changing your diet and exercise routine, and going to medical appointments are more likely to be successful with the support of family and friends. However, lifestyle changes can also place a lot of stress on family members, particularly if the changes made are drastic ones. Family members are at risk for feeling upset or overwhelmed and, at times, resentful because of these changes.

The financial costs of scleroderma (e.g., the costs of medical appointments, medical supplies, medications not covered by insurance) can also cause stress for both you and your family members. Medical appointments can also be costly due to distance required for travel to an appointment and disruption of work schedules. And, lastly, severe illness leading to disability and the inability to complete day-to-day tasks or to go to work can cause both financial and emotional stress.

Some family members (including caretakers, romantic partners, and your children) face huge challenges when you are diagnosed with scleroderma. Most family members will feel a certain amount of responsibility for your health, but this burden is often greater for caretakers and partners. Additionally, although all relationships with family and friends can be strained by the additional stress of managing scleroderma, romantic relationships can be further stressed by scleroderma's impact on intimacy and family planning (Levis et al, 2011). Scleroderma can make sexual intimacy more challenging and can affect planning for pregnancy. Those with scleroderma are at high risk of depression and anxiety and this can affect partners, as well (Kwakkenbos et al, 2012). The final group of individuals who can become particularly stressed are children (especially young children) of individuals with scleroderma who might not be able to fully understand the illness and its management. Children can become confused, curious, worried, or afraid when they see parents in pain or fatigued, taking medications, or when skin changes occur in a parent's body. Children might become fearful that they will lose their parent, particularly if they observe complications of scleroderma.

In sum, several aspects of scleroderma—including the initial diagnosis and management, the lifestyle changes necessary to manage scleroderma, and the investment of time and money to reduce the risk and to manage complications—can be stressful for you, for your family members, and for your friends. Fortunately, many resources are available to support your family members, friends, and caregivers. For the remainder of this chapter, we discuss how best to identify family members who are stressed as well as the resources available to help support them.

What Are Some Indicators That a Family Member Is Not Coping Well?

It is normal for family members to react to the diagnosis and management of scleroderma with stress, worry, anger, and sadness, particularly directly after they learn about your diagnosis. However, healthy management of these emotions is crucial for your well-being.

Everyone has a different ability to cope with stress and their emotions. Most people are able to manage stress well and will cope well when a family member is managing scleroderma. For those who struggle and have difficulty coping, additional support might be needed.

How will you know whether a family member is not coping well? Some people are more transparent about their emotions, and it is easier to determine whether they are not coping well; they express their thoughts and emotions openly. However, others are not as expressive, and you might need to rely on observing their actions and their physical signs of stress. You know your family members best, and you might already have an idea of which signs indicate that they might not be coping well based on how they have handled other stressful experiences. In this section, we discuss some signs that indicate when someone is not coping well. We cover both more common and subtle expressions and behaviors as well as rarer but more concerning signs.

Most often when family members are not coping well, you will see only small changes in the way they express their feelings, interact with others, and show physical signs of stress. Because people express themselves very differently, different peoples' reactions to the same situation can appear very differently. For instance, some people become more withdrawn or isolated, whereas others become more outspoken or attached. Some people might eat more in response to stress, whereas others eat less. Some people act as if they couldn't care less about things or begin to ignore problems, whereas others become overwhelmed or react more strongly than they normally would. This might show itself through anxiety, frustration, or impatience. Stress can be expressed physically (e.g., pain in the jaw from clenching or grinding teeth, tension in the muscles, nail biting, fidgeting) or by changes in sleep patterns. Physical complaints (e.g., headaches, dizziness, low energy, an upset stomach or digestive problems, aches and pains) can become more common in family members who do not typically express their emotions.

Although most people will not demonstrate extreme or severe signs of stress, it is important to be aware of these factors because they can be a sign of something more serious (such as a depressive disorder or an anxiety disorder). These signs include disturbances in eating and sleeping habits, a decrease in concentration ability, being less interested in or being less satisfied with normally enjoyable activities, making poor decisions, and not completing responsibilities (such as household chores, work, and school duties). In addition, tearfulness, outbursts, misbehavior, and temper tantrums (in children), or more aggressive behaviors (such as yelling or arguing) can arise. When distress increases, some people refuse to get out of bed, refuse to go to work or school, or use tobacco or alcohol to cope. If you notice any of these changes in a family member, you should consider reaching out for more support, as discussed later in this chapter.

It is important to remember that most family members cope well when challenged and rarely experience the aforementioned severe signs. In fact, you might find that scleroderma (and its treatment) can bring people closer together. However, it is important to know the signs of poor coping so that you can provide, or reach out for, extra support when needed. This is also particularly important for family members who have previously had extreme reactions to stress or for those with mental health disorders, because increased stress could lead to a return of, or worsening of, their symptoms.

What Are Some Ways to Improve Coping in Family Members?

When you are concerned that a family member or a loved one is not coping well, it should be addressed as soon as possible. The entire family can be affected if one member is not coping well, and this might affect the management of your scleroderma. Healthy and supportive family relationships as well as good communication are important for successful scleroderma management. Furthermore, if a family member is having symptoms suggestive of a psychiatric illness, such as a depressive disorder or an anxiety disorder, he or she should see a mental health professional who can provide effective treatment and prevent a worsening of symptoms.

Coping in your family members can be improved, both at home and through professional resources, by using education and understanding of scleroderma, finding ways for family members to be supportive or help in scleroderma management, addressing the family member's needs, improving communication, and seeking professional support.

One of the first steps in managing stress and emotional reactions (e.g., fear) is to gain a better understanding of scleroderma. Learning more about scleroderma, its complications, and its management can reduce anxiety and distress. Family members and friends do not need to become experts, but they should learn enough to feel comfortable supporting you in your illness. Increasing their knowledge of scleroderma can improve understanding and through this, family members can also gain a better idea of what it must be like for you to manage scleroderma. It can be particularly helpful for family and friends to understand scleroderma as it relates to you, such as what specific symptoms or complications you are experiencing and understanding your treatment plan. For example, they might become more patient with you when you need more time to do things, are unable to do things, when you are experiencing discomfort or fatigue, feeling more stressed, or didn't sleep well (Chapter 7 presents additional resources for learning more about scleroderma).

Another way to improve coping by your family members is to help them to feel useful as you deal with your disease. This can be a difficult area to address because what is helpful for one person might not be helpful for another. Some people with scleroderma will do well with reminders about treatment or receiving help from others, but other people might dislike being reminded or might not want assistance. You should encourage family members who show an interest and who want to be helpful to discuss with you your needs or wants ahead of time, especially if receiving their help could result in creating less stress for you.

It is also important to understand that allowing your family members to provide support or care can help your family members reduce their stress. For instance, one area that can create a lot of stress for family members is your reduced function due to pain, fatigue, physical changes, and, at times, depression. Family members often feel torn between trying to help with daily tasks and allowing their loved one to complete tasks themselves, particularly if their loved one is struggling with not being able to complete their own tasks. In this case, excessive stress can be reduced by communicating your wishes directly. It can help family members cope if they are able to assist without feeling guilty or fearful that you will become upset or irritated. In allowing a family member or friend to help it may even allow you to conserve energy to spend more time with them. This is just one example of how improving communication, working together, and resolving conflicts among family members can improve family relationships, coping, and scleroderma management.

When family members are providing support or helping with scleroderma management it can take a variety of forms. Family members might provide emotional support when you are feeling stressed or when you are having a difficult day. Or, they can help you more by taking you to an appointment or helping you to complete tasks that are difficult or tiring for you. Finally, family members can work with you toward remaining active and engaged. Ultimately, family members might feel more in control and cope better if they are a part of discussions about care and changes that will affect them. This is particularly helpful for children, who are often left out of these discussions.

Other ways to improve coping and family communication as well as to reduce conflicts can include obtaining professional help (such as through individual, couples, family, or group therapists and counselors). Family members can also reach out to a *primary care provider* (PCP) or *psychiatrist* for medication recommendations if needed. Professional resources can even help with mild symptoms, and it is best to seek help early. It is especially important to reach out for help when severe symptoms occur. Your rheumatology health care team and PCPs are good resources for referrals to professional support for family members. Health insurance companies can also provide a list of local mental health providers. One additional place to seek further support is through *support groups*, which we discuss in more detail in the next section.

Are Support Groups Available to Family Members?

Coping with the stress, emotions, and lifestyle changes that come with having a family member with scleroderma can be challenging. Some people might find that they prefer to handle problems on their own, with the support of family members and friends, or through professional support. Others might find it useful to speak with those in a similar position, such as other people who have family members with scleroderma or other rheumatic illnesses. Support groups and social media outlets (e.g., online forums, message boards, interest groups) are a familiar way for family members to get extra support from one another. These resources offer a place to discuss experiences and struggles and to obtain peer support and advice. This could include hearing about ways to provide support, to communicate, or to motivate family members with scleroderma. Support groups and social media groups can also serve as a place to learn more about other local and internet resources for you and your family members; you can also learn other people's opinions of these available resources.

Support groups come in a variety of forms, including in-person versus online groups, those with peer leaders versus outside facilitators, and those that have group discussions versus invited speakers. Some support groups are open to all family members and some are specifically designed for couples, caregivers, or children. Most in-person groups meet on a regular basis (e.g., weekly or monthly). Online groups might have 24/7 access, which might be better for those who have difficult schedules and who cannot get to an in-person group regularly. Online groups might also be better for those who do not live near in-person groups or for those who prefer to express themselves anonymously. It is important to note that support groups are different than *therapy groups*. Therapy groups are run by trained mental health professionals and serve as another helpful option for support.

The first step to take when thinking about joining a group is to consider what the goals of the group are and what aspects would make it more comfortable and easier for your participation. When looking for a support group, the best place to begin is to ask medical providers for recommendations, to check with local medical centers, or to look at the websites listed in Table 10-1. When feeling unsure whether a group is the right fit for you, it is always okay to attend a meeting or two to try it out.

Table 10-1: Recommended Resources for Support Through Groups and Social Networks

Organization	Website or Other Access Information
American College of Rheumatology (ACR)	simpletasks.org www.rheumatology.org
Arthritis Foundation	www.arthritis.org
Scleroderma Foundation	www.scleroderma.org
Scleroderma International Network	https://sclero.org/

When joining a support group or an online social media site, it is important to remember that other members of the group are not medical professionals. Therefore, individuals who use these resources should think carefully about the advice provided by others because it might not always be correct, reliable, or the best fit for their family member with scleroderma or for themselves. It is always best to ask a medical provider about information found online, particularly before making any changes to the scleroderma management. Medical providers have the education and training to help determine whether the information is accurate and appropriate for each individual's situation.

Summary

Scleroderma can dramatically affect the lives of the family members, caretakers, and friends of people with scleroderma. As a result, those closest to the person with scleroderma are at risk for becoming stressed. This stress can lead to difficulty coping with a family member's diagnosis and the management of his or her scleroderma. This chapter provided specific advice for identifying signs that a family member is not coping well, specific ways to improve coping, and recommendations for resources to provide support for family members.

GLOSSARY

4-7-8 breathing: A technique for breathing in air that involves breathing through your nose and holding the breath for the count of 4, holding your breath for a count of 7, and blowing it out forcibly through your mouth for a count of 8.

Academy of Nutrition and Dietetics: A professional organization focused on food, nutrition, dietetics, and health. Members include dietetics professionals with undergraduate and advanced degrees in nutrition and dietetics, which include registered dietitians, nutritionists, dietetics technicians, and students.

ACE-inhibitors: A type of blood pressure medication often used for the treatment of scleroderma renal crisis.

Acid reflux: A condition that occurs when acid from the stomach travels up into the esophagus causing irritation and pain.

Action stage: A stage in the Stages of Change Theory. In the action stage, you changed a problem behavior/routine in the past six months to a healthier and more acceptable behavior. Your efforts to maintain the new behavior will be ongoing to avoid returning to the problem behavior.

Acupuncture: A complementary and alternative medicine approach, commonly used in the practice of Chinese medicine or Eastern medicine. Acupuncture is practiced widely in the United States and can be combined with traditional Western medicine approaches. Acupuncture involves the placement of thin needles in strategic locations on the body depending on the symptoms and organs considered involved in the symptoms of the patient. Acupuncture is used to treat pain symptoms and many types of emotional, physical, and mental concerns.

Acute: An abrupt appearance of symptoms, often severe, that lasts for a short period of time.

Acyclovir: A medicine that is used for certain viral infections, like herpes.

Adaptive equipment: Devices that can be used to help you complete your activities of daily living when limitations exist.

Adrenaline: A stress hormone secreted by the body as part of the "fight or flight" response to fear, perceived threats, or other stressful situations. The hormone causes the heart rate to increase and allows the muscles to quickly respond to the situation by fleeing or taking other actions requiring exertion.

Aerosolized pentamidine: An inhaled medicine that prevents a bacterial lung infection called pneumocystis pneumonia.

Ambrisentan: An endothelin receptor antagonist medication used to treat pulmonary hypertension.

American Academy of Sleep Medicine (AASM): A professional organization dedicated to promoting optimal health through better sleep. Members include sleep medicine physicians, researchers, educators, and health care professionals.

American College of Rheumatology (ACR): A professional organization dedicated to advancing the profession of rheumatology and the care of patients with rheumatic diseases. Members include physicians, rheumatology health professionals, researchers, scientists, practice managers, and students who promote rheumatology through health care, education, research, and advocacy.

American College of Sports Medicine (ACSM): A professional organization dedicated to health and fitness, including exercise, through research, education, and practice. Members vary widely from physicians to personal trainers and from professors to students; they are trained in exercise physiology, exercise science, sports medicine, and health and fitness and help people live healthy, active lives.

American Council on Exercise (ACE): A professional organization dedicated to certifying exercise professionals and health coaches. The organization sets the standards for professional expectations and offers examinations that evaluate a professional's knowledge level and competency. Certifications are provided to professionals who pass the ACE examination.

American Heart Association (AHA): An organization dedicated to fighting heart disease and stroke. The organization funds research, advocates for public policy, and offers educational tools to improve and save lives. It offers public health education, including training in cardiopulmonary resuscitation (CPR) to health care professionals.

Amlodipine: A vasodilator medication that is used to treat Raynaud phenomenon. It is also a blood pressure medication.

Amphetamine/dextroamphetamine (Adderall): A medicine that is typically used for attention deficit disorder.

Amputation: The removal of part of a limb (arm or leg), finger, or toe by surgery, injury, or illness.

Ancillary study: A lab test or medical test that is performed to help in disease evaluation and management.

Angiotensin: A substance produced by the kidneys that increases blood pressure.

Angiotensin converting enzyme inhibitors (ACE-I): Medicines typically used to reduce blood pressure by blocking an enzyme that increases blood pressure. This medication is used to treat scleroderma renal crisis.

Angiotensin receptor blockers (ARBs): Medicines typically used to reduce blood pressure by blocking a receptor (to angiotensin) that would normally increase blood pressure.

Anti-centromere antibodies: Self-reactive antibodies, or autoantibodies, targeting the centromere structure of cells, which is detectable in the blood of some women with scleroderma, particularly in limited scleroderma.

Antifibrotic medication: A medication that works to reduce the formation and buildup of scar tissue in those with scleroderma.

Anti-PM-Scl antibody: An antibody that can be seen in people with scleroderma and sometimes in patients with muscle inflammation.

Anti-RNA Polymerase III: An antibody that can be seen in people with scleroderma and is associated with the development of diffuse skin disease and with potential scleroderma renal crisis development.

Anti-Scl-70 antibody (Anti-topoisomerase I): An antibody that can be seen in people with scleroderma. It is associated with diffuse skin disease and potential interstitial lung disease development.

Anti-Th/To antibody: An antibody that can be seen in people with scleroderma and is associated with pulmonary hypertension as well as diffuse skin disease.

Anti-topoisomerase I antibody: Another term for anti-Scl-70 antibody.

Anti-U1-RNP antibody: An antibody often seen in patients with mixed connective tissue disease.

Antibiotic: A class of medication that treats bacterial infections.

Antibodies: Proteins made by white blood cells (the immune system) to bind to and help remove foreign molecules in the body, including infectious organisms.

Antinuclear antibody (ANA): An antibody that can be seen in low levels in the general population and at higher levels in many patients with different types of autoimmune disease.

Anxiety: A feeling of being upset, nervous, and/or worried.

Arrhythmia: An abnormality in the electrical activity of the heart leading to an irregular heartbeat.

Arteriovenous malformation (AVM): A tangle of abnormal blood vessels connecting arteries and veins in the brain.

Artery: A vessel that carries blood within the body.

Arthritis: Inflammation of the joints.

Arthritis Foundation: An organization dedicated to the prevention, treatment, and cure for all forms of arthritis.

Aspiration: When food, stomach acid, or saliva goes down the airway.

Atherosclerotic: Pertaining to atherosclerosis, which is the progressive thickening and hardening of the walls of arteries from fatty deposits along the inner lining of these vessels.

Atherosclerotic cardiovascular disease (ASCVD): Progressive thickening and hardening of the walls of arteries from fatty deposits on their inner lining.

Atherosclerotic coronary artery disease (CAD): Progressive thickening and hardening of the walls of arteries in the heart from fatty deposits along the inner lining of these vessels.

Atovaquone: A medicine that helps to prevent malaria and some other infections such as Pneumocystis jiroveci pneumonia.

Autoantibody: A protein that is produced by the immune system that binds to proteins in your own body.

Autoimmune condition: *See* autoimmune disease.

Autoimmune disease: Any disease that is caused by the immune system being overly active, often due to the body's immune system mistakenly recognizing normal structures or molecules as foreign.

Autoimmune disorder: *See* autoimmune disease.

Autoimmune thyroid disease: A class of disorders involving immune-mediated inflammation or destruction of the thyroid gland.

Autologous stem cell transplantation (ASCT): A transplant of your own cells from your immune system into your own body. This treatment is being used to treat some people with scleroderma.

Avascular necrosis: Bone death caused most frequently by lack of blood flow and is often related to the use of steroid medications.

Azathioprine: An immune suppressing drug commonly used to treat lupus and, at times, to treat arthritis; safe to take during pregnancy.

Barium esophagram: A diagnostic test, also referred to as a barium swallow, that involves X-ray imaging after a person has swallowed a white, chalky solution that assists in obtaining clearer images of the esophagus, which is the passageway that attaches the mouth to the stomach.

Barrett's esophagus: A pre-cancerous condition in which a portion of the esophagus (the tube connecting your mouth to your stomach) is replaced by tissue that looks like the lining of the intestines.

B cell depletion therapy: A medical treatment that decreases the immune cells that make antibodies.

Behavior therapy: A form of psychotherapy, or talk therapy, that focuses on helping a person understand how changing his or her behaviors can affect thoughts and how they are feeling.

Bifidobacterium infantis: A friendly strain of lactic acid bacteria in the same group as Lactobacillus.

Biofeedback: A non-invasive approach in which electrodes or probes are placed on the body (e.g., finger, forehead, other muscles) while sitting relaxed, watching the visual display ("feedback") about biological measures ("bio") such as muscle tension, skin temperature, skin moisture, and blood flow. Biofeedback involves the mind–body connection, with the "bio" measures changing when the mental focus centers on changing these measures in the desired direction. Biofeedback training is offered by professionals who have specialized training.

Bisacodyl and senna: Medicines that act as stool softeners to treat constipation.

Bisphosphonates: A class of medicines that increase bone strength and reduce fractures.

Black box warning: The strictest warning put in the labeling of prescription drugs or drug products by the US Food and Drug Administration (FDA) when there is reasonable evidence of an association of a serious hazard with the drug.

Blood clot: A collection of clotting factors and cells in a blood vessel resulting in obstruction of blood flow.

B lymphocytes (B cells): Immune cells that produce antibodies.

Bone marrow: The sponge-like tissue inside bones where blood cells are made.

Bosentan: A medicine that treats pulmonary hypertension by blocking the endothelin receptor.

Calcinosis cutis: Deposits of calcium-containing material under the skin.

Calcium channel blockers: A class of medications that is used to disrupt the movement of calcium into the heart and blood vessel walls and is generally utilized to treat high blood pressure. This class of medication is also used to treat Raynaud phenomenon and digital ulcers by causing dilation of blood vessels to the hands and feet.

Capillary dilation: Abnormally enlarged small blood vessels that can be associated with Raynaud phenomenon and autoimmune diseases.

Captopril: A medicine that is an ACE-inhibitor that reduces blood pressure. It is one of the medications used to treat scleroderma renal crisis.

Cardiac: Relating to the heart.

Cardiologist: A physician specializing in conditions affecting the heart.

Cardiovascular disease: The narrowing or blockage of blood vessels, which can result in chest pain, a heart attack, or stroke.

Carpal tunnel syndrome: A condition in which the median nerve (one of the nerves that runs through the wrist into the hand) is compressed and causes numbness and tingling in the hand, particularly involving the thumb, index finger, middle finger, and a portion of the ring finger.

Case manager: A person, often a social worker or nurse, trained in planning, coordination, monitoring, and evaluation of medical services for a patient with emphasis on quality of care, continuity of services, and cost effectiveness.

Case reports: A published description of medical cases.

Cataracts: A condition characterized by clouding of the lens of the eye(s).

Centers for Disease Control (CDC): The health protection agency for the United States. The CDC analyzes trends and emerging situations and offers health information to the public and protects the nation from health threats.

Central line: A medical-grade plastic tube that provides access to the large veins of the body and can be used to administer intravenous fluids or medications.

Certified exercise physiologist (CEP): A health professional who specializes in exercise mechanics and the benefits of exercise. This person uses exercise to help patients or clients gain fitness, improve health, and maintain health goals. These professionals typically have an undergraduate and/or advanced degree in exercise physiology (and nutrition in some cases). CEPs are certified by either the American College of Sports Medicine or the American Council on Exercise.

Chemotherapy: A class of medications that uses chemicals that are toxic to rapidly growing cells, such as in the treatment of cancer.

Chest CT scan: A computerized scan of the chest.

Cholestyramine: A "bile acid-binding resin" medication that can be used to clear leflunomide from the body.

Chronic: Symptoms that persist for a long period of time and/or continue to recur.

Chronic kidney disease: A disorder characterized by abnormal function of the kidneys that persists for greater than three months (also called "chronic renal disease").

Chronic obstructive pulmonary disease (COPD): Chronic inflammatory pulmonary disease that causes reduced airflow in the lungs, which may be associated with difficulty breathing, cough, and wheezing. This disorder often occurs in people who smoke cigarettes.

Ciprofloxacin: An antibiotic that treats urine, skin, and blood infections. It is also used to treat small intestinal bacterial overgrowth.

Circulation: Movement of the blood through the body.

Cisapride: A medicine that increases movement of contents within the gastrointestinal system by stimulating serotonin receptors.

Classification criteria: A standardized set of signs, symptoms and laboratory or other test findings that are utilized to assist providers in defining a disease process, most commonly used to classify patients who will be entering a clinical trial (research study).

Clinical manifestations: Symptoms a patient reports and the findings on a physical exam that characterize a disease.

Clinical practice guidelines: Agreed upon ways in which medical providers monitor and treat a condition and its complications.

Clostridium difficile (C. diff): An infectious bacterium that causes diarrhea and often causes an infection in a person who has received one or more antibiotics.

Cognitive-behavioral therapy (CBT): A form of psychotherapy or talk-therapy that focuses on problem solving by identifying solutions to problems, challenging misconceptions and maladaptive thought processes, and modifying behaviors that are unproductive and destructive to produce more effective and health-promoting actions.

Colon: Part of the gastrointestinal tract called the large intestine.

Colonic hypomotility: Also known as colonic inertia; a motility disorder that results in slow transit time of stool in the large bowel and often results in the abnormal passage of stool.

Colonoscopy: A minimally invasive, diagnostic procedure that involves inserting a tube into the colon and allows for visualization of the large intestine and lower part of the small bowel. It is often used to screen for colon cancer.

Colorectal surgeon: A surgeon who specializes and treats diseases affecting the colon, anus, and rectum.

Complete blood cell (CBC) count: A lab test that reports the number of red blood cells, white blood cells, and platelets.

Computed tomography (CT) scan: Imaging study, involving radiation, often used to look at the internal organs, such as the heart, lungs, lymph nodes, and intestines.

Conceiving: Becoming pregnant with a child.

Conception: The process of becoming pregnant, when the egg is fertilized by the sperm.

Congenital abnormalities: Clinical manifestations that occur due to genetic makeup and are thus present from the time of birth.

Congestive heart failure: A condition in which the heart does not pump blood as strongly as it should.

Constipation: Difficulty in emptying the bowels, usually associated with hardened feces or stool.

Contemplation stage: A stage in the Stages of Change Theory. In the contemplation stage, you want to change a behavior or routine and might know you need to change a behavior, although you feel uncertain about your readiness and ability to make the necessary changes.

Contractures: Essentially muscles or tendons that have remained too tight for too long, becoming shorter and limiting the ability of a limb or digit to straighten out.

Coronary artery disease (CAD): Decreased blood flow to the heart that results from the hardening of arteries.

Corticosteroids: A group of steroid medications that have anti-inflammatory effects.

Cuticular hemorrhage: Bleeding of the small blood vessels within the nailfold, at the base of the cuticle, that can be seen in people with scleroderma.

Cyclophosphamide: A medication that is a type of chemotherapy that potently reduces the immune system function and has been used to treat lung disease associated with scleroderma.

Cystic fibrosis: A hereditary disease that affects the lungs ad digestive system, where thick and sticky mucus can clog the lungs and obstruct the pancreas.

Dapsone: A medication that is frequently used to treat rashes.

Defecography: A form of medical imaging that uses X-rays to visualize the anatomy and functioning of the anus, rectum, and pelvic floor.

Dentist: A medical provider who specializes in the diagnosis, prevention, and treatment of diseases and conditions of the oral cavity.

Depression: Feelings of sadness, lacking enjoyment in usual activities, and possible disturbances in appetite and sleep.

Depressive symptoms: Symptoms of sadness and lack of enjoyment in daily activities.

Dermatologist: Physician skilled in the diagnosis and treatment of skin conditions.

Diabetes: Also called diabetes mellitus, this is a group of diseases that affects how a person's body utilizes sugar, which is called glucose, and results in inappropriate metabolism and elevated blood glucose.

Diaphragmatic breathing: A type of breathing that involves contraction of the diaphragm, a muscle located between the thoracic cavity and the abdominal cavity.

Diclofenac: A non-steroidal anti-inflammatory drug (NSAID) used to treat pain.

Dietitians: Professionals trained in the science of nutrition and dietetics. They have completed an undergraduate or advanced degree program that meets the standards of their professional organization (Academy of Nutrition and Dietetics) and the accreditation organization (The Accreditation Council for Education in Nutrition and Dietetics). Many dietitians will be eligible to take an additional examination to become a Registered Dietitian.

Diffuse scleroderma: A type of scleroderma with involvement of more areas of skin involved.

Diffuse skin disease: A variant of scleroderma characterized by more extensive and potentially aggressive skin thickening, including the upper arms, thighs, and torso.

Digital pits: Small indentations on the fingertips resulting from decreased blood flow to the fingertip tissue due to Raynaud phenomenon.

Digital sympathectomy: A procedure in which the hand surgeon cuts the tiny nerves to the smallest arteries in the fingers to improve blood flow.

Digital ulcers: Open sores in the skin that occur on the fingers and often result from Raynaud phenomenon.

Dilate: The action of enlarging, particularly when a round object becomes enlarged (like a blood vessel).

Disease-modifying antirheumatic drugs (DMARDs): Medications such as methotrexate that reduce inflammation in rheumatic diseases.

Diuretics: A class of medication that typically reduces blood pressure by increasing urine production.

Domperidone: A medication that helps to increase movement and contraction of the gastrointestinal system.

Drug-induced lupus: A type of disease characterized by rashes, joint pains, and other possible manifestations of lupus that occurs as a result, or adverse effect, of taking certain medications.

Dysmotility: A disorder that develops when there is impairment of the muscles of the digestive system that changes their speed of functioning and strength. This results in irregular movement of the gastrointestinal tract, often causing symptoms such as acid reflux, constipation, bloating, and/or diarrhea.

Dyspareunia: Painful sexual intercourse.

Dysphagia: Difficulty swallowing properly.

Echo/Doppler study: An ultrasound.

Echocardiogram: A test that utilizes ultrasound (high-frequency sound waves) to evaluate the heart pump function as well as each of the valves and major blood vessels leading from the heart to the body.

Electrocardiogram (EKG): A medical test that detects, records, and measures the heart's electrical activity. It is useful in making a diagnosis of heart rhythm disturbances, a heart attack, and other conditions.

Electromyogram (EMG) with nerve conduction study: A medical test that is utilized to measure the electrical activity as well as the speed in which nerves function and send signals within a specific muscle or group of muscles.

Enalapril: A medicine that is an ACE-inhibitor that reduces blood pressure.

En coup de sabre: A sub-type of localized scleroderma, characterized by thickening of one part of the skin, typically in a line and involving the face.

Endoscope: An illuminated optical, slender tubular instrument used to look deep into the body, used in procedures called endoscopy.

Endoscopy: A minimally invasive, diagnostic procedure that involves inserting a tube into the food pipe (esophagus), stomach, and initial portion of your small intestine.

Endothelin: A molecule that acts to decrease the size of a blood vessel.

Endothelin receptor antagonists (ERAs): A class of medication that treats pulmonary hypertension by blocking the endothelin receptor, hence causing dilation of blood vessels.

Endothelin receptor blockers (ERBs): *See* ERAs.

Enteric-coated: A coating on a medication that is a special substance that delays dissolution (dissolving) of the medication until it is past the stomach.

Environmental factors: Elements in the environment that may influence the development of disease, such as infections, toxins, chemicals, foods.

Enzyme: A substance that facilitates chemical reactions.

Eosinophilic fasciitis: A skin condition, resembling scleroderma, that causes hardening of the skin and can often have an orange peel–like appearance. This condition typically does not involve the fingers.

Epigenetic: Non-genetic influences that change gene expression.

Epoprostenol: A prostacyclin analog medication that treats pulmonary hypertension by mimicking a substance called prostaglandin, resulting in dilation of blood vessels.

Erectile dysfunction (ED): The inability of a man to maintain an erection that is adequate to sustain satisfying sexual activity.

Ergonomics: Adjustments made in the design of the physical space, such as in the workplace, to improve comfort and avoid risks of discomfort or problems with posture.

Esophageal dilation: The procedure involving placement of a balloon through an endoscope to dilate or stretch the food pipe (esophagus) to treat a stricture.

Esophageal stricture: Narrowing of the esophagus, which is the passageway that attaches the mouth to the stomach.

Esophageal ulceration: A painful sore located in the lining of the lower part of the esophagus, usually as a result of a bacterial infection.

Esophagus: The tube that connects the mouth to the stomach.

Etanercept: A medicine that suppresses the immune system by blocking tumor necrosis factor-alpha (TNF-α) and preventing it from binding to the TNF receptor.

European League Against Rheumatism (EULAR): Non-governmental organization that coordinates health professionals and scientific societies in Europe.

Exercise tolerance: The ability of a person to endure exercise.

Fertility: The ability to conceive or reproduce.

Fertility preservation specialist: A provider who is trained in techniques to preserve your fertility in the face of conditions or treatments that reduce fertility.

Fetus: An unborn baby between 8 weeks post conception through date of birth.

Fiber laxatives: Medicines that increase the frequency of bowel movements by increasing the bulkiness of stool.

Fibrosis: Scar tissue composed of substances such as collagen. Fibrosis can involve the skin or various internal organs and is responsible for many of the symptoms in scleroderma.

Fingertip ulcers: Sores on the ends of your fingers, often resulting from Raynaud phenomenon.

First-degree relative: One's immediate blood-related family members (father, mother, siblings, and children).

Flexion contractures: Bent limbs or digits, that one cannot straighten using one's own muscle power.

Fluoxetine: A medicine that typically is used to treat depression by increasing a substance called serotonin.

FODMAP diet: A diet that focuses on minimizing the ingestion of Fermentable Oligosaccharides, Disaccharides, Monosaccharides and Polyols, which might be poorly absorbed by some individuals.

Folic acid: Folate, a B vitamin, that is often taken by people who are taking methotrexate. It helps to reduce side effects from methotrexate.

Food and Drug Administration (FDA): A federal agency of the US Department of Health and Human Services that is responsible for the protection and promotion of public health, including the control and supervision of prescription medications.

Forced vital capacity: The total amount of air exhaled during the FEV test.

Functional residual capacity: The volume of air (measured on pulmonary function testing) that remains in the lungs after passively exhaling (breathing out).

Gangrene: When lack of blood flow causes death of tissue.

Gastric antral vascular ectasia (GAVE): A disorder, also known as watermelon stomach, that is a rare but significant cause of chronic gastrointestinal bleeding or iron deficiency anemia, which can occur in patients with scleroderma.

Gastroenterologist: A physician skilled in the diagnosis and treatment of digestive tract diseases, including esophageal, stomach, and bowel diseases.

Gastroesophageal reflux disease (GERD): A digestive disorder that occurs when gastric acid (from the stomach) flows from the stomach back into the esophagus or mouth.

Gastrointestinal (GI): The organ system involved in digesting food.

Gastroparesis: A condition that affects the normal movement of the muscles in the stomach and reduces a patient's ability to propel food from the stomach forward into the small intestine.

Generalized morphea: A coalescence of single patches of morphea (localized hardening of the skin). This condition is not associated with internal organ involvement.

Genes: A unit of heredity, made up of DNA, which is passed from parent to child.

Genetic factors: Elements within your DNA that can contribute to an inherited risk of disease and thus might influence the development of disease.

Gestational diabetes: Diabetes that develops during pregnancy.

Glaucoma: A condition caused by increased pressure inside the eyeball.

Glucocorticoids: A class of corticosteroid medications that are highly anti-inflammatory and suppress the immune system.

Gluten: According to the Celiac Disease Foundation, gluten is the name for proteins found in wheat products that can be found under the names of wheat, wheatberries, durum, emmer, semolina, spelt, farina, farro, graham, Kumut, Khorasan wheat, and einkorn. Barley, rye, and triticale also contain gluten. Gluten is commonly found in many processed foods because it helps foods maintain their shape.

Gold standard: Best approach.

Gynecologist: A medical doctor who specializes in the health of and treats diseases of the female reproductive system and organs; in addition to seeing patients in the office, many also perform surgery.

Gynecomastia: A disease characterized by increasing size of breast tissue. This can occur in men and women.

H_2 blockers: A class of medicines that works on a receptor in the stomach to decrease acid production.

Health Assessment Questionnaire: A specific screening tool that compiles and measures results pertaining to general health topics and patient function, typically filled out by the patient.

Heartburn: A condition in which the acid from the stomach irritates the esophagus and causes symptoms of chest and/or throat pain.

Heart failure: A condition in which the heart does not pump as strongly or effectively as it should.

Hemorrhagic cystitis: A condition in which there is sudden onset of blood in the urine (hematuria) and irritative bladder symptoms.

High-resolution computed tomography (HRCT): A form of medical imaging, computed tomography (CT), that utilizes specific techniques to enhance the image resolution to evaluate health problems, most commonly lung disease.

High-risk pregnancy: Any pregnancy that is deemed to be at a higher-than-average risk of an adverse outcome for any reason.

HLA molecules: Molecules on the surface of some immune cells that carry foreign substances and present them to other immune cells to activate a part of the immune system.

Hormonal contraceptives: A class of medicine that prevents pregnancy.

Huntington disease: A progressive brain disorder that causes uncontrolled movements, emotional problems, and impaired thinking.

Hydrogen breath test: A diagnostic test that measures the level of hydrogen in the breath and is utilized in the diagnostic process of several gastrointestinal conditions, including small intestinal bacterial overgrowth (SIBO).

Hydroxychloroquine: An anti-malarial medication commonly used in low doses to treat arthritis and lupus.

Hypertension: Elevated blood pressure over a standard normal level, which varies by age and pregnancy status.

Hypnosis: A non-invasive therapeutic technique that first involves a professional, specially trained in hypnosis, putting you into a deep state of relaxation and mental focus. During this deep state, you become more suggestible to ideas, such as breaking bad habits or making positive changes.

Ibuprofen: A non-steroidal anti-inflammatory drug (NSAID), available over-the-counter, used to treat pain.

Iloprost: A prostacyclin analog medication used to treat pulmonary hypertension.

Imaging tests: Tests that provide information in the form of pictures about the inside of your body; these can include X-rays, CT scans, and MRI scans.

Immune modulator: A class of medicine that decreases the activity of the immune system.

Immune system: A defense system within the body that involves many structures and processes to protect and fight against diseases. This system helps to clear away damaged cells.

Immune system activation: When the immune system begins to fight an infection.

Immunogenic: Any substance that is stimulating to the immune system.

Immunoglobulins: A class of proteins that bind to other proteins and helps the body to respond to infection, inflammation, and vaccinations.

Immunosuppressant (or immune suppressing medication): A medication that decreases the activity of the immune system; often used in autoimmune diseases to decrease the damage caused by an overly active immune system.

IMPRESS study: An Italian study performed to evaluate pregnancy outcomes in people with scleroderma. This study found that most women with scleroderma who became pregnant had stable scleroderma disease throughout the pregnancy. Heartburn worsened and Raynaud phenomenon improved in the study population.

Incontinence: Loss of the ability to hold urine or stool inside the body.

Inflammation: The body's biological response to something that is perceived as harmful and can occur on a short-term (acute) or long-term (chronic) basis, and it is characterized by certain cells that cause redness, swelling, and/or warmth.

Inflammatory muscle disease: A group of diseases that involve chronic muscle inflammation.

Inflammatory process: The body's response to injury or disease. The body produces mediators or chemicals to help repair the damage from injury or disease.

Internal organ involvement: Conditions affecting the organs within the body, such as the heart, lungs, stomach, kidneys, liver, and/or intestines.

Internal organs: Parts of the body that are underneath the skin and are important for the proper function of the human body (examples include the heart, lungs, stomach, kidneys, liver, and intestines).

Internal organ screening studies: Tests that are performed to learn whether a condition is affecting the organs within the body, such as the heart, lungs, stomach, kidneys, liver, and/or intestines.

Interstitial lung disease (ILD): A group of diseases that causes scarring or fibrosis of the lungs leading to lung stiffness, difficulty breathing, and impaired oxygen exchange.

Intestinal motility: The movement of food through the digestive system.

Intraocular pressure: The pressure inside the eyeball.

Intrauterine device (IUD): A device that is inserted into the uterus to deliver a medicine or is used as a mechanism for contraception.

Intrauterine growth retardation (IUGR): A fetus who has insufficient growth while in the uterus; generally, a fetus with a weight below the 10th percentile for the gestational age.

Intravenous (IV): Located inside the venous system.

Irritable bowel syndrome: A group of disorders that involves chronic inflammation of the digestive tract characterized by symptoms including abdominal pain, cramping, bloating, or constipation.

Ischemia: An inadequate supply of blood to an organ or part of the body.

Joint contracture: Inability to fully straighten a joint completely.

Joint imaging: Medical imaging of the joint structure, often in the hands and/or feet but can include any joint(s), that is utilized to assess the structure of the joints as well as to monitor joint disease.

Kidney failure: A reduction in, or lack of, kidney function from various causes.

Kidney function: The way the kidney works, involving regulation of body fluids, urinary concentration, acid-base balance, and excretion of wastes and toxins.

Kidneys: Two bean-shaped organs in the body that are located on each side of the spine just below the rib cage and are involved in the removal of waste and extra water from the bloodstream into the urine.

Lactation: The period during which a woman is breastfeeding.

Lactobacillus: A friendly bacteria that normally lives in our digestive tract without causing disease.

Lactose malabsorption: A condition that interferes with the ability to fully digest the sugar (lactose) which is a component of milk and some other dairy products.

Laxatives: A class of medications that increases the frequency of bowel movements.

Leflunomide: An immune suppressing medication commonly used to treat arthritis associated with autoimmune diseases.

Left ventricular ejection fraction: The percentage of the volume of blood within the left ventricle of the heart that is pumped out in one contraction. This measurement can be used to evaluate for the presence of heart failure.

Lesions: A wound, ulcer, abscess, or tumor.

Licensed clinical social worker (LCSW): A social worker who has met specific state licensing requirements to provide diagnostic assessments and ongoing therapies to address emotional and mental health concerns.

Limitations in mobility: Not being able to move around easily or perform usual activities.

Limited scleroderma: A sub-type of scleroderma characterized by skin thickening that may involve the skin on the face and is otherwise restricted to the lower arms (below the elbows) and/or lower legs (below the knees).

Linear scleroderma: A sub-type of localized scleroderma, linear scleroderma is often a streak of hard, waxy skin that develops on the arms, legs, or forehead and is more common in children.

Lisinopril: A medicine that is an ACE-inhibitor that decreases blood pressure.

Liver: The largest, solid internal organ and gland in the body. The liver is located on the right side of the abdomen and assists with digestion.

Localized scleroderma: Scleroderma involvement solely of the skin (also called morphea), without any systemic manifestations or organ involvement.

Losartan: A type of medication in the class of angiotensin receptor blockers (ARBs) that reduces blood pressure by blocking angiotensin. It can also be used to treat Raynaud phenomenon.

Low-residue diet: A diet that limits high-fiber foods, like whole grain breads and cereals, nuts, seeds, dried fruit, and vegetables.

Luminal distention: The state of the inner space or a cavity of a tubular organ (e.g., intestine) being enlarged from internal pressure.

Lymphoma: A type of cancer that is characterized by an increase in the number of lymph cells and size of tissues that are involved in fighting infections, such as the lymph nodes and spleen.

Magnetic resonance imaging (MRI): A form of medical imaging that utilizes powerful magnets, radio waves, and a computer to produce detailed images of the inside of the body to diagnose or monitor various health concerns.

Maintenance stage: A stage in the Stages of Change Theory. In the maintenance stage, you have successfully changed a problem behavior or routine to a more accepted behavior *and* have successfully gone without relapse or return to the problem behavior. This change has been maintained between 6 months and 5 years.

Major depressive disorder (MDD): A disease characterized by decreased mood, sleep changes, decreased interest in pleasurable activities, appetite changes, poor concentration, decreased energy.

Malabsorption: Imperfect absorption of food and nutrients by the small intestine.

Malnutrition: Lack of adequate nutrition due to a poor diet or inability to absorb nutrients.

Mammogram: A screening test involving X-rays to evaluate for evidence of breast cancer.

Maternal fetal medicine (MFM): A branch of medicine focused on caring for the mother and fetus before, during, and after pregnancy, particularly in women with chronic medical conditions, fetuses determined to have abnormalities, and "high-risk" pregnancies.

Meditation: The practice of focusing your mind on one thing to keep your mental focus on the present, such as focusing on your breath, a body sensation, or a word or phrase. This practice allows you to move your mind away from outside distractions and interruptions.

Methotrexate: An immune suppressing drug commonly used to treat rheumatoid arthritis and occasionally used to treat various manifestations of scleroderma.

Methylphenidate (Ritalin): A medication that treats attention deficit disorder.

Metronidazole: An antibiotic that is often used to treat infections in the digestive system.

Microbiome: The collection of microorganisms living in or on the human body.

Mindfulness-based stress reduction (MBSR): A formal eight-week, stress-reduction therapy developed and studied by Dr. Jon Kabat-Zinn to treat anxiety, depression, chronic pain, and stress. Mindfulness is the Buddhist practice of focusing the mind on the breath, each step, or other point of focus. The MBSR approach helps develop skills to allow your mind to let go of normal emotional reactions to stressful events and instead allow the body to relax and change your thoughts regarding a situation, which serves to reduce your body's physiological stress responses.

Minute ventilation: The volume of air that is inhaled or exhaled in one minute; this can be measured on pulmonary function testing.

Miscarriage: The expulsion of the fetus before it is viable and able to survive independently, before the 28th week of gestation.

mm Hg: A measurement unit for pressure as recorded with blood pressure.

Modified Rodnan Skin Score: A standardized measure completed by an evaluating health care provider that is used to determine skin thickness in people with scleroderma.

Morphea: Also known as localized scleroderma; a rare skin condition that causes painless, discolored patches on your skin, typically on your abdomen, chest, or back. It is not associated with internal organ involvement.

Motility study/esophageal manometry: A diagnostic test that is utilized to assess and measure the function of the esophagus and the valve between the esophagus and stomach.

Multidisciplinary: Multiple different medical specialties.

Multiple sclerosis: A chronic, often progressive disease that involves sheaths of nerves in the central nervous system (i.e., brain and spinal cord).

Muscle biopsy: A medical procedure that involves removal of a small piece of tissue and cells from a specific muscle(s) that is then closely examined by a pathologist to assist with the diagnostic process for diseases involving muscle tissue.

Musculoskeletal: Part of the body that involves the joints, muscles, ligaments, tendons, and bones.

Mycophenolate mofetil (CellCept®): An immune suppressing medication that can be used to treat some manifestations of scleroderma.

Mycophenolate sodium (Myfortic®): A form of mycophenolic acid that is enteric coated to make it more tolerable than mycophenolate mofetil, in terms of gastrointestinal side effects.

Mycophenolic acid (MPA): An immune suppressing medication that can be used to treat some manifestations of scleroderma.

Mycophenolate mofetil: An immune suppressing medication that can be used to treat some manifestations of scleroderma.

Myopathy or myositis: Inflammation of muscles, usually immune mediated, that can cause muscle weakness and muscle wasting.

Nailfold capillaries: Small blood vessels that are at the base of the fingernails, near the cuticles. These are often abnormal in people with scleroderma.

Nailfold capillaroscopy: Evaluation of the small blood vessels, called capillaries, at the base of the fingernails, behind the cuticles, by use of a magnifying device.

Naproxen: A non-steroidal anti-inflammatory drug (NSAID) used to treat a variety of pains, available over-the-counter.

Neonatal death: Death of an infant during the first 28 days of life.

Nephrologist: Medical subspecialist who is skilled in the diagnosis and treatment of kidney diseases.

Nicotine: A chemical that is highly addictive and contained in all tobacco products, including e-cigarettes. Nicotine is absorbed into the lungs when smoking tobacco, and in the mouth when chewing tobacco. Nicotine use can lead to nicotine dependence and the need to continue to use a certain amount of nicotine to avoid withdrawal symptoms. Nicotine acts as a stimulant and disturbs sleep. Use of nicotine constricts the blood vessels throughout the body and worsens many medical conditions, including Raynaud phenomenon, diabetes, and high blood pressure.

Nicotine replacement therapy (NRT): NRT represents various types of nicotine replacement products, used to help you stop smoking or chewing tobacco without experiencing nicotine withdrawal symptoms. Products include nicotine patches, nicotine gum, nicotine lozenges, nicotine inhaler, and nicotine nasal spray. NRT products contain nicotine without the other known additives and chemicals found in tobacco products. Some of these products can be obtained over-the-counter without a doctor's prescription.

Nicotine withdrawal: Because nicotine is an addictive chemical, withdrawal symptoms are common with nicotine abstinence. There are a set of unpleasant withdrawal symptoms experienced during the first several days to few weeks after you abruptly stop using nicotine (found in all tobacco products). These include cravings that last about 15 to 20 minutes, anxiety, restlessness, difficulty sleeping, irritability, mood changes, and increased appetite.

Nifedipine: A vasodilator medication that is used to treat Raynaud phenomenon. It is also a blood pressure medication.

Nintedanib: A medication that reduces fibrosis and has been shown to slow the rate of declining lung function in those with scleroderma-associated interstitial lung disease.

Nitric oxide/nitrates: A substance that acts on blood vessels to dilate them (increase their size).

Non-steroidal anti-inflammatory drugs (NSAIDs): A class of medications used to treat pain by reducing inflammation without suppressing the immune system, available over-the-counter at lower doses.

Normotensive scleroderma renal crisis: Kidney problems associated with scleroderma in the absence of hypertension.

Nurse practitioner (NP): An advanced practice nurse trained to assess patient needs, order and interpret diagnostic and laboratory tests, diagnose illness and disease, prescribe medications, and formulate treatment plans.

Obstetrician: A physician specializing in caring for women during pregnancy, the birth of the baby, and after pregnancy.

Obstructive sleep apnea (OSA): A sleep disorder in which breathing repeatedly stops for at least 10 seconds at a time during sleep.

Occupational therapist: A health professional who is skilled in the evaluation and treatment of the recuperation of physical and mental illnesses through the use of everyday activities. These professionals are dedicated to helping people live their lives as independently as possible. They teach you ways to make everyday tasks easier that have become difficult due to a disability or injury. They offer strategies to accomplish tasks without pain or discomfort, like dressing, cooking, cleaning, or bathing so that you can live your life to the fullest. Occupational therapists hold a state license to treat patients and work closely with physicians and the other health care team members. A variety of techniques are utilized to develop, recover, or maintain meaningful, daily activities that generally involve the upper extremities or small joints and muscles.

Occupational therapy: A disciple to develop, recover, or maintain meaningful activities, physical and motor skills, and enhance self-esteem and a sense of accomplishment.

Octreotide: A medication that causes increased movement or motility within the digestive system.

Ophthalmologist: A physician specialized to manage diseases of the eye.

Organ rejection: When the receiving body reacts with inflammation to a transplanted organ.

Organs: The internal structures of the body such as the heart, lungs, and kidneys are responsible for all bodily functions.

Organ systems: Different internal parts of the body that have the potential to be involved by disease.

Orthopedic surgeon: A physician specialized to perform corrective surgery for most large and small joints.

Osteonecrosis: Bone death resulting from any cause.

Osteoporosis: Decreased density and strength of the bone that is associated with an increased risk for fracture.

Oxygen: An element that is required for humans (and other living organisms) to breathe, which can also be provided by supplementing through a nasal cannula or mask to assist the lungs.

Oxygen saturation: The percentage of hemoglobin (the molecule within our red blood cells that carries oxygen) that contains oxygen.

Pain specialist: Physician or other health professional who is skilled in the management and treatment of pain.

Palpitations: A symptom felt by a person characterized by a strong, fast, or irregular heartbeat.

Parasympathetic nervous system: The part of the involuntary nervous system that serves to slow the heart rate, enhance activity in the intestines and glands, and relax sphincter muscles.

Patient-reported outcome measures (PROMS): Results from questionnaires or screening tools that are completed by patients with a focus on the person's report of his/her own health status and/or health-related quality of life.

Peau d'orange: Abnormal skin with the appearance of looking like an orange peel.

Penile erection: When the penis fills with blood.

Pericardial effusion: A collection of fluid surrounding the heart.

Pericarditis: Inflammation of the lining that surrounds the heart.

Pericardium: The thin lining surrounding the heart.

Periodontal care: Care for gum diseases.

Peripheral/proximal: Situated away from (peripheral), versus closer to (proximal), the center of the body.

Peripheral vascular disease (PVD): A gradually progressive disorder of the circulation caused by narrowing, blockage, or spasm of the blood vessels.

Pharmacist: A professional trained to dispense prescription medications and provide education to patients about how to take their medications.

pH monitoring with impedance: A technique used to diagnose gastroesophageal reflux disease.

Phosphodiesterase 5 inhibitors: A class of medications that decreases blood pressure in the lungs by blocking phosphodiesterase breakdown.

Phosphodiesterase inhibitors: A group of medications that are used to block one or more of the five sub-types of the enzyme phosphodiesterase, resulting in blood vessel dilation; they are generally utilized to treat pulmonary artery hypertension and sometimes digital ulcers.

Physiatrist: A physical medicine and rehabilitation (PM and R) physician who treats a wide variety of conditions affecting the brain, spinal cord, nerves, bones, joints, ligaments, muscles, and tendons.

Physical health: How well you are feeling in terms of your body and its usual functions.

Physical therapists: Professionals dedicated to helping people regain physical functioning and reduce pain and disability following an injury, surgery, or other type of limitation. This person develops exercise plans and recommends safe exercises that will strengthen and improve overall functioning, which allows you to gain and/or restore physical function to your maximum capacity. Physical therapists hold a state license to treat patients and work closely with physicians and the other health care team members.

Physical therapy: Also known as physiotherapy, a discipline that treats acute or chronic pain, soft tissue injuries, arthritis, gait disorders, and musculoskeletal impairments.

Pitting scars: Small indentations or scars on the tip of the fingertips, often occurring after severe Raynaud phenomenon or after a digital ulcer.

Placebo: An inactive drug that resembles a study drug (used in studies to compare the outcomes between placebo-treated groups and study drug-treated groups).

Placenta: The structure within a pregnant woman's uterus that forms along with the fetus and is responsible for providing nutritional support from the mother's blood to the fetus through the umbilical cord.

Placental blood vessels: The fetal-placental circulation that allows the umbilical arteries to carry deoxygenated blood and nutrient-depleted fetal blood from the fetus to the villous core fetal vessels.

Pneumocystis carinii pneumonia: An outdated term that refers to a type of lung infection caused by the bacteria *pneumocystis jiroveci*.

Pneumocystis jiroveci pneumonia: A type of lung infection caused by the bacteria *pneumocystis jiroveci*.

Pneumonia: An infection of the lungs.

Polyethylene glycol (Miralax®): A type of medication that increases the frequency of bowel movements.

Polyps: Abnormal overgrowth of cells in tissue, which are generally small and flat or mushroom-like stalks.

Precancerous: A condition that if left untreated could develop into cancer.

Precision medicine: An approach to patient care that allows doctors to select treatments that are most likely to help patients based on a genetic understanding of their disease.

Preconception counseling: A discussion with a physician or other health professional to help plan for pregnancy, including discussing any risks and interventions that might be needed prior to conception.

Precontemplation stage: A stage in the Stages of Change Theory. In the precontemplation stage, you are not thinking about making any changes in a behavior/routine and see no problem with a behavior that others might consider a problem. You might defend your behavior to others.

Prednisone: A medication targeting the immune system that is commonly used to treat various types of inflammation in autoimmune diseases.

Preeclampsia: A serious medical condition in pregnant women that can occur any time after 20 weeks of gestation until after delivery and is characterized by high blood pressure as well as protein in the urine. This condition threatens the health of both mother and baby.

Premature or preterm birth: Infants born before 37 weeks of gestation.

Preparation stage: A stage in the Stages of Change Theory. In the preparation stage, you are getting ready to change a problem behavior or routine, by learning the steps needed to implement the change, making plans for when (i.e., the date) you will make the change and setting up contingency plans to be successful.

Priapism: A painful penile erection.

Primary care physician (PCP): A medical doctor skilled in the diagnosis and treatment of a broad range of medical conditions who can coordinate patient access to a variety of health care services.

Primary care provider: Physician or health professional skilled in the diagnosis and treatment of a broad range of medical conditions who often coordinates patient's care with other specialized care providers.

Primary Raynaud phenomenon: Cold-induced, well-demarcated color changes in the fingertips that occur in people without an underlying disorder associated with this condition.

Probenecid: A medicine that increases the secretion of uric acid from the kidneys to prevent gout.

Probiotics: A microorganism introduced into the body for its potentially beneficial qualities.

Productive: A cough that brings up phlegm (mucous).

Productivity: The ability to be effective and accomplish your project(s).

Professional medical society: Groups of medical professions from a given discipline.

Progressive multifocal leukoencephalopathy (PML): An infection caused by the JC virus (John Cunningham virus) in the brain that might rarely occur in people taking strong medicines that inhibit the immune system.

Progressive muscle relaxation (PMR): A relaxation technique that is designed to ease anxiety and stress and promote sleep. PMR is taught by creating tension in certain muscle groups and then relaxing that muscle group, noticing the different states of tension and relaxation. The tense–relax technique progresses throughout the body until all the muscles have become relaxed. When a muscle is tensed and then relaxed, a deeper state of relaxation is achieved.

Promotility agents: Drugs (e.g., metoclopramide, cisapride) that increase the contractile force and accelerate the transit within the gastrointestinal tract.

Promotility drugs: A group of medications that are utilized to promote the movement of ingested material/food through the gastrointestinal system as well as assist with decreasing gastroesophageal reflux symptoms.

Prospective: A type of research study that involves enrolling individuals before a particular event occurs and following them through that event and beyond. For example, a study enrolling women before they become pregnant and then following them through their pregnancies would be considered a prospective study during pregnancy.

Prostacyclin: A molecule that results in increased size (dilation) of blood vessels in the body.

Prostacyclin analogs: A group of medications that are used to bind to a prostaglandin receptor and are utilized to treat pulmonary artery hypertension (PAH) by causing dilation of blood vessels.

Prostaglandin: A lipid with diverse hormone-like effects, that influences the contraction and relaxation of smooth muscle, the dilation and constriction of blood vessels, the control of blood pressure, and the modulation of inflammation.

Proton pump inhibitor (PPI): A class of medications that decrease stomach acid by working on a proton pump of acid in the stomach lining. These medications are used to treat gastroesophageal reflux disease.

Psychiatrist: A physician specialized to manage various mental illnesses and to prescribe medications.

Psychological health: How well you are feeling in terms of your thoughts and mood.

Psychologist: A specialist trained in various forms of counseling, including cognitive-behavioral therapy. This specialist is not able to prescribe medications.

Psychosis: A disorder in which a person sees something or hears something that is not physically present.

Psyllium husk: A type of digestive fiber that increase stool bulk.

Puffy fingers: When the fingers become swollen, often in the early stages of scleroderma.

Pulmonary arterial hypertension (PAH): A type of high blood pressure that affects the blood vessels in a person's lungs and can lead to respiratory symptoms.

Pulmonary fibrosis: Scarring of the lungs.

Pulmonary function tests (PFTs): Tests that are used to assess the quality of a person's ability and quality of breathing to characterize respiratory disorders.

Pulmonary function tests (PFTs) with spirometry and diffusion capacity: Tests performed that measure how well the lungs work by inhaling and exhaling into a machine. The purpose of these tests is to measure the amount of air movement with each breath as well as the lung volumes and ability of air to pass through the lung tissue.

Pulmonary hypertension: A type of high blood pressure that affects the blood vessels in a person's lungs and can lead to respiratory symptoms.

Pulmonary pressures: Measurements of the pressure in the lung arteries that are utilized as a diagnostic tool for pulmonary artery hypertension (PAH).

Pulmonary rehabilitation: A therapeutic program that assists with the improvement in an individual's ability to breathe and is most often utilized for someone who has chronic lung and breathing problems.

Pulmonologist: A physician skilled in the diagnosis and treatment of lung disease.

Purple striae: Purple lines that develop on the skin as a result of extreme or rapid stretching of the skin due to medications or a medical condition.

Radiograph (X-ray): A form of medical imaging that uses a type of electromagnetic radiation to diagnose and monitor disease or trauma. It is commonly used to assess the lungs, bones, and joints.

Randomized controlled trials (RCTs): Research studies that involve comparing a treatment with a placebo; in such studies patients and researchers often do not know which they are receiving. Results of RCTs are considered the strongest and most reliable type of data.

Raynaud phenomenon: A condition in which the blood vessels undergo reversible spasm when exposed to the cold or stress leading to poor blood flow to the fingers and toes, causing the fingers to appear white, blue, and often red and flushed as it resolves. The fingers, toes, tongue, and tip of your nose can be affected.

Raynaud phenomenon symptoms: Symptoms related to the blood vessel changes that occur in response to the cold (see Raynaud phenomenon).

Raynaud's condition score: A specific screening tool that is used to determine the difficulty people have with Raynaud phenomenon as well as how this disease affects peoples' activities and daily functioning.

Receptors: Molecules that act when another molecule binds to it.

Rectal manometry/anorectal manometry: A diagnostic test that measures and evaluates the strength of the rectal and anal muscles.

Reflux/gastroesophageal reflux disease (GERD): A disease that occurs when stomach acid flows back into the esophagus, which is the passageway that attaches the mouth to the stomach.

Registered dietitian: A health care professional with expertise in food and nutrition.

Relapse: A stage in the Stages of Change Theory. The relapse stage is when you return to a problem behavior or routine after you had adopted a healthier and more acceptable behavior for a brief or long-lasting period. This stage requires you to return to an earlier stage of change to implement additional strategies to help prevent another failed attempt to change a problem behavior.

Relaxation techniques: Any method that promotes a relaxed physiological and mental state, a sense of peacefulness and inner calm. There are a number of relaxation techniques that ease muscle tension, anxiety, and stress, such as progressive muscle relaxation, meditation, mindfulness, slow deep breathing, and 4-7-8 breathing.

Renal crisis: *See* Scleroderma renal crisis.

Renal failure: A condition characterized by failure of the kidneys to perform their normal function. In the most serious cases, dialysis might be required.

Research studies: Studies in which subjects are assigned to one of more interventions to evaluate the effects of those interventions on health-related or behavioral outcomes.

Rheumatic diseases: Conditions characterized by an overactive immune system, such as involving autoantibody formation or inflammation which can occur in the skin, internal organs and/or connective tissues of the body, including joints, ligaments, bones, tendons, and muscles.

Rheumatic disorder: Medical condition that affects the immune system and/or the musculoskeletal system. There can be involvement of the skin, internal organs, joints, bones, muscles, and other body tissues, such as ligaments and tendons.

Rheumatoid arthritis: An autoimmune disease characterized by pain, swelling, and inflammation of predominantly the smaller joints of the body.

Rheumatologist: A physician specializing in the care of patients with autoimmune diseases as well as conditions affecting the joints (arthritis), muscles, and bones.

Rifampin: A medication that treats certain bacterial infections.

Right heart catheterization: An invasive test using a catheter to measure pressures within the heart and lungs performed as a diagnostic tool for pulmonary hypertension.

Riociguat: A medication that decreases blood pressure by stimulating guanylate cyclase and is used to treat pulmonary arterial hypertension (PAH).

Risk factors: Things that increase the chances of a person developing a disease or condition.

Rituximab: A medication that works by removing B cells from the body.

RNA polymerase III antibodies: A self-reactive antibody, or autoantibody, that can be found in people with scleroderma. The presence of this autoantibody is predictive of the development of more extensive (diffuse) skin involvement and a risk for scleroderma renal crisis (SRC).

Rodnan skin score: A scoring system to measure the thickness of the skin in different parts of the body.

Scleredema: A rare, self-limiting skin condition defined by progressive thickening and hardening of the skin, usually on the upper back, neck, shoulders, and face.

Sclerodactyly: Tightening and thickening of the skin of the fingers and toes.

Scleroderma-specific antibodies: A specific set of antibodies that are commonly associated with systemic sclerosis and are a part of classification criteria, including anti-centromere, anti-RNA polymerase III, and anti-topoisomerase I.

Scleroderma en coup de sabre: Long crease of fibrotic skin that often occurs around the head and neck, characteristically involving the forehead. Named after a saber.

Scleroderma renal crisis (SRC): A life-threatening complication of scleroderma that presents with sudden onset of severe hypertension accompanied by rapidly progressive renal failure, congestive heart failure, anemia, and confusion.

Scleromyxedema: Considered a mimic of scleroderma, this is a fibrotic condition of the skin that presents as a waxy appearance.

Screening tests: Blood or other laboratory testing performed to evaluate for internal organ abnormalities related to disease.

Secondary Raynaud phenomenon: Cold-induced, well-demarcated color changes in the fingertips that occur in people with an underlying disorder associated with this condition (such as scleroderma).

Selective serotonin re-uptake inhibitor (SSRI): A class of medication that treats depression by allowing for increased serotonin.

Serotonin: A molecule that acts on brain tissue and has a general effect of decreasing depression.

Serotonin receptor (SSR): A molecule that can bind to serotonin.

Sexual dysfunction: Any difficulty experienced by an individual or couple with normal sexual desire and function.

Sicca symptoms: Dryness of the eyes and mouth.

Sickle cell anemia: An inherited form of anemia, in which there aren't enough healthy red blood cells to carry adequate amounts of oxygen throughout your body.

Sign: An objective finding that is detected by a health care provider on the physical examination of a patient.

Sildenafil: A medication that dilates blood vessels by inhibiting phosphodiesterase and is used to treat erectile dysfunction, pulmonary hypertension, severe Raynaud phenomenon, and digital ulcers.

Sjogren syndrome: An autoimmune disease commonly affecting the salivary and tear glands, causing dry eyes and dry mouth.

Sleep clinic: An office in which providers specialize in the diagnosis and management of sleep disorders such as obstructive sleep apnea.

Sleep study: A diagnostic test that records specific breathing and body activity while someone sleeps. This is utilized to identify sleep disorders.

Small bowel dysmotility: A motility disorder that results in slow transit time of food materials throughout the small bowel, which can result in bacterial overgrowth and malabsorption.

Small for gestational age (SGA): Newborns who are smaller than the 10th percentile for the gestational age at which they were born.

Small intestinal bacterial overgrowth (SIBO): The presence of excessive bacteria in the small intestine, often implicated as the cause of chronic diarrhea and malabsorption. Symptoms can include bloating, abdominal pain, and diarrhea.

Social adjustment: The process by which an individual adjusts to the demands, values, or standards of society so as to feel and be accepted by society.

Solid organ transplants: The intentional act of removing a body part from one person to place in another person.

Specialized scleroderma center: A medical clinic designed to provide comprehensive care specifically for people with scleroderma.

Speech therapist: A medical professional who works to prevent, assess, diagnose, and treat speech, language, social communication, cognitive communication, and swallowing disorders.

Spider veins: Dilated blood vessels on the surface of the skin.

Spirometry: A common office test used to assess how well your lungs work by measuring how much air you inhale, how much you exhale, and how quickly you exhale.

SSA and SSB autoantibodies: Specific sets of antibodies that are commonly associated with Sjogren's syndrome.

Stages of Change: A process of adaptation and change that moves through precontemplation, contemplation, preparation, action, maintenance, and termination.

Stem cells: Cells that have the ability to morph into any type of blood cell.

Stem cell transplant: A medical procedure to replace a person's immune system by stem cells, derived from the same person or another person, in order to promote the development of a healthier immune system.

Steroids: A class of medications that inhibits the immune system.

Stillbirth: The birth of an infant after at least 28 weeks of gestation who has died in the womb.

Stomach: An internal organ involved in digesting food, where food goes after it travels through the mouth and esophagus.

Stool blood test: A test to evaluate for the presence of microscopic amounts of blood in the stomach, intestines, or colon.

Stool studies: Various diagnostic tests to examine stool for the detection and identification of bacteria, viruses, and other germs that can cause abnormal bowel movements.

Stricture: A narrowing that develops in a tubular structure, like the esophagus; this can result from gastroesophageal reflux.

Subcutaneous (SC): Something located under the skin.

Subspecialist: A physician who has trained in a specialized area of a field such as within internal medicine. This can include a rheumatologist, pulmonologist, or a cardiologist, among others.

Support group: A group of people with an illness or interest in common who meet to offer help to one another by sharing experiences and thoughts.

Surgeon: Physician skilled in treating medical conditions through performing operations.

Sympathetic nervous system: Part of the nervous system that serves to accelerate heart rate, constrict blood vessels, and raise blood pressure.

Symptoms: Subjective evidence of a physical condition or disturbance observed or reported by a patient, such as pain or fatigue.

Syncope: Fainting.

Systemic form of scleroderma: A form of scleroderma in which the disease has spread beyond the skin to involve internal organs, such as the lungs, gastrointestinal tract, kidneys, blood vessels, and/or heart.

Systemic lupus erythematosus (SLE): Often called simply "lupus." A chronic autoimmune disease that can affect many different internal organs and commonly causes rashes and arthritis.

Systemic scleroderma: A chronic connective tissue disease involving the hardening of the skin and dysfunction of the internal organs (e.g., lungs, kidneys, blood vessels, gastrointestinal tract).

Systemic sclerosis: Another name for scleroderma, a condition characterized by blood vessel abnormalities, skin and organ fibrosis.

Systemic sclerosis sine scleroderma: A sub-type of scleroderma with fibrosis of internal organs without skin thickening.

Tacrolimus: A medicine that inhibits the immune system by blocking calcineurin.

Tadalafil: A vasodilator medicine that treats pulmonary hypertension, Raynaud phenomenon, digital ulcers, and erectile dysfunction by blocking phosphodiesterase 5.

Tai chi: An ancient Chinese practice that promotes mental and physical well-being that involves doing movements or exercises that are gentle, slow, and controlled. These movements can be done sitting or standing.

Telangiectasias: Small, dilated blood vessels that are near the surface of the skin that can develop anywhere on the body but are most commonly found on the face and hands in people with systemic sclerosis.

Telmisartan: A type of medication in the class of angiotensin receptor blockers (ARBs) that reduces blood pressure by blocking angiotensin. It can also be used to treat Raynaud phenomenon.

Tendon: A flexible, strong band of tissue that attaches muscle to bone.

Tendon friction rubs: Leathery, rubbing sensations felt over the tendon as the tendon moves with the joint going through its motion.

Teratogenic: A substance that can cause damage to the unborn child, commonly referring to medications taken by the mother that can lead to abnormalities in the fetus.

Therapeutic alliance: The helping alliance between a health care professional and a client or patient.

Therapy group: A group of patients who come together regularly under the guidance of a therapist to talk about problems and difficult experiences.

Thyroid disease: A group of diseases that causes the thyroid gland to become over- or under-active and results in a multitude of symptoms of disrupted metabolism.

Tissue: An aggregate of cells, usually of one kind, that coalesce to form the building blocks of skin and organs.

Titration: A way to slowly and carefully adjust a medication dose.

Tobacco cessation: Stopping smoking cigarettes.

Toxic: Poisonous.

Transdermal patches: A type of medicine delivery involving a patch that goes on the skin.

Transrectal ultrasound: A form of medical imaging that uses high-frequency sound waves to produce dynamic images of organs in the pelvis and to diagnose causes of incontinence.

Transtheoretical approach: A model of behavior change that assesses an individual's readiness to act on a new and healthier behavior, and provide strategies, or processes to guide the individual.

Trimethoprim-sulfamethoxazole: An antibiotic medicine that treats or prevents a variety of infections. It contains sulfa and may be used to treat *Pneumocystis jirovecii*.

Tuberculosis: Bacteria that grow very slowly and cause infection in the lungs but that can spread to the bones, joints, skin, and other organs.

U1RNP antibody: A self-reactive antibody, or autoantibody, targeted at the U1RNP molecule, which is detectable in the blood of some people with scleroderma.

Ultrasound: A form of medical imaging that uses high-frequency sound waves to produce dynamic images of a body's tissues, organs, and blood flow to diagnose or monitor various health concerns.

University of California Los Angeles Gastrointestinal Tract 2.0 (UCLA GIT 2.0): A specific screening tool that is used to determine categorical severity of gastrointestinal symptoms in people with systemic sclerosis.

Upper endoscopy, esophagogastroduodenoscopy (EGD): A procedure by which a lighted tubular instrument is used to look within the body to evaluate the esophagus, stomach and duodenum (first part of the small intestines).

Upregulating: The process by which the production of something increases, especially in genetics.

Urologist: A physician who specializes and treats diseases associated with the urinary tract and male reproductive organs.

Vaccines: A treatment containing part of an infectious disease that is given to a person to prevent a future infection by that disease.

Valacyclovir: A medicine that treats certain viral infections, like herpes.

Vascular: Relating to the blood vessels, which are also responsible for many of the symptoms in scleroderma.

Vascular disease: Also known as vasculopathy; pathological conditions related to the blood vessels.

Vasculature: The circulatory/cardiovascular/vascular system within the body that allows the blood to circulate and move various vital components to and from cells in the body.

Vasculopathy: A general term used to describe any disease affecting blood vessels.

Vasoconstriction: A condition resulting in a decrease in or narrowing of the size of a blood vessel, typically increasing the pressure and decreasing blood flow.

Vasodilation: Improved blood flow occurs when there is widening of blood vessels.

Vasodilators: Medications that open (dilate) blood vessels.

Very low birth weight: Newborns weighing less than 1,500 g (3.3 lbs).

Viral hepatitis: Infection of the liver by one of several viruses such as Hepatitis A, Hepatitis B, or Hepatitis C.

Visceral hypersensitivity: A condition of extreme internal physical sensitivity (e.g., in the gut).

Water retention: Fluid buildup in the body often causing swelling in the legs.

Wheat dextrin (Metamucil and Benefiber): A type of digestive fiber that is derived from wheat.

White blood cell (WBC): Type of blood cell that fights infections.

X-ray: A form of medical imaging that uses a type of electromagnetic radiation to diagnose and monitor disease or trauma. It is commonly used to assess the lungs, bones, and joints.

Xifaxan: A medicine derived from rifamycin, an antibiotic, that treats diarrhea.

Yoga: A type of exercise for improved flexibility that involves moving the body into different positions or postures while relaxing the mind and focusing on gentle breathing.

REFERENCES

1. Abalos E, Cuesta C, Grosso AL, et al: Global and regional estimates of preeclampsia and eclampsia: A systematic review. *European Journal of Obstetrics and Gynecology, and Reproductive Biology.* 2013; 170(1): 1–7.
2. Amaral TN, Peres FA, Lapa AT, et al: Neurologic involvement in scleroderma: A systematic review. *Seminars in Arthritis and Rheumatism.* 2013; 43(3): 335–347.
3. American Academy of Sleep Medicine. Health Sleep Habits. http://www.sleepeducation.org/essentials-in-sleep/healthy-sleep-habits Accessed June 25, 2018.
4. American Heart Association. American Heart Association Recommendations for Physical Activity in Adults. http://www.heart.org/HEARTORG/HealthyLiving/PhysicalActivity/FitnessBasics/American-Heart-Association-Recommendations-for-Physical-Activity-in-Adults_UCM_307976_Article.jsp#.Wy_33y2ZNE4. Accessed June 24, 2018.
5. American Psychiatric Association. (2013). *Diagnostic and Statistical Manual of Mental Disorders.* 5th ed. Washington, DC.
6. Antonucci R, Zaffanello M, Puxeddu E, et al: Use of non-steroidal anti-inflammatory drugs in pregnancy: Impact on the fetus and newborn. *Current Drug Metabolism.* 2012 May 1; 13(4): 474–490.
7. Arthritis Foundation. 7 Dynamic Warm Ups. https://www.arthritis.org/living-with-arthritis/exercise/workouts/simple-routines/dynamic-stretching.php?_ga=2.173382886.493862312.1529848779-1004891772.1528604627. Accessed June 8, 2018.
8. Arthritis Foundation. Weight Training 101. https://www.arthritis.org/living-with-arthritis/exercise/how-to/weight-training-for-beginners.php. Accessed June 8, 2018.
9. Arthritis Foundation. A New Way to Stretch. https://www.arthritis.org/living-with-arthritis/exercise/how-to/stretching-benefits.php. Accessed June 8, 2018.

10. Arthritis Foundation. Exercise: How Much is Enough? https://www.arthritis.org/living-with-arthritis/exercise/how-to/how-much-is-enough.php. Accessed June 8, 2018.

11. Avouac J, Airo P, Meune C, et al: Prevalence of pulmonary hypertension in systemic sclerosis in European caucasians and meta-analysis of 5 studies. *Journal of Rheumatology*. 2010; 37(11): 2290–2298.

12. Bar-Gil Shitrit A, Grisaru-Granovsky S, Ben Ya'acov E, et al: Management of inflammatory bowel disease during pregnancy. *Digestive Diseases and Sciences*. 2016; 61: 2194–2204.

13. Barnes J, Mayes M: Epidemiology of systemic sclerosis: Incidence, prevalence, survival, risk factors, malignancy, and environmental triggers. *Current Opinions in Rheumatology*. 2012;24: 165–170.

14. Bartlett, S, Haaz, C, Mill, C, et al: Yoga in rheumatic diseases. *Current Rheumatology Reports*. 2013; 15: 1–14.

15. Bassel M, Hudson M, Taillefer SS, et al: Frequency and impact of symptoms experienced by patients with systemic sclerosis: Results from a Canadian National Survey. *Rheumatology* (Oxford). 2011; 50(4): 762–767.

16. Baubet T, Ranque B, Taieb O, et al: Mood and anxiety disorders in systemic sclerosis patients. *La Presse Medicale*. 2011; 40(2): e111–e119.

17. Bellando-Randone S, Matucci-Cerinic M: Very early systemic sclerosis and pre-systemic sclerosis: Definition, recognition, clinical relevance and future directions. *Current Rheumatology Reports*. 2017; 19(10): 65.

18. Benrud-larson LM, Haythornthwaite JA, Heinberg LJ, et al: The impact of pain and symptoms of depression in scleroderma. *Pain*. 2002; 95(3): 267–275.

19. Black CM: Scleroderma—clinical aspects. *Journal of Internal Medicine*. 1993; 234(2): 115–118.

20. Bolster MB, Silver RM. Clinical features of systemic sclerosis. In: Hochberg MC, Silman AJ, Smolen JS, Weinblatt ME, Weisman MH, eds. *Rheumatology*, 6th edition. Philadelphia: Elsevier Ltd; 2014; 1165-1176.

21. Bosello S, De Santis M, Lama G, et al: B cell depletion in diffuse progressive systemic sclerosis: Safety, skin score modification and IL-6 modulation in an up to thirty-six months follow-up open-label trial. *Arthritis Research & Therapy*. 2010; 12(2): R54.

22. Bosello SL, De Luca G, Rucco M, et al: Long-term efficacy of B cell depletion therapy on lung and skin involvement in diffuse systemic sclerosis. *Seminars in Arthritis & Rheumatology*. 2015; 44(4): 428–436.

23. Bossini-Castillo L, Lopez-Isac E, Martin J: Immunogenetics of systemic sclerosis: Defining heritability, functional variants and shared-autoimmunity pathways. *Journal of Autoimmunity*. 2015; 64: 53–65.

24. Bruni C, Raja J, Denton CP, et al: The clinical relevance of sexual dysfunction in systemic sclerosis. *Autoimmunity Reviews*. 2015; 14(12): 1111–1115.

25. Burt RK, Shah SJ, Dill K, et al: Autologous non-myeloablative haemopoietic stem-cell transplantation compared with pulse cyclophosphamide once per month for systemic sclerosis (ASSIST): An open-label, randomised phase 2 trial. *Lancet*. 2011; 378(9790): 498–506.

26. Carlson DA, Hinchcliff M, Pandolfino JE: Advances in the evaluation and management of esophageal disease of systemic sclerosis. *Current Rheumatology Reports*. 2015; 17(1): 475.

27. Centers for Disease Control. Quitting Smoking. https://www.cdc.gov/tobacco/data_statistics/fact_sheets/cessation/quitting/index.htm. Accessed June 20, 2018.

28. Chakravarty EF, Khanna D, Chung L: Pregnancy outcomes in systemic sclerosis, primary pulmonary hypertension, and sickle cell disease. *Obstetrics and Gynecology*. 2008; 111(4): 927–934.

29. Chen JS, Roberts CL, Simpson JM, et al: Pregnancy outcomes in women with rare autoimmune diseases. *Arthritis and Rheumatology*. 2015; 67(12): 3314–3323.

30. Chifflot H, Fautrel B, Sordet C, et al: Incidence and prevalence of systemic sclerosis: A systematic literature review. *Seminars in Arthritis & Rheumatology*. 2008; 37(4): 223–235.

31. Chung L, Shapiro L, Fiorentino D, et al: MQX-503, a novel formulation of nitroglycerin, improves the severity of Raynaud's phenomenon: A randomized, controlled trial. *Arthritis and Rheumatism*. 2009; 60(3): 870–877.

32. Coghlan JG, Galie N, Barbera JA, et al: Initial combination therapy with ambrisentan and tadalafil in connective tissue disease-associated pulmonary arterial hypertension (CTD-PAH): Subgroup analysis from the AMBITION trial. *Annals of Rheumatic Diseases*. 2017; 76(7): 1219–1227.

33. Collins J, Mazor Y, Jones M, et al. Efficacy of anorectal biofeedback in scleroderma patients with fecal incontinence: A case-control study. *Scandinavian Journal of Gastroenterology*. 2016; 51: 1433–1438.

34. Curtis JR, Westfall AO, Allison J, et al: Population-based assessment of adverse events associated with long-term glucocorticoid use. *Arthritis Care & Research*. 2006; 55(3): 420–426.

35. Cutolo M, Sulli A, Secchi ME, et al: Nailfold capillaroscopy is useful for the diagnosis and follow-up of autoimmune rheumatic diseases. A future tool for the analysis of microvascular heart involvement? *Rheumatology.* 2006; 45: 43–46.

36. Daoussis D, Liossis SN, Tsamandas AC, et al: Experience with rituximab in scleroderma: Results from a 1-year, proof-of-principle study. *Rheumatology* (Oxford). 2010; 49(2): 271–280.

37. Daoussis D, Liossis SN, Tsamandas AC, et al: Effect of long-term treatment with rituximab on pulmonary function and skin fibrosis in patients with diffuse systemic sclerosis. *Clinical and Experimental Rheumatology.* 2012; 30(2 Suppl 71): S17–22.

38. Daoussis D, Melissaropoulos K, Sakellaropoulos G, et al: A multicenter, open-label, comparative study of B-cell depletion therapy with Rituximab for systemic sclerosis-associated interstitial lung disease. *Seminars in Arthritis & Rheumatology.* 2017; 46(5): 625–631.

39. Delaney S, Colantonio D, Ito S: Methotrexate in breast milk. *Birth Defects Research.* 2017; 109(SI): 711.

40. Denton CP, Black CM: Scleroderma—clinical and pathological advances. *Best Practices & Research: Clinical Rheumatology.* 2004; 18(3): 271–290.

41. Denton CP, Khanna D: Systemic sclerosis. *Lancet.* 2017; 390(10103): 1685–1699.

42. Desbois AC, Cacoub P: Systemic sclerosis: An update in 2016. *Autoimmunity Reviews.* 2016; 15(5): 417–426.

43. Distler O, Highland KB, Gahlemann M et al: Nintedanib for systemic sclerosis-associated interstitial lung disease. *New England Journal of Medicine.* 2019; 380: 2518-2528.

44. Dourmishev LA, Guleva DV, Miteva LG: Intravenous immunoglobulins for treatment of connective tissue diseases in dermatology. *Wiener Medizinische Wochenschrift.* (1946). 2018; 168(9–10): 213–217.

45. Dowman L, Hill C, Holland A: Pulmonary rehabilitation for interstitial lung disease. *Cochrane Database of Systematic Reviews.* 2014; 6:(10).

46. Dubos M, Ly K, Martel C, et al: Is rituximab an effective treatment of refractory calcinosis? *British Medical Journal Case Reports.* 2016.p11.bcr2015213179 doi: 10.113b/bcr-2015-213179.

47. Dunn L, Greer R, Flenady V, et al: Sildenafil in pregnancy: A systematic review of maternal tolerance and obstetric and perinatal outcomes. *Fetal Diagnostics and Therapeutics.* 2017; 41(2): 81–88.

48. Dziadzio M, Denton CP, Smith R, et al: Losartan therapy for Raynaud's phenomenon and scleroderma: Clinical and biochemical findings in a fifteen-week, randomized, parallel-group, controlled trial. *Arthritis & Rheumatology.* 1999; 42(12): 2646–2655.

49. Ebata S, Yoshizaki A, Fukasawa T, et al: Unprecedented success of rituximab therapy for prednisolone- and immunosuppressant-resistant systemic sclerosis-associated interstitial lung disease. *Scandinavian Journal of Rheumatology.* 2017; 46(3): 247–252.

50. Evans DL, Charney DS, Golden RN, et al: Mood disorders in the medically ill: Scientific review and recommendations. *Biological Psychiatry.* 2005; 58: 175–189.

51. Faezi ST, Paragomi P, Shahali A, et al: Prevalence and severity of depression and anxiety in patients with systemic sclerosis. *Journal of Clinical Rheumatology.* 2017; 23: 80–86.

52. Farge D, Burt RK, Oliveira MC, et al: Cardiopulmonary assessment of patients with systemic sclerosis for hematopoietic stem cell transplantation: Recommendations from the European Society for Blood and Marrow Transplantation Autoimmune Diseases Working Party and collaborating partners. *Bone Marrow Transplant.* 2017; 52(11): 1495–1503.

53. Fernandez-Codina A, Simeon-Aznar CP, Pinal-Fernandez I, et al: Cardiac involvement in systemic sclerosis: Differences between clinical subsets and influence on survival. *Rheumatology International.* 2017; 37(1): 75–84.

54. Fiore MC, Jaén CR, Baker TB, et al: Treating Tobacco Use and Dependence: 2008 Update. Clinical Practice Guideline. Rockville, MD: U.S. Department of Health and Human Services. Public Health Service. May 2008. https://www.ncbi.nlm.nih.gov/books/NBK63952/. Accessed June 24, 2018.

55. Frank D, Khorshid L, Kiffer J, et al: Biofeedback in medicine: Who, when, why and how? *Mental Health Family Medicine.* 2010; 7: 85–91.

56. Frech TM, Khanna D, Maranian P, et al: Probiotics for the treatment of systemic sclerosis-associated gastrointestinal bloating/distention. *Clinical and Experimental Rheumatology.* 2011; 29(2 Suppl 65): S22–25.

57. Frech T, Khanna D, Markewitz B, et al: Heritability of vasculopathy, autoimmune disease, and fibrosis: A population-based study of systemic sclerosis. *Arthritis & Rheumatism.* 2010; 62(7): 2019–2116.

58. Freedman R, Ianni P, Wenig P. Behavioral treatment of Raynaud's phenomenon in scleroderma. *Journal of Behavioral Medicine.* 1984; 7: 343–353.

59. Gabrielli A, Avvedimento EV, Krieg T: Scleroderma. *New England Journal of Medicine.* 2009; 360(19): 1989–2003.

60. Galie N, Humbert M, Vachiery J-L, et al: 2015 ESC/ERS Guidelines for the diagnosis and treatment of pulmonary hypertension: The joint task force for the diagnosis and treatment of pulmonary hypertension of the European Society of Cardiology (ESC) and the European Respiratory Society (ERS): Endorsed by: Association for European Paediatric and Congenital Cardiology (AEPC), International Society for Heart and Lung Transplantation (ISHLT). *European Respiratory Journal.* 2015; 45(4): 903–975.

61. Galie N, Olschewski H, Oudiz RJ, et al: Ambrisentan for the treatment of pulmonary arterial hypertension: Results of the ambrisentan in pulmonary arterial hypertension, randomized, double-blind, placebo-controlled, multicenter, efficacy (ARIES) study 1 and 2. *Circulation.* 2008; 117(23): 3010–3019.

62. Giuggioli D, Lumetti F, Colaci M, et al: Rituximab in the treatment of patients with systemic sclerosis. Our experience and review of the literature. *Autoimmunity Reviews.* 2015; 14(11): 1072107–8.

63. Greco C, Nakajima C, Manzi S: Updated review of complementary and alternative medicine treatments for systemic lupus erythematosus. *Current Rheumatology Reports.* 2013; 15: 1–13.

64. Greco C, Rudy T, Manzi S: Effects of a stress-reduction program on psychological function, pain, and physical function of systemic lupus erythematosus patients: A randomized controlled trial. *Arthritis and Rheumatology (Arthritis Care Research).* 2004; 51: 625–634.

65. Gyger G, Barron M: Systemic sclerosis: Gastrointestinal disease and its management. *Rheumatic Disease Clinics of North America.* 2015; 41: 459–473.

66. Harrison B, Silman A, Hider S, et al: Cigarette smoking as a significant risk factor for digital vascular disease in patients with systemic sclerosis. *Arthritis and Rheumatism.* 2002; 46: 3312–3316.

67. Herrick AL: Therapeutic implications from the pathogenesis of Raynaud's phenomenon. *Expert Review of Clinical Immunology.* 2017; 13(7): 723–735.

68. Hinchcliff M, Toledo DM, Taroni JN, et al: Mycophenolate mofetil treatment of systemic sclerosis reduces myeloid cell numbers and attenuates the inflammatory gene signature in skin. *Journal of Investigative Dermatology.* 2018; 138(6): 1301–1310.

69. Hinchcliff M, Varga J: Managing systemic sclerosis and its complications. *The Journal of Musculoskeletal Medicine.* 2011; 28(10): 380.

70. Hinchcliff M, Whitfield ML: Molecular stratification by gene expression as a paradigm for precision medicine in systemic sclerosis. In: Varga J, Denton CP, Wigley F, et al, eds. *Scleroderma: From Pathogenesis to Comprehensive Management. Management and Outcome Assessment.* 2nd ed.: New York: Springer Science; 2017: pp. 657–672.

71. Ho K, Reveille J: The clinical relevance of autoantibodies in scleroderma. *Arthritis Research & Therapy.* 2003; 5: 80–93.

72. Horváth J, Bálint Z, Szép E, et al: Efficacy of intensive hand physical therapy in patients with systemic sclerosis. *Clinical and Experimental Rheumatology.* 2017; 35: 159–166.

73. Hudson M, Lo E, Hercz D, et al: Cigarette smoking in patients with systemic sclerosis. *Arthritis and Rheumatism.* 2011; 63: 230–238.

74. Hui K, Johnston M, Brodsky M, et al: Scleroderma, stress and CAM utilization. *Evidence-Based Complementary and Alternative Medicine.* 2009; 6: 503–506.

75. Hurabielle C, Allanore Y, Kahan A, et al: Flare of calcinosis despite rituximab therapy. *Seminars in Arthritis & Rheumatology.* 2014; 44(2): e5–6.

76. Ionica FE, Mogoanta L, Nicola GC, et al: Antifibrotic action of telmisartan in experimental carbon tetrachloride-induced liver fibrosis in Wistar rats. *Romanian Journal of Morphology and Embryology = Revue Roumaine de Morphologie et Embryologie.* 2016; 57(4): 1261–1272.

77. Irish L, Kline C, Gunn H, et al: The role of sleep hygiene in promoting public health: A review of empirical evidence. *Sleep Medicine Reviews.* 2015; 22: 23–36.

78. Jacobson BC, Somers SC, Fuchs CS, et al: Body-mass index and symptoms of gastroesophageal reflux in women. *New England Journal of Medicine.* 2006; 354(22): 2340–2348.

79. Jaeger VK, Walker UA: Erectile dysfunction in systemic sclerosis. *Current Rheumatology Reports.* 2016; 18: 49.

80. Jaeger V, Wirz E, Allanore Y, et al: Incidences and risk factors of organ manifestations in the early course of systemic sclerosis: A longitudinal EUSTAR study. *Plos One.* 2016 Oct 5; 11(10): e0163894. doi: 10.1371/journal.pone.0163894. ecollection 2016.

81. Jewett LR, Kwakkenbos L, Delisle VC, et al: Psychosocial issues and care for patients with systemic sclerosis. *Scleroderma.* 2016; 615–621.

82. Jordan S, Distler JH, Maurer B, et al: Effects and safety of rituximab in systemic sclerosis: An analysis from the European Scleroderma Trial and Research (EUSTAR) group. *Annals of Rheumatic Diseases.* 2015; 74(6): 1188–1194.

83. Kabat-Zinn J: *Full Catastrophe Living: Using the Wisdom of Your Body and Mind to Face Stress, Pain, and Illness.* 15th Anniversary ed. New York: Delta Trade Paperback/Bantam Dell; 2005.

84. Kasifoglu T, Bilge S, Yildiz F, et al: Risk factors for malignancy in systemic sclerosis patients. *Clinical Rheumatology.* 2016; 35: 1529–1533.

85. Khan K, Zamora J, Lamont RF, et al: Safety concerns for the use of calcium channel blockers in pregnancy for the treatment of spontaneous preterm labour and hypertension: A systematic review and meta-regression analysis. *Journal of Maternal-Fetal and Neonatal Medicine.* 2010 Sep; 23(9): 1030–1038.

86. Khanna D: Assessing disease activity and outcomes in systemic sclerosis. In: Hochberg M, Gravallese E, Silman A, et al: *Rheumatology.* 7th ed.: Philadelphia, PA. Elsevier; 2019: pp. 1263–1269.

87. Khanna D, Nagaraja V, Gladue H, et al: Measuring response in the gastrointestinal tract in systemic sclerosis. *Current Opinion in Rheumatology.* 2013; 25(6): 700–706.

88. Khanna D, Serrano J, Berrocal V, et al: A randomized controlled trial to evaluate an internet-based self-management program in systemic sclerosis. *Arthritis Care and Research.* 2018 May 9. doi: 10.1002/acr.23595. [epub ahead of print]

89. Khor CG, Chen XL, Lin TS, et al: Rituximab for refractory digital infarcts and ulcers in systemic sclerosis. *Clinical Rheumatology.* 2014; 33(7): 1019–1020.

90. Khouri C, Gailland T, Lepelley M, et al: Fluoxetine and Raynaud's phenomenon: Friend or foe? *British Journal of Clinical Pharmacology.* 2017; 83(10): 2307–2309.

91. Kim WG, Yong SD, Yook SJ, et al: Comparison of black carbon concentration and particle mass concentration with elemental carbon concentration for multi-walled carbon nanotube emission assessment purpose. *Carbon.* 2017; 122: 228–236.

92. Korn JH, Mayes M, Matucci Cerinic M, et al: Digital ulcers in systemic sclerosis: Prevention by treatment with bosentan, an oral endothelin receptor antagonist. *Arthritis and Rheumatism.* 2004; 50(12): 3985–3993.

93. Kowal-Bielecka O, Fransen J, Avouac J, et al: Update of EULAR recommendations for the treatment of systemic sclerosis. *Annals of the Rheumatic Diseases.* 2017; 76(8): 1327–1339.

94. Kucharz EJ, Kopec-Medrek M: Systemic sclerosis sine scleroderma. *Advances in Clinical and Experimental Medicine.* 2017; 26(5): 875–880.

95. Kwakkenbos L, Delisle VC, Fox RS, et al: Psychosocial aspects of scleroderma. *Rheumatic Disease Clinics of North America.* 2015; 41(3): 519–528.

96. Kwakkenbos L, van Lankveld GJM, Vonk MC, et al: Disease-related and psychosocial factors associated with depressive symptoms in patients with systemic sclerosis, including fear of progression and appearance self-esteem. *Journal of Psychosomatic Research.* 2012; 72(3): 199–204.

97. Lafyatis R, Kissin E, York M, et al: B cell depletion with rituximab in patients with diffuse cutaneous systemic sclerosis. *Arthritis & Rheumatology.* 2009; 60(2): 578–583.

98. Laing TJ, Gillespie BW, Toth MB, et al: Racial differences in scleroderma among women in Michigan. *Arthritis & Rheumatology*. 1997; 40(4): 734–742.

99. Langevitz P, Buskila D, Lee P, et al: Scleroderma hypertensive renal crisis and the changing pattern of mortality in systemic sclerosis (Scleroderma). *Nephron*. 1991; 57(1): 111–112.

100. Leask A: When there's smoke there's . . . scleroderma: Evidence that patients with scleroderma should stop smoking. *Journal of Cell Communication and Signaling*. 2011; 5: 67–68.

101. Lee JJ, Pope J: Diagnosis and management of systemic sclerosis: A practical approach. *Drugs*. 2016; 76: 203–213.

102. Lepri G, Avouac J, Airo P, et al: Effects of rituximab in connective tissue disorders related interstitial lung disease. *Clinical and Experimental Rheumatology*. 2016; 34 Suppl 100(5): 181–185.

103. Levis B, Hudson M, Knafo R, et al: Rates and correlates of sexual activity and impairment among women with systemic sclerosis. *Arthritis Care & Research*. 2011; 64(3): 640–650.

104. Magge S, Lembo A: Low-FODMAP diet for treatment of irritable bowel syndrome. *Gastroenterology and Hepatology*. 2012; 8: 739–745.

105. Marie I, Gehanno J: Environmental risk factors of systemic sclerosis. *Seminars in Immunopathology*. 2015; 37: 463–473.

106. Marie A, Leroi A-M, Gourcerol G, et al: Lactose malabsorption in systemic sclerosis. *Alimentary Pharmacologic Therapeutics*. 2016; 44: 1123–1133.

107. Mariette X, Cazals-Hatem D, Warszawki J, et al: Lymphomas in rheumatoid arthritis patients treated with methotrexate: A 3-year prospective study in France. *Blood*. 2002; 99(11): 3909–3915.

108. Matucci-Cerinic M, Denton CP, Furst DE, et al: Bosentan treatment of digital ulcers related to systemic sclerosis: Results from the RAPIDS-2 randomised, double-blind, placebo-controlled trial. *Annals of the Rheumatic Diseases*. 2011; 70(1): 32–38.

109. Mayes M, Assassi S: Classification and epidemiology of scleroderma. In: Hochberg M, Silman A, Smolen J, et al: *Rheumatology*. 6th ed.: Philadelphia, PA: Elsevier; 2015: pp. 1153–1158.

110. Mayes MD, Bossini-Castillo L, Gorlova O, et al: Immunochip analysis identifies multiple susceptibility loci for systemic sclerosis. *American Journal of Human Genetics*. 2014 Jan 2; 94(1): 47–61.

111. Mayes MD, Ho KT: Understanding and managing scleroderma. *Scleroderma Foundation*. May 15, 2018.

112. McMahan Z, Hummers L: Systemic sclerosis: Challenges for clinical practice. *Nature Reviews Rheumatology*. 2013; 9: 90–103.

113. McNearney TA, Reveille JD, Fischbach M, et al: Pulmonary involvement in systemic sclerosis: Associations with genetic, serologic, sociodemographic, and behavioral factors. *Arthritis & Rheumatology*. 2007; 57(2): 318–326.

114. Melina V, Craig W, Levin S: Position of the Academy of Nutrition and Dietetics: Vegetarian Diets. *Journal of Academic Nutrition Diet*. 2016; 116: 1970–1980.

115. Melsens K, Vandecasteele E, Deschepper E, et al: Two years follow-up of an open-label pilot study of treatment with rituximab in patients with early diffuse cutaneous systemic sclerosis. *Acta Clinica Belgica*. 2018; 73(2): 119–125.

116. Methotrexate 2017 [Available from: https://mothertobaby.org/fact-sheets/methotrexate-pregnancy/].

117. Milette K, Thombs BD, Maiorino K, et al: Challenges and strategies for coping with scleroderma: Implications for a scleroderma-specific self-management program. *Disability and Rehabilitation*. 2018; 1–10: Epub: 0.1080/09638288.2018.

118. Mitchell K, Kaul M, Clowse ME: The management of rheumatic disease in pregnancy. *Scandinavian Journal of Rheumatology*. 2010 Mar; 39(2): 99–108.

119. Mohammed AGA, Alshihre A, Al-Homood IA: Rituximab treatment in patients with systemic sclerosis and interstitial lung disease. *Annals of Thoracic Medicine*. 2017; 12(4): 294–297.

120. Molberg O, Hoffmann-Vold AM: Interstitial lung disease in systemic sclerosis: Progress in screening and early diagnosis. *Current Opinion in Rheumatology*. 2016; 28(6): 613–618.

121. Morrisroe K, Frech T, Schniering J, et al: Systemic sclerosis: The need for structured care. *Best Practice & Research Clinical Rheumatology*. 2016; 30: 3–21.

122. Morrisroe KB, Nikpour M, Proudman SM: Musculoskeletal manifestations of systemic sclerosis. *Rheumatic Disease Clinics of North America*. 2015; 41(3): 507–518.

123. Morrisroe K, Sudararajan V, Stevens W, et al: Work productivity in systemic sclerosis, its economic burden and association with health-related quality of life. *Rheumatology*. 2018; 57: 73–83.

124. Mosca L, Benjamin EJ, Berra K, et al: Effectiveness-based guidelines for the prevention of cardiovascular disease in women—2011 update: A guideline from the American Heart Association. *Circulation*. 2011; 123: 1243–1262.

125. Nagaraja V, McMahan Z, Getzug T, et al: Management of gastrointestinal involvement in scleroderma. *Current Treatment Outpatient Rheumatology*. 2015; 1: 82–105.

126. Nakamura K, Yoshizaki A, Takahashi T, et al: The first case report of fatal acute pulmonary dysfunction in a systemic sclerosis patient treated with rituximab. *Scandinavian Journal of Rheumatology.* 2016; 45(3): 249–250.

127. Nguyen C, Ranque B, Baubet T, et al: Clinical, functional and health-related quality of life correlates of clinically significant symptoms of anxiety and depression in patients with systemic sclerosis: A cross-sectional survey. *PLoS One.* 2014;9(2): e90484.

128. Numajiri H, Yoshizaki A, Ebata S, et al: Successful treatment with rituximab in a Japanese patient with systemic sclerosis-associated interstitial lung disease resistant to oral steroid and cyclophosphamide. *Journal of Dermatology.* 2018 Jun; 45(6): e140–e141.

129. Okamoto M, Okano A, Akamatsu S, et al: Rituximab is effective for steroid-refractory sclerodermatous chronic graft-versus-host disease. *Leukemia.* 2006; 20(1): 172–173.

130. Olsson KM, Channick R: Pregnancy in pulmonary arterial hypertension. *European Respiratory Review.* 2016 Dec; 25(142): 431–437.

131. Ornish D, Brown S, Scherwitz L, et al: Can lifestyle changes reverse coronary heart disease? The Lifestyle Heart Trial. *Lancet.* 1990; 336: 129–133.

132. Parker J, Smarr K, Buckelew S, et al: Effects of stress management on clinical outcomes in rheumatoid arthritis. *Arthritis and Rheumatology.* 1995; 38: 1807–1818.

133. Pattanaik D, Brown M, Postlethwaite BC, et al: Pathogenesis of systemic sclerosis. *Frontiers in Immunology.* 2015; 6: 272.

134. Pauling JD, Frech TM, Domsic RT, et al: Patient participation in patient-reported outcome instrument development in systemic sclerosis. *Clinical & Experimental Rheumatology.* 2017 Sep-Oct; 35 Suppl 106(4): 184–192.

135. Penn H, Howie AJ, Kingdon EJ, et al: Scleroderma renal crisis: Patient characteristics and long-term outcomes. *QJM.* 2007; 100(8): 485–494.

136. Pischon N, Hoedke D, Kurth S, et al: Increased periodontal attachment loss in patients with systemic sclerosis. *Journal of Periodontology.* 2016; 763–771.

137. Pisoni CN, D'Cruz DP: The safety of mycophenolate mofetil in pregnancy. *Expert Opinion on Drug Safety.* 2008; 7(3): 219–222.

138. Poole JL, Brewer C, Rossi K, et al: Factors related to oral hygiene in persons with scleroderma. *International Journal of Dental Hygiene.* 2005; 3: 13–17.

139. Poole J, Conte C, Brewer C, et al: Oral hygiene in scleroderma: The effectiveness of a multi-disciplinary intervention program. *Disability and Rehabilitation.* 2010; 379–384.

140. Poormoghim H, Andalib E, Almasi AR, et al: Systemic sclerosis and calcinosis cutis: Response to rituximab. *Journal of Clinical Pharmacy and Therapeutics*. 2016; 41(1): 94–96.

141. Pope JE: Pulmonary arterial hypertension in scleroderma: Care gaps in screening. *Arthritis Research & Therapy*. 2017; 19.

142. Prado G, Allen R, Trevisani V, et al: Sleep disruption in systemic sclerosis (scleroderma) patients: Clinical and polysomnographic findings. *Sleep Medicine*. 2002; 3: 341–345.

143. Prochaska J, Norcross J, DiClemente C: *Changing for Good: A Revolutionary Six-Stage Program for Overcoming Bad Habits and Moving Your Life Positively Forward*. New York: Harper Collins; 1994.

144. Revenson T, Schiaffino K, Majerovitz D, et al: Social support as a double-edge sword: The relation of positive and problematic support to depression among rheumatoid arthritis patients. *Social Science Medicine*. 1991; 33: 807–813.

145. Richard N, Hudson M, Gyger G, et al: Clinical correlates of faecal incontinence in systemic sclerosis: Identifying therapeutic avenues. *Rheumatology*. 2017; 56: 581–588.

146. Rimoldi SF, Scherrer U, Messerli FH: Secondary arterial hypertension: When, who, and how to screen? *European Heart Journal*. 2014; 35(19): 1245–1254.

147. Rirash F, Tingey PC, Harding SE, et al: Calcium channel blockers for primary and secondary Raynaud's phenomenon. *The Cochrane Database of Systematic Reviews*. 2017; 12: Cd000467.

148. Ryu RJ, Easterling TR, Caritis SN, et al: Prednisone pharmacokinetics during pregnancy and lactation. *Journal of Clinical Pharmacology*. 2018; 58(9): 1223–1232.

149. Saketkoo LA, Magnus JH, Doyle MK: The primary care physician in the early diagnosis of systemic sclerosis: The cornerstone of recognition and hope. *American Journal of the Medical Sciences*. 2014; 347(1): 54–63.

150. Sakkas LI, Simopoulou T, Katsiari C, et al: Early systemic sclerosis-opportunities for treatment. *Clinical Rheumatology*. 2015; 34(8): 1327–1331.

151. Salazar G, Mayes MD: Genetics, epigenetics, and genomics of systemic sclerosis. *Rheumatic Disease Clinics of North America*. 2016 Aug 1; 41(3): 345–366.

152. Sampios-Barros PD, Samara AM, Marques Neto JF: Gynaecologic history in systemic sclerosis. *Clinical Rheumatology*. 2000; 19(3): 184–187.

153. Sandhu D, Fass R: Current trends in the management of gastroesophageal reflux disease. *Gut and Liver*. 2018; 12: 7–16.

154. Sanges S, Riviere S, Mekinian A, et al: Intravenous immunoglobulins in systemic sclerosis: Data from a French nationwide cohort of 46 patients and review of the literature. *Autoimmunity Reviews*. 2017; 16(4): 377–384.

155. Sari A, Guven D, Armagan B, et al: Rituximab experience in patients with long-standing systemic sclerosis-associated interstitial lung disease: A series of 14 patients. *Journal of Clinical Rheumatology: Practical Reports on Rheumatic & Musculoskeletal Diseases*. 2017; 23(8): 411–415.

156. Saunders P, Tsipouri V, Keir GJ, et al: Rituximab versus cyclophosphamide for the treatment of connective tissue disease-associated interstitial lung disease (RECITAL): Study protocol for a randomised controlled trial. *Trials*. 2017; 18(1): 275.

157. Savelkoul M, Post M, de Whitte L, et al: Social support, coping, and subjective well-being in patients with rheumatic diseases. *Patient Education Counseling*. 2000; 39: 205–218.

158. Scleroderma Foundation. Eating well with scleroderma. http://www.scleroderma.org/site/DocServer/NUTRITION_FINAL.pdf?docID=1462. Accessed June 22, 2018.

159. Scleroderma Foundation. Raynaud Phenomenon. http://www.scleroderma.org/site/DocServer/Raynaud.pdf?docID=322. Accessed June 22, 2018.

160. Shah SJ, Kahan A: Cardiac Involvement. In: Wigley F, Denton C, Varga J, eds.: *Scleroderma: From Pathogenesis to Comprehensive Management*. New York: Springer Science + Business, LLC; 2012.

161. Shah AA, Wigley FM: My approach to the treatment of scleroderma. *Mayo Clinic Proceedings*. 2013; 88(4): 377–393.

162. Shang P, Liu T, Liu W, et al: Telmisartan improves vascular remodeling through ameliorating prooxidant and profibrotic mechanisms in hypertension via the involvement of transforming growth factor-beta1. *Molecular Medicine Reports*. 2017; 16(4): 4537–4544.

163. Showalter K, Hoffmann A, DeCredico N, et al: Complementary therapies for patients with systemic sclerosis. *The Journal of Scleroderma and Related Disorders*. 2018; under review.

164. Simms R: Localized scleroderma and scleroderma-like syndromes. In: Hochberg M, Silman A, Smolen J, et al: *Rheumatology*. 6th ed. Philadelphia, PA. Elsevier; 2015: pp. 1219–1223.

165. Smith V, Van Praet JT, Vandooren B, et al: Rituximab in diffuse cutaneous systemic sclerosis: An open-label clinical and histopathological study. *Annals of Rheumatic Diseases*. 2010; 69(1): 193–197.

166. Sobanski V, Giovannelli J, Lynch BM, et al: Characteristics and survival of anti-U1 RNP antibody-positive patients with connective tissue disease-associated pulmonary arterial hypertension. *Arthritis and Rheumatology*. 2016; 68(2): 484–493.

167. Sobanski V, Launay D, Depret S, et al: Special considerations in pregnant systemic sclerosis patients. *Expert Review of Clinical Immunology*. 2016; 12(11): 1161–1173.

168. Sobanski V, Launay D, Hachulla E, et al: Current approaches to the treatment of systemic-sclerosis-associated pulmonary arterial hypertension (SSc-PAH). *Current Rheumatology Reports*. 2016; 18(2): 10.

169. Soh MC, Nelson-Piercy C. High-risk pregnancy and the rheumatologist. *Rheumatology* (Oxford). 2015 Apr; 54(4): 572–587.

170. Sporbeck B, Mathiske-Schmidt K, Jahr S, et al. Effect of biofeedback and deep oscillation on Raynaud's phenomenon secondary to systemic sclerosis: Results of a controlled prospective randomized clinical trial. *Rheumatology International*. 2012; 32: 1469–1473.

171. Steen VD: Pregnancy in women with systemic sclerosis. *Obstetrics and Gynecology*. 1999; 94(1): 15–20.

172. Steen VD, Conte C, Day N, et al: Pregnancy in women with systemic sclerosis. *Arthritis and Rheumatism*. 1989; 32(2): 151–157.

173. Steen VD, Medsger TA: Fertility and pregnancy outcome in women with systemic sclerosis. *Arthritis and Rheumatism*. 1999; 42(4): 763–768.

174. Steen T, Medsger T: Case-control study of corticosteroids and other drugs that either precipitate or protect from the development of scleroderma. *Arthritis & Rheumatism*. 1998; 41(9): 1613–1619.

175. Stefanantoni K, Sciarra I, Iannace N, et al. Occupational therapy integrated with a self-administered stretching program on systemic sclerosis patients with hand involvement. *Clinical and Experimental Rheumatology*. 2016; 34 Suppl 100(5): 157–161.

176. Sullivan KM, Goldmuntz EA, Keyes-Elstein L, et al: Myeloablative autologous stem-cell transplantation for severe scleroderma. *New England Journal of Medicine*. 2018; 378(1): 35–47.

177. Taraborelli M, Ramoni V, Brucato A, et al: Successful pregnancies but a higher risk of preterm births in patients with systemic sclerosis: An Italian multicenter study. *Arthritis and Rheumatism*. 2012; 64(6): 1970–1977.

178. Tashkin DP, Elashoff R, Clements PJ, et al: Cyclophosphamide versus placebo in scleroderma lung disease. *New England Journal of Medicine*. 2006; 354(25): 2655–2666.

179. Tashkin DP, Roth MD, Clements PJ, et al: Mycophenolate mofetil versus oral cyclophosphamide in scleroderma-related interstitial lung disease (SLS II): A randomised controlled, double-blind, parallel group trial. *Lancet Respiratory Medicine.* 2016; 4(9): 708–719.

180. Thiebaut M, Launay D, Rivière S, et al: Efficacy and safety of rituximab in systemic sclerosis: French retrospective study and literature review. *Autoimmunity Reviews.* 2018; 17(6): 582–587.

181. Thombs BD, Taillefer SS, Hudson M, et al: Depression in patients with systemic sclerosis: A systematic review of the evidence. *Arthritis & Rheumatology.* 2007; 57(6): 1089–1097.

182. Thombs BD, van Lankveld W, Bassel M, et al: Psychological health and well-being in systemic sclerosis: State of the science and consensus research agenda. *Arthritis Care Research.* 2010; 62(8): 1181–1189.

183. Toussirot E, Bereau M: The risk of progressive multifocal leukoencephalopathy under biological agents used in the treatment of chronic inflammatory diseases. *Inflammation & Allergy Drug Targets.* 2014; 13(2): 121–127.

184. van den Hoogen FH, Boerbooms AM, Swaak AJ, et al: Comparison of methotrexate with placebo in the treatment of systemic sclerosis: A 24 week randomized double-blind trial, followed by a 24 week observational trial. *British Journal of Rheumatology.* 1996; 35(4): 364–372.

185. van den Hoogen F, Khanna D, Fransen J, et al: Classification criteria for systemic sclerosis: An ACR-EULAR Collaborative Initiative. *Arthritis & Rheumatism.* 2013; 65(11): 2737–2747.

186. van den Hoogen F, Khanna D, Fransen J, et al: 2013 Classification Criteria for Systemic Sclerosis: An American College of Rheumatology/European League Against Rheumatism Collaborative Initiative. *Annals of Rheumatic Diseases.* 2013; 72(11): 1747–1755.

187. van Laar JM, Farge D, Sont JK, et al: Autologous hematopoietic stem cell transplantation vs. intravenous pulse cyclophosphamide in diffuse cutaneous systemic sclerosis: A randomized clinical trial. *Journal of the American Medical Association.* 2014; 311(24): 2490–2498.

188. Vilela VS, Maretti GB, Gama LM, et al: Rituximab for the therapy of systemic sclerosis: A series of 10 cases in a single center. *Revista Brasileria de Reumatologia Engl Ed.* 2016; 56(5): 458–463.

189. Walker UA, Clements PJ, Allanore Y, et al: Muscle involvement in systemic sclerosis: Points to consider in clinical trials. *Rheumatology.* 2017; 56: V38–V44.

190. Walker UA, Tyndall A, Ruszat R: Erectile dysfunction in systemic sclerosis. *Annals of Rheumatic Diseases.* 2009; 68: 1083–1085.

191. Walter K, Dilger C: Ibuprofen in human milk. *British Journal of Clinical Pharmacology.* 1997; 44: 211–212.

192. Wang C: Role of Tai Chi in the treatment of rheumatologic diseases. *Current Rheumatology Reports.* 2012; 14: 598–603.

193. Wiernik PH, Duncan JH: Cyclophosphamide in human milk. *Lancet.* 1971; 1(7705): 912.

194. Wigley FM, Wise RA, Seibold JR, et al: Intravenous iloprost infusion in patients with Raynaud phenomenon secondary to systemic sclerosis. A multicenter, placebo-controlled, double-blind study. *Annals of Internal Medicine.* 1994; 120(3): 199–206.

195. Williams D, Davidson J: Chronic kidney disease in pregnancy. *British Medical Journal.* 2008; 336(7637): 211–215. www.toxnet.nlm.nih.gov/newtoxnet/lactmed. Accessed, December 5, 2018.

196. Yocum D, Hodes R, Sundstrom W, et al: Use of biofeedback training in treatment of Raynaud's disease and phenomenon. *Journal of Rheumatology.* 1985; 12: 90–93.

197. Young A, Namas R, Dodge C, et al: Hand impairment in systemic sclerosis: Various manifestations and currently available treatment. *Current Treatment Options in Rheumatology.* 2016; 2(3): 252–269.

198. Yuen HK, Weng Y, Bandyopadhyay D, et al: Effect of a multi-faceted intervention on gingival health among adults with systemic sclerosis. *Clinical and Experimental Rheumatology.* 2011; 29: S26–S32.

199. Zhang QZ, Liu YL, Wang YR, et al: Effects of telmisartan on improving leptin resistance and inhibiting hepatic fibrosis in rats with non-alcoholic fatty liver disease. *Experimental and Therapeutic Medicine.* 2017; 14(3): 2689–2694.

INDEX

4-7-8 breathing, 101

A

acid reflux, 6, 12, 104–105
ambrisentan, 58, 60
American Academy of Dermatology, 80
American College of Rheumatology (ACR), 18, 75, 80, 82, 115
amlodipine, 27, 58
anal leakage, 28, 40
anger, 66
angiotensin converting enzyme (ACE) inhibitor, 7, 45, 52
angiotensin receptor blockers (ARBs), 36
anti-centromere antibodies (ACA), 18, 20
antinuclear antibodies (ANA), 18, 26
anti-PM-Scl, 18
anti-RNA Polymerase III antibody, 18
anti-Scl-70 antibody, 18, 20
anti-Th/To antibodies, 18
anti-topoisomerase I, 18
anti-U1-RNP, 20
anxiety, 7, 75
arrhythmias, 6
arthralgias/arthritis, 46
Arthritis Foundation, 78, 82, 115
aspiration, 6, 27
assessment and diagnosis
  diagnosis, 18, 24
  history, 12–14
  overview of, 12
  physical exam, 14–17
  practical considerations following, 69
  reporting symptoms to your doctor, 24, 28, 67, 76
  screening tests, 25–29, 70
  second opinions, 74–75
  sharing your diagnosis and prognosis, 68–69, 110
atherosclerotic cardiovascular disease (ASCVD), 96
atherosclerotic coronary artery disease (CAD), 96
autoantibodies, used in diagnosis, 18
autoimmune disease
  blood tests for, 4
  family history of, 14
  genetic factors, 62
  screening for, 26
autologous stem cell transplantation (ASCT), 35, 42
azathioprine, 58, 59

B

Barrett's esophagus, 6, 38
biofeedback, 100
blood pressure
　aggressive control of, 45
　safe thresholds, 7
bosentan, 27, 58, 60
breastfeeding, 57, 61–62

C

calcinosis, 3, 14
calcium channel blockers, 27, 36, 58, 60
CALM app, 100
capillary dilation, 16
captopril, 45
cardiac disease, 54
cardiac signs and symptoms, 6
carpal tunnel syndrome, 70
case managers, 93
chronic kidney disease, 52
classification criteria, 18, 24, 74
Cleveland Clinic, 78
clinical manifestations, 2
clinical practice guidelines, 75
complications
　associated with pregnancy, 50–51
　avoiding, 28–29
　lifestyle changes to lessen, 96–104
　managing fear of developing, 70
congestive heart failure, 6
coping skills, 111–114
corticosteroids, 20
counselors, 75
cuticular hemorrhage, 16
cyclophosphamide, 32, 41, 51, 58, 60

D

dentists, 91
depression
　coping with, 66
　incidence of, 7, 75
　treatment for, 67, 76
dermatologic signs and symptoms, 3
dermatologists, 91
diabetes, 19, 26
diagnosis. *See* assessment and diagnosis
diaphragmatic breathing, 101
diet, 97–98, 103–106
diffuse scleroderma, 2, 16, 26
digital ulcers
　assessment and diagnosis, 18
　avoiding, 101
　effects of pregnancy on, 51
　sexual dysfunction related to, 50
　treatment for, 36, 38, 42, 60
dysmotility, 6
dyspareunia, 8
dysphagia, 13

E

echocardiograms, 25
education resources
　articles and videos, 81–82
　finding reliable, 78–80
　local library and internet, 77
　medical societies and organizations, 80–81
　professional counselors, 75
　rheumatologists, 74
　second opinions, 74–75
　social media, 82–83

education resources *(continued)*
  specialized scleroderma centers, 76
  support groups, 81
electrocardiogram (EKG), 26
electromyograms, 26
elevated blood pressure, 7
emotional responses
  anger, 66
  depression, 7, 66
  fear, 66, 70
  professional counseling for, 75
  reducing stress, 70, 100–104, 110–115
  regaining your emotional equilibrium, 68
  self-blame, 66
  sharing with support network, 67, 69
  sharing your diagnosis, 68–69
employment issues, 70
en coup de sabre, 2
endothelin receptor antagonists, 27, 58, 60
endothelin receptor blockers (ERBs), 38, 44
environmental factors, 20
eosinophilic fasciitis, 19
epigenetics, 62
epoprostenol, 43, 58, 61
esophageal strictures, 6, 27, 38
esophageal ulcerations, 38
European League Against Rheumatism (EULAR), 18
exercise, 97, 104–106

F

family members
  coping strategies for, 113–115
  discussing your illness with, 110
  risk of stress in, 110–112
  signs of stress in, 111–112
  support groups for, 114–115
fatigue, 3
fear, 66, 70
fecal soilage, 28
feelings, sharing with support network, 67
fertility, 50. *See also* pregnancy; reproductive health

fibrosis, 2, 9
flexion contractures, 8, 16
FODMAP diet, 98, 103

G

gastric antral vascular ectasia (GAVE), 18, 20, 27
gastroenterologists, 24, 89
gastroesophageal reflux disease (GERD), 38, 97, 104
gastrointestinal (GI) manifestations
  managing with diet, 97, 103–105
  signs and symptoms, 6, 27
  treatment, 38–41
General Health Assessment Questionnaire, 24
generalized morphea, 2
genetic factors, 21, 62–63
glucocorticoids, 46
gynecologists, 90

H

"hardening of the skin", 2
health assessment questionnaires, 24
health care team
  case managers and social workers, 93
  dentists, 91
  dermatologists, 91
  gastroenterologists, 89
  nephrologists, 89
  nurse practitioners, 92–93
  ophthalmologists, 91
  pharmacists, 92–93
  physical and occupational therapists, 90, 92–93
  primary care providers (PCPs), 86
  psychologists and psychiatrists, 90–91
  pulmonologists, 89–90
  registered dieticians, 92–93
  rheumatologists, 87–88
  surgeons, 91–92
  urologists and gynecologists, 90–91

heartburn, 6, 12, 27
high-resolution computed tomography (CT), 25
history and physical, 12–18
HLA molecules, 62
hydrogen breath test, 27
hydroxychloroquine, 59

I

iloprost, 27, 58, 61
immunoglobulins, 34
incontinence, 6
insurance coverage, 27
internet resources
  finding reliable, 77–79
  list of professional organizations, 78–79
interstitial lung disease (ILD), 5, 25, 41, 52, 53
intrauterine growth retardation (IUGR), 56
IV immunoglobulin (IVIg), 34

J

joint contractures, 7, 88, 91, 97, 105
joint imaging, 25

K

kidneys. *See* renal system

L

lactose malabsorption, 98
laxatives, 40
leflunomide, 58, 59
library resources, 77
licensed clinical social workers (LCSWs), 29, 93
lifestyle changes
  benefits of, 96
  diet, 97–98, 103–105
  exercise, 97, 104–106
  strategies for successful, 96
  stress reduction, 100–104, 110–115

support systems for, 106–107
tobacco use, 98–99
limited scleroderma, 2, 16, 26
linear scleroderma, 2, 19
localized scleroderma, 2, 19
loved ones. *See* family and friends
low blood glucose. *See* hypoglycemia
low-residue diet, 40

M

macitentan, 27
magnetic resonance imaging (MRI), 26
major depressive disorder (MDD), 66
maternal fetal medicine (MFM), 50
Mayo Clinic, 78
meditation, 70
Medline, 78
mental health providers, 76
methotrexate, 33, 58, 59
microbiome, 63
mindfulness-based stress reduction (MBSR), 100
miscarriage, 54
mobility limitations, 50, 66–68, 70, 88, 92
Modified Rodnan Skin Score, 25
morphea, 2, 19
muscle biopsies, 26
muscle relaxation exercises, 71
musculoskeletal system complications
  signs and symptoms, 7
  treatment, 46
mycophenolate mofetil, 41, 58, 60
mycophenolic acid (MPA), 33
myositis, 46

N

nailfold capillaries, 12, 25
National Institute of Arthritis and Musculoskeletal and Skin Diseases (NIAMS), 80
National Organization of Rare Disorders (NORD), 78

neonatal death, 56
nephrologists, 89
nicotine replacement therapy (NRT), 99
nifedipine, 27, 58
nitrates, 37
normotensive scleroderma renal crisis (normotensive SRC), 42, 45
NSAIDs, 58–59
nurse practitioners, 92

O

obstructive sleep apnea (OSA), 25
online questionnaires, 24
ophthalmologists, 91
organ involvement, risk factors for, 19–20

P

palpitations, 6
patient education. *See* education resources
patient questionnaires, 24
patient reported outcome measures, 24
"peau d'orange" appearance, 19
pericardial effusion, 6
pericarditis, 6
pharmacists, 92
phosphodiesterase-5 inhibitors (PD-5I), 27, 36, 44, 58, 60
physical and occupational therapists, 90, 92, 97
physical examination, 14–17
pneumonia, 6
precision medicine, 32
pre-conception counseling, 50
prednisone, 20, 45, 58–59
preeclampsia, 52
pregnancy. *See also* reproductive health
  breastfeeding, 61–62
  contraindication for ACE inhibitors, 52
  contraindication for cyclophosphamide, 32
  contraindication for methotrexate, 33
  contraindication for mycophenolic acid, 33
  health risks to fetus, 54–56
  health risks to mother, 51–54
  inheritability of scleroderma, 62
  medications and their safety, 57–61
  potential complications, 50–51
premature births, 53, 55
primary care provider (PCP), 86–87
primary Raynaud phenomenon, 4
probiotics, 40
professional counseling, 75
professional medical societies, 80
prognosis, 68
progressive muscle relaxation exercises, 71
prostacyclin analogs, 27, 38, 43, 58, 61
proton pump inhibitors (PPIs), 38
psychiatric care, 75, 90–91
psychiatric signs and symptoms, 7, 29
psychological interventions, 70, 90
puffy fingers, 3, 12
pulmonary arterial hypertension (PAH), 20, 25, 42
pulmonary complications
  signs and symptoms, 5
  treatment, 40–45
pulmonary fibrosis, 5
pulmonary function tests (PFTs), 25
pulmonary hypertension, 5, 52, 53–54
Pulmonary Hypertension Association, 78
pulmonologists, 24, 89

Q

questionnaires, 24

R

Raynaud phenomenon
  ischemia resulting in gangrene, 38
  precautions to minimize, 101
  symptoms of, 4
  treatment, 27, 35–38
rectal incontinence, 40
reflux, 27
registered dietitians, 92
relaxation exercises, 71
renal crisis
  increased risk with high dose steroids, 42

pregnancy and, 52
risk of, 20
screening tests for, 26
symptoms of, 7
treatment, 45
renal system complications
　signs and symptoms, 7
　treatment, 45–46
reproductive health. *See also* pregnancy
　contraceptives and MPA, 33
　contraindications for methotrexate, 34
　sexual dysfunction, 8, 13, 28, 50
　sterility due to cyclophosphamide, 32, 51
rheumatic diseases, 18, 74
rheumatologists
　education resources offered by, 74
　follow-up visits with, 8, 88
　initial evaluation by, 12, 24, 87
riociguat, 45
rituximab, 34, 41
Rodnan Skin Score, 16

S

scleredema, 19
sclerodactyly, 3, 8
scleroderma
　appearance changes, 8
　assessment and diagnosis, 12–19
　cause of, 2, 66
　classification criteria, 18, 74
　complications of, 8
　genetic factors, 21, 62–63
　risk factors for developing, 2
　risk factors for organ involvement, 19–20
　signs and symptoms of, 3–8
　types of, 2, 19
scleroderma en coup de sabre, 19
Scleroderma Foundation, 79, 82, 115
Scleroderma International Network, 79, 82, 115
scleroderma renal crisis (SRC)
　pregnancy and, 52

risk of, 20
screening tests for, 26
symptoms of, 7
treatment, 45
Scleroderma Research Foundation, 79
scleroderma-specific antibodies, 26
scleromyxedema, 19
screening tests, 25–29, 70
secondary Raynaud phenomenon, 4
second opinions, 74–75
selective serotonin re-uptake inhibitor (SSRI), 37
self-blame, 66
self-care, 29, 76
sexual dysfunction, 8, 13, 28, 50
sicca symptoms, 13
signs and symptoms
　cardiac, 6
　constitutional, 3
　dermatologic, 3
　gastrointestinal, 6
　musculoskeletal, 7
　of inability to cope, 111–112
　psychiatric, 7, 29
　pulmonary, 5
　recognizing, 8
　renal, 7
　reporting to your doctor, 24, 28, 67, 76
　symptom management, 28
　vascular, 4
sildenafil, 27, 44, 58, 60
Sjogren syndrome, 13, 26
skin thickening
　effects on quality of life, 3
　sexual dysfunction due to, 50
　treatment, 32–35
sleep disturbances, 102
sleep studies, 25
small for gestational age (SGA) infants, 56
small intestinal bacterial overgrowth (SIBO), 13, 27, 39
smoking cessation, 98

social media, 82–83
specialized scleroderma centers, 76
"spider veins", 14
stem cell transplantation, 32, 35, 42
stillbirth, 56
stress, reducing, 70, 100–104, 110–115
strictures, 6, 27, 38
suicide, 67
support groups, 29, 67, 68, 81–82, 114–115
surgeons, 91
symptom management, 28
syncope, 6
systemic sclerosis, 2, 19
systemic sclerosis sine scleroderma, 2

T

tadalafil, 27, 44, 58, 60
telangiectasias, 3, 8, 12, 14, 25
tendon friction rubs, 7, 16
teratogenic medications, 52
therapists, 75
thyroid disease, 26
tobacco use, 20, 70, 98
topical nitrates, 37
treatment
  depression, 76
  discussing changes with your doctor, 51, 80
  gastrointestinal (GI) manifestations, 38–40
  muscle and joint symptoms, 46–47
  overview of, 32
  pulmonary complications, 40–45
  Raynaud phenomenon, 35–38
  renal complications, 45–46
  screening tests guiding, 27
  skin thickening, 32–35

U

urologists, 90

V

vascular signs and symptoms, 4, 9

W

"watermelon stomach", 27
WebMD, 79
workplace issues, 70

Y

yoga, 71